Palgrave Studies in African Leadership

Series Editors
Faith Ngunjiri
Concordia College
Moorhead, MN, USA

Nceku Nyathi
De Montfort University
Leicester, UK

Almost every continent has solid representation in the field of leadership studies except for Africa, despite its rapid growth. A groundbreaking series, Palgrave Studies in African Leadership fills a gap in the production of knowledge and scholarly publishing on Africa and provides a much needed outlet for the works of scholars interested in African leadership studies around the world. Where many studies of leadership in Africa focus solely on one country or region, this series looks to address leadership in each of the different regions and countries of the continent. This comes at a time when business and academic discourse have begun to focus on the emerging markets across Africa. The wide-ranging scholarly perspectives offered in this series allow for greater understanding of the foundation of African leadership and its implications for the future. Topics and contributors will come from various backgrounds to fully explore African leadership and the implications for business, including scholars from business and management, history, political science, gender studies, sociology, religious studies, and African studies. The series will analyze a variety of topics including African political leadership, women's leadership, religious leadership, servant leadership, specific regions, specific countries, specific gender categories, specific business entities in Africa, and more.

More information about this series at
http://www.palgrave.com/gp/series/14652

Claude-Hélène Mayer
Lynette Louw • Christian Martin Boness
Editors

Managing Chinese-African Business Interactions

Growing Intercultural Competence in Organizations

Editors
Claude-Hélène Mayer
Department of Management
Rhodes University
Grahamstown, South Africa

Lynette Louw
Department of Management
Rhodes University
Grahamstown, South Africa

Christian Martin Boness
Department of Management
Rhodes University
Grahamstown, South Africa

Palgrave Studies in African Leadership
ISBN 978-3-030-25184-0   ISBN 978-3-030-25185-7   (eBook)
https://doi.org/10.1007/978-3-030-25185-7

© The Editor(s) (if applicable) and The Author(s), under exclusive licence to Springer Nature Switzerland AG 2019
This work is subject to copyright. All rights are solely and exclusively licensed by the Publisher, whether the whole or part of the material is concerned, specifically the rights of translation, reprinting, reuse of illustrations, recitation, broadcasting, reproduction on microfilms or in any other physical way, and transmission or information storage and retrieval, electronic adaptation, computer software, or by similar or dissimilar methodology now known or hereafter developed.
The use of general descriptive names, registered names, trademarks, service marks, etc. in this publication does not imply, even in the absence of a specific statement, that such names are exempt from the relevant protective laws and regulations and therefore free for general use.
The publisher, the authors and the editors are safe to assume that the advice and information in this book are believed to be true and accurate at the date of publication. Neither the publisher nor the authors or the editors give a warranty, express or implied, with respect to the material contained herein or for any errors or omissions that may have been made. The publisher remains neutral with regard to jurisdictional claims in published maps and institutional affiliations.

Cover illustration: © Alex Linch / shutterstock.com

This Palgrave Macmillan imprint is published by the registered company Springer Nature Switzerland AG.
The registered company address is: Gewerbestrasse 11, 6330 Cham, Switzerland

Foreword

A three-day summit in China in November 2006 marked the beginning of a strategic relationship between China and Africa, as well as significant growth in Chinese foreign direct investment and in China's general presence in Africa (Bräutigam, 2009, p. 2). Even though China's presence on the continent has led to significant development and growth in Africa's infrastructure and manufacturing sector (Ma Mung, 2008, p. 96), the relationship between these countries has raised concerns, criticism and even accusations of neo-colonialism (Shen & Taylor, 2012, p. 693).

My experience of living in South Africa for over 25 years and working in many other countries—including Namibia, Swaziland and the Democratic Republic of the Congo, just to mention a few—has equipped me with a good understanding of the importance and complexity of China-Africa relations, which deserve in-depth study and analysis, not only by academia but also by other interested parties. In this regard, I would like to offer my congratulations to the Department of Management at Rhodes University for pursuing their interest in the study of Chinese-African intercultural interactions, in particular, the exploration of some practical issues concerning Chinese entities in the African cultural and business context. This book essentially addresses the main conflict areas in China-Africa relations, including cultural differences, impact on local trade and commerce, and the presence of a diverse workforce resulting from the migration of Chinese workers (Adisu, Sharkey, & Okoroafo, 2010, p. 7).

I like the approach adopted by the academics and authors in using case studies to demonstrate accomplishments in managing Chinese-African business interactions. Authors with different backgrounds and expertise from a variety of countries have brought us true stories of Chinese enterprises in a wide range of African countries: Tanzania, Zambia, Uganda, Namibia, Mozambique, Rwanda, Angola, South Sudan, Cameroon, Zimbabwe and South Africa. The observations and investigations in these business cases should be a good reflection of how intercultural interaction between the Chinese and Africans on the African continent can be enhanced to improve organisational success. We must acknowledge, however, the existing differences between business environments, traditional cultures and local legislation in various African countries. Success in selected countries and organisations does not necessarily mean the success of Chinese involvement in Africa as a whole.

The approaches and methodologies applied by the authors are appropriate to the subject and purpose of the research, which aims to bring practical insight and suggest competent ways to deal with intercultural interactions in Chinese-African organisations. The conclusions and recommendations derived from these case studies are more convincing than pure theoretical and literature probes. As the saying goes: action speaks louder than words.

I would like to use the opportunity to thank and congratulate all the authors, the editors and the Department of Management at Rhodes University for their great effort and dedication in carrying out this task and presenting a quality intellectual product to the readers, who will certainly find value and benefit in the texts contained in this book.

Johannesburg, South Africa   Shengfei Gan
May 2019

References

Adisu, K., Sharkey, T., & Okoroafo, S. C. (2010). The impact of Chinese Investment in Africa. *International Journal of Business and Management*, 5(9), 3–9.

Bräutigam, D. (2009). *Dragon's Gift: The Real Story of China in Africa*. Oxford: Oxford University Press.

Ma Mung, E. (2008). Chinese Migration and China's Foreign Policy in Africa. *Journal of Chinese Overseas, 4*(1), 91–109.

Shen, S., & Taylor, I. (2012). Ugandan Youths' Perceptions of Relations with China. *Asian Perspective, 36*(4), 693–723.

Acknowledgements

We would like to thank Rhodes University's Department of Management for hosting the project "Chinese organisations in sub-Saharan Africa", for Rhodes University assisting us in all of our research endeavours in different countries in Africa, for supporting us financially and with our vision. Special thanks go to Mr Trevor Amos, who heads the department.

Further, we would like to thank our cooperation partners in different African countries who supported us in conducting our research projects in various organisations and countries. In particular, we thank Samuel Kussaga and Moses Hella in Tanzania, who contributed to our research projects in South Africa and who assisted us in analysing and interpreting the data.

For language and technical editing, we would like to thank Mrs Ruth Coetzee, who has worked for us reliably for several years on different papers, articles and chapters, and also on this book project.

We acknowledge, with thanks, the seed funding for this project provided by the Sandisa Imbewu Fund at Rhodes University. This benefited the research for Chaps. 4 and 16.

The financial assistance of the National Research Foundation of South Africa for Grant No. 93636 towards the research for Chaps. 5, 9 and 12 is hereby acknowledged. Opinions expressed in these chapters and conclusions arrived at are those of the authors and are not necessarily attributed to the National Research Foundation.

Contents

Part I Cultural Insights into Chinese-African Management 1

1 Introduction 3
   Claude-Hélène Mayer

2 Chinese Cultural Concepts and Their Influence on Management 19
   Zhaoyi Liu

3 African Cultural Concepts and Their Influence on Management 37
   Samukele Hadebe and Dion Nkomo

Part II Intercultural Training Cases: Dealing with International Communication, Cooperation and Negotiation 59

4 Case 1: Dealing with Organisational Strategies in the Tanzanian-Chinese Chalinze Water Project 61
   Christian Martin Boness

5 Case 2: "Not who I am, not what I mean": Intercultural Communication in Chinese-South African Interactions 71
Fungai B. Chigwendere

6 Case 3: Dealing with Organisational Structures, Decision-Making and Participation in the Zambian Textile Industry 85
Christian Martin Boness, Naiming Wei, and Claude-Hélène Mayer

7 Case 4: A Negotiation Between Chinese and Namibian Organisations in Namibia 101
Haiyan Zhang, Chen Ni, and Liusheng Wang

8 Case 5: How to Make Friends in Rwanda: A Chinese Tea Ceremony 111
Christian Martin Boness

Part III Intercultural Training Cases: Entrepreneurship, Management Styles, Language and Identity 125

9 Case 6: Setting Up Small, Medium and Micro Enterprises by Chinese Entrepreneurial Immigrants in Maputo, Mozambique 127
Mattheus Johannes Louw, Lynette Louw, and Fiona Geyser

10 Case 7: Managing a Chinese-Angolan National Housing Project in Angola's Capital, Luanda 135
Christian Martin Boness, Naiming Wei, and Claude-Hélène Mayer

11 Case 8: Language, Culture and Power in the Chinese-South African Telecommunications Sector 149
June Sun

12 Case 9: Transforming Employee Conflicts in a Chinese Construction Firm in Kampala, Uganda 161
Sidney Muhangi

Part IV Intercultural Training Cases: International Human Resource Management 169

13 Case 10: Sharing Knowledge in a Sudanese Oil Refinery Through Cultural and Language Trainings 171
Christian Martin Boness

14 Case 11: Working Conditions in a Chinese-Ugandan Communications Company 179
Christian Martin Boness and Naiming Wei

15 Case 12: Managing a Chinese-South African Restaurant in Port Elizabeth, South Africa 191
Zhaoyi Liu

Part V Intercultural Training Cases: Management Practices and Employment Relations 203

16 Case 13: Employee Perceptions of a Chinese Heavy-Machinery-Importing Organisation Operating in Uganda 205
Lynette Louw, Katherine Burger, and Mattheus Johannes Louw

17 Case 14: Hiring and Firing in the Chinese-Zimbabwean Mining Industry 215
Christian Martin Boness

18 Case 15: Managing Chinese-Cameroonian Daily Interactions in a Company in Douala, Cameroon 225
Jocelyne Kenne Kenne

19 Case 16: A Cross-cultural Conference in the Mozambique Confucius Institute 233
Christian Martin Boness and Naiming Wei

Index 247

Notes on Contributors

Christian Martin Boness holds a master's degree in Theology and a doctorate in Pedagogics from Georg-August-Universität Göttingen, Germany. He lectures at higher education institutions in various countries and is an international consultant and mediator in business organisations. He is also a researcher associated with the project "Chinese organisations in sub-Saharan Africa". He has lived and worked in Scandinavia, Tanzania and South Africa, and he specialises in negotiation tactics, mediation and conflict management across cultures, particularly in business organisations and institutions of higher education. His research focuses on the development of educational models for intercultural school curricula and on managing intercultural conflict.

Katherine Burger holds honours degree in the field of cross-cultural management, from Rhodes University, South Africa. Her work experience includes four years in a leadership position at South Africa's largest private asset management company. She is now a self-employed enthusiast in people development and aims to freelance and consult in the talent management field. She enjoys assisting students and recent graduates with personal development in bridging the divide between studying and the first steps of their careers.

Fungai B. Chigwendere is a PhD graduate from Rhodes University in South Africa, developed a sustained interest in cross-cultural management, having been a researcher and project coordinator for a groundbreaking project "Management of People and Change in Africa" while at the ESCP-EAP European School of Management Studies in Oxford. She is a member of the Rhodes University research project on Chinese organisations in sub-Saharan Africa, which aims, through cross-cultural collaborative research, to better understand the way Chinese organisations are being managed in African countries.

Fiona Geyser is a former Rhodes University graduate. She holds a Bachelor of Social Science in Management and Organisational Psychology and an honours degree in Management, where she concentrated her research on Chinese entrepreneurial immigrants' small business ventures in Mozambique. Her research interests include immigrant entrepreneurship, management styles, language and communication. Her preliminary research findings were presented at the Southern African Institute for Management Scientists (SAIMS) Conference 2017 in Bloemfontein.

Samukele Hadebe is a senior researcher with a special focus on worker education and trade unions at the Chris Hani Institute, Johannesburg, South Africa. Previous positions include serving as director of the Centre for Public Engagement in Zimbabwe, director of Public Policy Research Institute of Zimbabwe, founding director of the Confucius Institute at the University of Zimbabwe and Deputy Dean of the Faulty of Arts. He is the chief editor of the first monolingual Ndebele dictionary, *Isichazamazwi SesiNdebele*.

Jocelyne Kenne Kenne is a PhD candidate at the University of Bayreuth, Germany. She has a master's degree in Linguistics and Intercultural Communication from the University of Siena, Italy. She is working on her PhD thesis in Linguistics, titled "Language and interaction in a Chinese community in Cameroon". Her research interests include intercultural communication, language contact, second language acquisition and the field of pragmatics.

Zhaoyi Liu is a PhD candidate and research associate at Rhodes University, specialising in research on Chinese organisations' development in South Africa. Her own business operations include projects between South African and Chinese governments, and localisation and development consultation for Chinese enterprises and organisations in South Africa. Her experience of local business management and consulting in South Africa provides her with insight into the problems and situations that Chinese enterprises face in this country.

Lynette Louw is a Professor in the Raymond Ackerman Chair, the former Head of the Management Department, and Deputy Dean of the Faculty of Commerce at Rhodes University, South Africa. She received her Doctor Commercii (Business Management) degree at the Nelson Mandela University in South Africa. Her areas of speciality are strategic management, international organisational behaviour and cross-cultural management. Internationally she has experience with higher education institutions in the Netherlands, Germany, Uganda and China. She also serves on the editorial board of rated national and international journals. She is the research leader in Africa of an extensive research project on Chinese management in Africa, in collaboration with colleagues in the UK and China.

Mattheus Johannes Louw is a senior lecturer in the Department of Management at Rhodes University, South Africa. He obtained his MBA degree in Human Resource Management from the University of Stellenbosch, South Africa. He is responsible for teaching Human Resource Management and Leadership at undergraduate and postgraduate levels. He also has experience in lecturing at universities in China, the Netherlands and Germany. His research areas include human resource management and intercultural management.

Claude-Hélène Mayer is Professor of Industrial and Organisational Psychology at the University of Johannesburg, an adjunct professor at the European University, Viadrina and Frankfurt (Oder), Germany, and a senior research associate at Rhodes University in South Africa. She holds a PhD in Psychology (University of Pretoria), a PhD in Management (Rhodes University), a doctorate in Political Sciences from Georg-August University in Germany and a Habilitation with a Venia Legendi (Europa Universität Viadrina, Germany) in psychology with focus on work, organisational and cultural psychology. She has published numerous monographs, text collections, accredited journal articles and special issues on transcultural mental health, sense of coherence, shame, culture and health, transcultural conflict management and mediation, women in leadership in culturally diverse work contexts, constellation work, coaching and psychobiography.

Sidney Muhangi attained his Bachelor's degree in Business Administration at Makerere University, Uganda, and an honours in Management at Rhodes University, South Africa. He is both a Mandela Rhodes and a Commonwealth scholar who is pursuing an MSc in Global Food Security and Development at Nottingham Trent University in the UK. He also has a passion for management research, social development and agribusiness.

Chen Ni is an assistant at the College of Foreign Studies in Nantong University, Jiangsu, China. She holds a bachelor's degree in Linguistics. Her interests focus on intercultural communication.

Dion Nkomo (PhD) is an associate professor at Rhodes University's School of Languages and Literatures. His academic interests include lexicography, translation, terminology, language planning and policy, multilingualism and higher education studies. He holds a C2 rating from the National Research Foundation and is a member of the Academy of Science of South Africa. Previously, he worked under the African Languages Lexical Project (University of Zimbabwe) and the Multilingualism Education Project (University of Cape Town).

June Sun holds a BA in Politics and International Relations from the University of Cambridge, and an MPhil in International Development from the University of Oxford. She has worked in the UK government, in journalism and as a technology market analyst. She is working as an international development technology consultant at Vera Solutions, providing technology solutions for social impact organisations. She is based in London, UK.

Liusheng Wang is an associate professor in the Department of Psychology at Nantong University in Jiangsu, China. He holds a PhD in Psychology from East China Normal University and has published books and journal articles in the areas of emotion, shame, embodied cognition, development of adolescents and cultural differences.

Naiming Wei holds a PhD degree in Electrical Engineering from the University Erlangen-Nürnberg in Germany. He has extensive international business experience and offers training for joint ventures and international companies in the area of leadership development, management performance improvement and intercultural communication. At Technische Hochschule Nürnberg Georg Simon Ohm, he is a professor in the Faculty of Business Administration for Strategic Management.

Haiyan Zhang is an associate professor at Nantong University, China. She holds a doctoral degree in Early Childhood Education, which she obtained from Jackson State University, USA. She has published several articles on comparative studies between Chinese and American educational systems, and articles concerning intercultural communication.

PART I

Cultural Insights into Chinese-African Management

CHAPTER 1

Introduction

Claude-Hélène Mayer

1.1 Introduction

Growing engagement of Chinese global investment, aid and trade in Africa has led to increased business interaction, organisational cooperation and trade between Chinese and African organisations and employees in southern Africa (BBC News, 2015). These international Chinese-African employee interactions, which take place at governmental, private or community engagement levels, have increased the scientific interest in Chinese-African cooperation and interaction significantly during the past years (Bird & Fang, 2009; Brewster, Carey, Grobler, Holland, & Wärnich, 2008; Mayer, Boness, Louw, & Louw, 2016).

Increasing intercultural and international research has identified the need for growing successful intercultural communication, interaction and organisational strategies, as well as human resource management in international cooperation to manage differences and conflict and to focus on similarities and synergies of members of different cultural origin and groups (Mayer, 2008a; Samovar, Porter, McDaniel, & Roy, 2014). Although Chinese and African people have conducted trade and led intercultural relations for many centuries (Mayer, Boness, & Louw, 2017),

C.-H. Mayer (✉)
Department of Management, Rhodes University, Grahamstown, South Africa

© The Author(s) 2019
C.-H. Mayer et al. (eds.), *Managing Chinese-African Business Interactions*, Palgrave Studies in African Leadership,
https://doi.org/10.1007/978-3-030-25185-7_1

these relatively new forms of intercultural employee interactions should be based on an in-depth understanding of cultural aspects and business behaviours of the individuals, teams and organisations involved. Several researchers have described the many challenges that Chinese organisations experience in global expansion and in intercultural management and leadership (Wang, Freeman, & Zhu, 2013). Others, however, note that Chinese-African cooperation in terms of dialogue and understanding has improved significantly during the past 15 years (Ni, 2015).

An in-depth understanding of cognition, affect and behaviour within the intercultural realms can lead to an increased intercultural understanding and intercultural competence and therefore lead to improved and more relaxed and successful intercultural interactions (Mayer, 2008b). In culturally diverse intercultural communication situations, the process of intercultural communication and how it is conducted are critical factors in establishing and maintaining cooperative and effective intergroup relations (Gudykunst, 1986; Hall, 1976; Mayer et al., 2016; Spencer-Rodgers & McGovern, 2002). Spencer-Rodgers and McGovern (2002) point out that differences in cognition—such as those expressed in values, norms, fundamental epistemologies, beliefs and thoughts—influence negative stereotypes. Further, along the process of intercultural communication, the experience of differences in affect and behaviour can impact negatively on intercultural communication itself. Such experiences include differences in emotional expression, perception and behaviour, involving how language, customs and communication styles are understood, expressed and used. Other studies have agreed with and expanded on this research, showing that perceived differences at cognitive, affective and behavioural levels can lead to lowered work effectiveness (Moreland, Levine, & Wingert, 2013). This may eventually result in negative overall evaluations of members of "the other group" (Spencer-Rodgers & McGovern, 2002).

Chinese-African management interactions are growing rapidly within China as well as within southern African countries (African Economic Outlook, 2014). However, recent studies in southern African contexts have shown that Chinese-African intercultural interactions are accompanied by stereotypes and cultural prejudices (Handley & Louw, 2016), which influence the management of employees, as well as the employee engagement, organisational dynamics and the success of the organisation (Jackson, Louw, & Zhao, 2013; Park & Alden, 2013).

Currently, many international and intercultural management and business interactions seem to bring with them verbal, non-verbal and paralingual misinterpretations—and are therefore based on misunderstandings rather than on mindful and interculturally competent interactions. On both sides, Chinese-African employees and managers who are involved in business interactions strive to flourish in local, organisational and global cooperation initiatives (Mayer et al., 2017). However, employees receive hardly any guidance or training to improve their intercultural business cooperation. Consequently, researchers have drawn attention to the need for developing new intercultural training tools for the Chinese-African context of organisational and individual cooperation (Xing, Liu, Tarba, & Cooper, 2016), since cooperation still presents serious challenges (Wang et al., 2013) and often causes frustration, unsuccessful interactions, intercultural prejudices and stereotyping (Mayer et al., 2016).

To increase their intercultural competence in short-, medium- and long-term interactions, Chinese and African employees can benefit from intercultural training (Xing et al., 2016). Xing et al. (2016) explain that intercultural learning can take place when members of both cultures are able to take cultural concepts into account, which might lead them to recognise similarities. Writers such as Handley and Louw (2016) suggest that Chinese and African leadership examine and compare the concepts of Confucianism in the Chinese cultural context and *Ubuntu* in the African cultural context (Xing et al., 2016).

During the past years, research projects and information concerning Chinese-African employee interactions and human resource management have grown (Xing et al., 2016); however, practical and applied training materials which provide insights into how to manage Chinese-African interactions successfully are rather rare, since research of Chinese investment in Africa has been studied primarily according to international trade and political economy perspectives (Kaplinsky & Morris, 2009). The need, however, for considering Chinese-African relationships in organisations and business has been pointed out before (Kamoche, Chizema, Mellahi, & Newenham-Kahindi, 2012). This seems to be particularly important when considering mutual benefits and development beyond international aid and trade (Bräutigam, 2009; Bräutigam & Tan, 2011).

This book responds to the call for practical intercultural insights and competent ways of dealing with intercultural interactions in international management, with special regard to Chinese-African organisational and business interaction. In Chaps. 2 and 3, Chinese and African culture-specific concepts of management and leadership are introduced and discussed, before specific case studies are presented.

1.2 Managing Intercultural Interactions Successfully

In international management, organisations can be defined as social, complex, open, adaptive and autopoietic systems (Mayer, 2011), which are seen as a product of the complex interaction of the environment and various intra-organisational factors such as human resources and their interrelations and management (Glasl, 1994; Mayer, Tonelli, Oosthuizen, & Surtee, 2018). Usually, organisations are embedded in supra-systems such as societies while containing subsystems such as individuals and subcultural groups. At the same time, organisations are viewed as complex and dynamic, made up of constantly changing relationships between the entities involved. Challenges within organisational systems are usually dealt with in culturally based ways in terms of their approaches and outcomes (International Council for Science, 2002). A particular challenge is the management of consistency, order and understanding in international management and intercultural interactions because supra-systems of the host society of the organisation, as well as cognition, affect, and behavioural orientations of individuals and subgroups inside organisations vary (Mayer, 2011). Further, individuals in organisations are influenced by their own identities and values, by the organisational culture and by the organisational structures and dynamics (Mayer, 2008a). The values, identities, organisational culture and structures within international and intercultural management and organisational settings become increasingly complex and need to be reflected and constantly re-evaluated so as to create a dynamic and inclusive culture in which motivational levels and well-being are high (Mayer & Krause, 2011).

In international management, it is assumed that managers need special abilities to cope with international and intercultural challenges (Mayer, 2011). These management competences—defined as sets of knowledge, skills, behaviours and attitudes which individuals need to work effectively (Hellriegel et al., 2007)—are in six key areas of communication, planning and administration, teamwork, strategic action, global awareness and emotional intelligence with self-management.

Communication competences include informal and formal communication and negotiation. Planning refers to the areas of time and project management, financial management and problem-solving, while teamwork competence emphasises designing teams, providing supportive environments and managing team dynamics. Strategic action highlights the understanding of industry and organisations when taking strategic actions. Global awareness competences are based on cultural knowledge and understanding, openness and sensitivity. Finally, emotional intelligence and self-management competences deal with integrity and ethical conduct, personal drive and resilience, balancing work and life issues, self-awareness and development, as well as spiritual intelligence (Hellriegel et al., 2007, pp. 23–35).

Within the context of intercultural management, culture can be defined as consisting of "the derivatives of experience, more or less organized, learned or created by the individuals of a population, including those images or encodements and their interpretations (meanings) transmitted from past generations, from contemporaries, or formed by individuals themselves" (Schwartz, 1992, p. 324). Culture is thereby seen as a construct through which individuals and groups create cultural boundaries, as well as in-groups and out-groups which are dynamic and changeable. M. Bennett (personal communication, April 30, 2017) defines culture in a very broad sense as "the coordination of meaning and action within a bounded group". Using this definition of culture, one can speak about organisational culture but also about individual and culture-specific group culture and membership. Awareness of these different forms of culture is important with regard to this book, which refers to intercultural interactions on various levels. In intercultural interactions, these constructed boundaries are usually experienced and crossed, and intercultural spaces are created in which intercultural interaction and communication take place.

1.3 INTERCULTURAL COMPETENCES

Managing organisations across nations and cultures involves information and knowledge of the cultural backgrounds (Hofstede, 1995). During the past decades, globalisation has brought a wider range of cultures into closer contact with each other than ever before; cultural boundaries are shifting, leading to increasing social and cultural transformation (UNESCO, 2013) and hybrid cultures.

Cultural aspects shape individuals' dispositions regarding their experiences and their interpretation of communication and interactions, as well as potential conflict (Mayer & Louw, 2012). Culture also shapes the goals of interactions and the interpretations of communicative acts (Gudykunst, 2005; Gudykunst & Kim, 1997). It is a challenge for individuals and organisations to see cultural diversity as a resource which should be responded to by increasing intercultural competences (UNESCO, 2009, 2013). Therefore, it is a priority for organisations and their employees—particularly in international and intercultural contexts—to understand the cultural aspects involved and to develop intercultural competences that help organisations to flourish (Lloyd & Härtel, 2003).

The term "competence" is difficult to define; scholars such as Deardorff (2009) explain that, in the intercultural context, the term has been equated with understanding, relationship development, satisfaction, effectiveness, appropriateness and adaptation, as well as with skills and abilities. These "equations have [also] been criticised" from different perspectives (Deardorff, 2009, p. 6). It is problematic that competences are defined through cultural lenses and cannot be defined as an overall universal concept. They are always seen as being based on cultural perspectives and contexts; they are never culture-neutral concepts (Spitzberg, 2007).

Various competences are considered critical to making capable global leaders in intercultural work contexts (see, e.g. Rosen, Digh, Singer, & Phillips, 2000). Leiba-O'Sullivan (1999) suggests that these competences include:

- Personal literacy (understanding and valuing oneself)
- Social literacy (engaging and challenging others)
- Business literacy (focusing and mobilising one's organisation)
- Cultural literacy (valuing and leveraging cultural differences and/or transcultural competent managers)

Other researchers such as Lloyd and Härtel (2003) refer to multidimensional facets of intercultural competences (see also Leung, Ang, & Tan, 2014; Schnabel, Kelava, van de Vijver, & Seifert, 2015). Expertise in the following areas plays a major role in intercultural competence:

Dissimilarity openness requires the appreciation of cultural differences and openness to resolving intercultural conflicts (Ting-Toomey, 2007).

Intercultural conflict-handling expertise (Ting-Toomey, 2007) impacts greatly on individuals and organisations (Mayer, 2008a, b), particularly in groups and organisations which consist of a culturally diverse workforce (Barak, 2013) and in which individuals are affected by increased complexity arising from cultural influences (Okech, Pimpleton-Gray, Vannatta, & Champe, 2016).

Emotion management skills help to deal with affect based on the experiences of value differences, thereby building increased emotional intelligence (Goleman, 1995). Emotional intelligence helps to manage stress and insecurities in a calm and relaxed manner to avoid counterproductive activities (Jordan, Ashkanasy, & Härtel, 2002), to comprehend situations emotionally (Mayer & Salovey, 1994) and thereby to increase mental health and well-being (Mayer, 2011). Emotional intelligence has been identified as one of the most important leadership competences in managing change and sustainability, organisational vision and diverse teams (Goleman, Boyatzkis, & McKee, 2013).

Intercultural communication ability is critical as part of intercultural competences since knowledge of language and verbal and non-verbal communication are highly important in both managing difference and coding and decoding messages (Martin & Nakayama, 2015).

Tolerance for ambiguity is a significant intercultural competence, which supports individuals in managing ambiguous and multilayered complex situations without requiring additional objective information (Hammer, 2015). It further assists in being receptive to new information about the self and others (Gudykunst & Kim, 1997). The higher one's tolerance for ambiguity is, the more comfortable individuals feel in unfamiliar situations (Lloyd & Härtel, 2003).

Cultural understanding is a key competence in the development of intercultural relationships, communication success and effectiveness (Pellowski, 2016). Michelle, Bateman, Gerrity, and Myint (2017) emphasise that cultural understanding contributes positively to identity development and to bridging transitions and change, while Berardo and Deardorff (2012) point out that a deep cultural understanding leads to an increase in respect and is essential in managing the experience of differences.

Information processing skills are important with regard to intercultural information processing attitudes and cognitive styles (Gudykunst & Kim, 1997), as well as regarding interpersonal communication skills and competences in highly complex and intercultural contexts (Sabee, 2015). Individuals with higher cognitive complexity tend to form more extensive and differentiated impressions of others, are better in representing the behavioural variability of others and seek out unique features of the environment more frequently than do individuals with lower cognitive complexity. They therefore hold a greater capacity to develop an understanding of different cultural systems (Yum, 1982).

Self-management skills are likely to improve intercultural interactions (Moran, Abramson, & Moran, 2016). Individuals with high self-management skills are likely to be more flexible in their behaviour and response to demanding situations. They are more capable of sharing information and enhancing performance (Lloyd & Härtel, 2003).

All of these competences support individuals in building intercultural identities and the ability to deal with intercultural situations and interactions successfully, while staying mentally healthy and well (Mayer, 2011). Employees in international organisations particularly require cognitive, affective and behavioural resources to cope with intercultural challenges, as they build their intercultural identity and thereby contribute to healthy and peaceful intercultural work environments.

The case studies presented in this book aim to increase the reader's intercultural competence by providing a growing insight into cultural mechanisms, perspectives, concepts and ideas, emotional and behavioural options. The general categories of intercultural competences outlined here can help to analyse the cases and understand the cultural insights presented.

1.4 Aim and Purpose of the Book

The main aim of this book is to provide guidance in understanding and establishing successful Chinese-African business interactions and cooperation in African countries. Accordingly, the purpose is to improve Chinese-African employee interactions, to contribute to an increased intercultural understanding and improvement of work-based relationships.

By reading these challenging case studies, the reader can develop an awareness of cultural perspectives within Chinese organisations that are investing in southern Africa. Chinese and African perspectives on the cases are presented so as to improve the reader's ability to understand multiple perspectives in a particular situation and to identify the most applicable solutions in dealing with cases in an interculturally competent way. As the training cases are explored, the reader can develop ideas and hypothesise about the cultural backgrounds, which influence the interactions in the described context. Chinese and African perspectives on the cases are presented and possible solutions and ideas for best practice from a perspective of intercultural competence are given.

Employees of Chinese and African descent can find ideas in this book about ways to understand and manage intercultural interactions successfully in organisations. However, it is not only employees and human resource managers who can benefit from learning how to guide and manage interactions on the basis of a multiple cultural understanding. The book is also useful for readers who would like to increase their general understanding of intercultural business communication and cooperation, and gain insights into intercultural challenges in intercultural and international organisations. Valuable insights are offered to students in the fields of industrial and organisational psychology, economics, management, human resource management, engineering and cultural sciences to develop an understanding of the challenges taking place in globalised, contemporary workplaces. Organisational consultants, intercultural and international human resource managers and trainers in diversity and intercultural management will also profit from using this book for consulting and training purposes in Chinese and African organisations.

The book is a practical tool to be used to gain insights into basic cultural concepts within Chinese-African encounters to increase the quality of intercultural interactions of Chinese and African cooperation within organisations. It further provides examples of challenges that can occur in these interactions and how to deal with them from differently defined cultural perspectives.

1.5 Contents of the Book and How to Use It

The book is divided into five parts and 19 chapters. Chapter 1 provides a short introduction to intercultural management and intercultural competences, and Chaps. 2 and 3 offer insights into cultural concepts relevant in Chinese and African management. Thereafter, Chaps. 4–19 each describe cases and provide the reader with a deep analysis of research-based real-case scenarios of Chinese-African cultural and business interaction. These cases usually expose intercultural challenges to the cognitive understanding of the situation, affective challenges (i.e. in emotional understanding and knowledge of the situation) and describe the behavioural aspects of the situation.

The case descriptions offer the reader situational cases experienced by Chinese and African employees who have worked in tight intercultural interactions in Chinese organisations in southern Africa. The cases deal with experiences on different levels, referring to individual, group-based or organisation-related experiences gained through interpersonal interactions. The contexts of the cases are provided within the case descriptions.

Table 1.1 Case overview

Case	Theme	Work context	Country
Dealing with international communication, cooperation and negotiation			
1	Dealing with organisational strategies in the Tanzanian-Chinese Chalinze Water Project	Water supply and treatment	Tanzania
2	"Not who I am, not what I mean": Intercultural communication in Chinese-African interactions	Mining, finance, IT and manufacturing	South Africa
3	Dealing with organisational structures, decision-making and participation in the Zambian textile industry	Textile industry	Zambia
4	A negotiation between Chinese and African companies in Namibia	General trading	Namibia
5	How to make friends in Rwanda: A Chinese tea ceremony	Florist and tin smelting	Rwanda
Entrepreneurship, management styles, language and identity			
6	Setting up small, medium and micro enterprises (SMMES) by Chinese entrepreneurial immigrants in Maputo, Mozambique	Retail sector entrepreneurs	Mozambique
7	Managing a Chinese-Angolan national housing project in Angola's capital, Luanda	Housing development	Angola
8	Language, culture and power in the Chinese-South African telecommunications sector	Telecommunications	South Africa
9	Transforming employee conflicts in a Chinese construction firm in Kampala, Uganda	Construction	Uganda
International human resource management			
10	Sharing knowledge in a Sudanese oil refinery through cultural and language trainings	Oil refinery	South Sudan
11	Working conditions in a Chinese-Ugandan communications company	Fibre optics	Uganda
12	Managing a Chinese-South African restaurant in Port Elizabeth, South Africa	Restaurant service industry	South Africa
Management practices and employment relations			
13	Employee perceptions of a Chinese heavy machinery importing organisation in Uganda	Importing	Uganda

(*continued*)

Table 1.1 (continued)

Case	Theme	Work context	Country
14	Hiring and firing in the Chinese-Zimbabwean mining industry	Mining	Zimbabwe
15	Managing Chinese-Cameroonian daily interactions in a company in Douala, Cameroon	Distributor organisation	Cameroon
16	A cross-cultural conference in the Mozambique Confucius Institute	Mining and coal procurement	Mozambique

The structure of the cases is as follows:

A case referring to a relevant Chinese-African intercultural interaction is described based on real experiences of Chinese and African employees. These experiences include the potential for conflict, which stems from the perceptions of either Chinese or African employees.

1. Following the description, questions referring to the case are framed, and readers are invited to respond to the questions.
2. Afterwards, perspectives on the case based on Chinese and African perceptions are explored, thereby providing the reader with cultural insights, perceptions and thought styles of individuals of either Chinese or African descent.
3. In a concluding step, possible solutions from both cultural perspectives are suggested. Based on these possible solutions, best practices are developed in terms of potential successful intercultural interaction.

All case descriptions follow a similar format and can be used in an autodidactical and/or in a group learning environment, such as in training or study groups or courses at high school or university level. Table 1.1 provides an overview of the cases presented in this book.

References

African Economic Outlook. (2014). *Trade Policies and Regional Integration in Africa*. Retrieved from http://www.africaneconomicoutlook.org/fileadmin/uploads/aeo/2014/PDF/Chapter_PDF/03_Chapter3_AEO2014_EN.light.pdf

Barak, M. E. M. (2013). *Managing Diversity. Towards a Globally Inclusive Workplace* (3rd ed.). Los Angeles: Sage.

BBC News. (2015, December 9). Zuma Says China-Africa Co-operation 'Win-Win'. Retrieved from http://www.bbc.com/news/world-africa-35018241

Berardo, K., & Deardorff, D. K. (2012). *Building Cultural Competence: Innovative Activities and Models*. Sterling, VA: Stylus Publishing.

Bird, A., & Fang, T. (2009). Cross Cultural Management in the Age of Globalization. (Editorial). *International Journal of Cross Cultural Management, 9*(2), 139–143.

Bräutigam, D. (2009). *The Dragon's Gift: The Real Story of China in Africa*. Oxford: Oxford University Press.

Bräutigam, D., & Tan, X. (2011). African Shenzhen: China's Special Economic Zones in Africa. *Journal of Modern African Studies, 49*(1), 27–35.

Brewster, C., Carey, L., Grobler, P., Holland, P., & Wärnich, S. (2008). *Contemporary Issues in Human Resource Management: Gaining a Competitive Advantage* (3rd ed.). Cape Town: Oxford University Press.

Deardorff, D. K. (Ed.). (2009). *The SAGE Handbook of Intercultural Competence*. Thousand Oaks, CA: Sage publications.

Glasl, F. (1994). *Das Unternehmen der Zukunft: Moralische Intuiion in der Gestaltung von Organisationen*. Stuttgart: Haupt Verlag.

Goleman, D. (1995). *Emotional Intelligence: Why It Can Matter More than IQ*. London: Bloomsbury.

Goleman, D., Boyatzkis, R., & McKee, A. (2013). *Primal Leadership. Unleashing the Power of Emotional Intelligence*. Boston, MA: Harvard Business Review Press.

Gudykunst, W. B. (Ed.). (1986). *Intergroup Communication*. Baltimore: E. Arnold.

Gudykunst, W. B. (2005). *Theorizing about Intercultural Communication*. Thousand Oaks, CA: Sage.

Gudykunst, W. B., & Kim, Y. Y. (1997). *Communicating with Strangers: An Approach to Intercultural Communication*. New York: McGraw-Hill.

Hall, E. T. (1976). *Beyond Culture*. Garden City, NJ: Anchor.

Hammer, M. R. (2015). The Developmental Paradigm for Intercultural Competence Research. *International Journal of Intercultural Relations, 48*, 12–13.

Handley, R. C., & Louw, M. J. (2016, September). *The Similarities and Differences between South African and Chinese Definitions and Descriptions of Leadership Style: A Mining Joint Venture Case Study*. Proceedings of the 28th Annual

Conference of the Southern African Institute of Management Scientists. Pretoria, South Africa.

Hellriegel, D., Jackson, S. E., Slocum, J., Staude, G., Amos, T., Klopper, H. H., et al. (2007). *Management* (2nd ed.). Cape Town: Oxford Southern Africa.

Hofstede, G. (1995). The Business of International Business Is Culture. In T. Jackson (Ed.), *Cross-cultural Management*. Boston: Butterworth Heinemann.

International Council for Science (ICSU). (2002). Resilience and Sustainable Development. Science Background Paper Commissioned by the Environmental Advisory Council of Swedish Government in Preparation for WSSD. *Series on Science for Sustainable Development*. No.3. Retrieved from http://www.icsu.org/2_resourcecentre/RESOURCE_list:base.php4?rub=8

Jackson, T., Louw, L., & Zhao, S. (2013). China in Sub-Saharan Africa: Implications for HRM Policy and Practice at Organizational Level. *The International Journal of Human Resource Management*, 24(13), 2512–2533.

Jordan, P. J., Ashkanasy, N. M., & Härtel, C. E. J. (2002). *Emotional Intelligence in Work Teams: Construct Definition and Measurement*. Paper presented at the 2nd Biennial Industrial and Organisational Psychology Conference, Melbourne, Australia.

Kamoche, K., Chizema, A., Mellahi, K., & Newenham-Kahindi, A. (2012). New Directions in the Management of Human Resources in Africa. *The International Journal of Human Resource Management*, 23(14), 2825–2834.

Kaplinsky, R., & Morris, M. (2009). Chinese FDI in Sub-Saharan Africa: Engaging with Large Dragons. *European Journal of Development Research*, 21(4), 551–569.

Leiba-O'Sullivan, S. (1999). The Distinction between Stable and Dynamic Cross-cultural Competencies: Implications for Expatriate Trainability. *Journal of International Business Studies*, 30(4), 709–725.

Leung, K., Ang, S., & Tan, M. L. (2014). Intercultural Competence. *Annual Review of Organizational Psychology and Organizational Behaviour*, 1, 489–519.

Lloyd, S., & Härtel, E. J. (2003, March). *The Intercultural Competencies Required for Inclusive and Effective Culturally Diverse Work Teams* (Working paper). Melbourne: Monash University.

Martin, J. N., & Nakayama, T. K. (2015). Reconsidering Intercultural (Communication) Competence in the Workplace: A Dialectical Approach. *Language and Intercultural Communication*, 15(1), 13–28.

Mayer, C.-H. (2008a). *Managing Conflict Across Cultures, Values and Identities: A Case Study in the South African Automotive Industry*. Stuttgart: Tectum.

Mayer, C.-H. (2008b). *Trainingshandbuch interkulturelle Mediation und Konfliktbearbeitung*. 2. Auflage. Münster: Waxmann.

Mayer, C.-H. (2011). *The Meaning of Sense of Coherence in Transcultural Management (Internationale Hochschulschriften Series)*. Münster: Waxmann.

Mayer, C.-H., Boness, C. M., & Louw, L. (2017). Perceptions of Chinese and Tanzanian Employees Regarding Intercultural Collaboration. *South African*

Journal of Human Resource Management, 15, a921. Retrieved from https://sajhrm.co.za/index.php/sajhrm/article/view/921/1304. https://doi.org/10.4102/sajhrm.v15i0.921

Mayer, C.-H., Boness, C. M., Louw, L., & Louw, M. J. (2016, September). *Intra- and Inter-group Perceptions of Chinese and Tanzanian Employees in Intercultural Cooperation*. Proceedings of the 28th Annual Conference of the Southern African Institute of Management Scientists. Pretoria, South Africa.

Mayer, C.-H., & Krause, C. (2011). Promoting Mental Health and Salutogenesis in Transcultural Organisational and Work Contexts. *International Review of Psychiatry, 23*(6), 495–500.

Mayer, C.-H., & Louw, L. (2012). Managing Cross-cultural Conflicts in Organizations. (Editorial). *International Journals of Cross Cultural Management, 12*(1), 3–8.

Mayer, C.-H., Tonelli, L., Oosthuizen, R. M., & Surtee, S. (2018). You Have to Keep Your Head on Your Shoulders': A Systems Psychodynamic Perspective on Women Leaders. *SA Journal of Industrial Psychology, 44*(0), a1424. Retrieved from https://sajip.co.za/index.php/sajip/article/view/1424/2214. https://doi.org/10.4102/sajip.v44i0.1424

Mayer, J., & Salovey, P. (1994). The Intelligence of Emotional Intelligence. *Intelligence, 17*(4), 433–442.

Michelle, L., Bateman, A., Gerrity, R., & Myint, H. H. (2017). Bridging Transitions Through Cultural Understanding and Identity. *Pedagogies of Educational Transitions, 16*, 29–42.

Moran, R. T., Abramson, N. R., & Moran, S. V. (2016). *Managing Cultural Differences* (9th ed.). London: Routledge.

Moreland, R. L., Levine, J. M., & Wingert, M. L. (2013). Creating the Ideal Group: Composition Effects at Work. In E. Witte & J. H. Davis (Eds.), *Understanding Group Behaviour. Small Group Processes and Interpersonal Relations* (Vol. 2, pp. 11–36). New York: Psychology Press, Taylor & Francis Group.

Ni, N. (2015). *Gaining Momentum: Johannesburg Summit to Consolidate China-Africa Partnership*. FOCAC Johannesburg Summit. [Special issue], 20–23.

Okech, J. E. A., Pimpleton-Gray, A. M., Vannatta, E., & Champe, J. (2016). Intercultural Conflict in Groups. *The Journal for Specialists in Group Work, 41*(4), 350–369.

Park, Y. J., & Alden, C. (2013). 'Upstairs' and 'Downstairs' Dimensions of China and the Chinese in South Africa. In The South African Human Rights Commission's Publication. *State of the Nation*. Retrieved from http://www.ru.ac.za/media/rhodesuniversity/content/sociology/documents/HSRC-SON_China,and,Chinese,in,SA_YJParkCAlden.doc

Pellowski, A. (2016). The Importance of Storytelling in Developing Cultural Understanding. In A. Y. Goldsmith, T. Heras, & S. Còrapo (Eds.), *Reading the*

World's Stories. An Annotated Biography of Intercultural Literature (pp. 7–8). London: Rowman & Littlefield.

Rosen, R., Digh, P., Singer, M., & Phillips, C. (2000). *Global Literacies: Lessons on Business Leadership and National Cultures.* New York, NY: Simon & Schuster.

Sabee, C. M. (2015). Interpersonal Communication Skill/Competence. *The International Encyclopedia of Interpersonal Communication.* Wiley & Sons.

Samovar, L., Porter, R., McDaniel, E., & Roy, C. (2014). *Intercultural Communication: A reader.* Boston: Cengage.

Schnabel, D., Kelava, A., van de Vijver, F. J. R., & Seifert, L. (2015). Examining Psychometric Properties, Measurement Invariance, and Construct Validity of a Short Version of the Test to Measure Intercultural Competence (TMIC-S) in Germany and Brazil. *International Journal of Intercultural Relations, 49,* 137–155. https://doi.org/10.1016/j.ijintrel.2015.08.00

Schwartz, T. (1992). Anthropology and Psychology. An Unrequired Relationship. In T. Schwartz, G. White, & G. Lutz (Eds.), *New Directions in Psychological Anthropology.* Cambridge: University Press.

Spencer-Rodgers, J., & McGovern, T. (2002). Attitudes toward the Culturally Different: The Role of Intercultural Communication Barriers, Affective Responses, Consensual Stereotypes, and Perceived Threat. *International Journal of Intercultural Relations, 26,* 609–631.

Spitzberg, B. H. (2007). *CSRS: The Conversational Skills Rating Scale: An Instructional Assessment of Interpersonal Competence. NCA Diagnostic Series* (2nd ed.). Annandale, VA: National Communication Association.

Ting-Toomey, S. (2007). Researching Intercultural Conflict Competence. *Journal of International Communication, 13,* 7–30.

UNESCO. (2009). World Report No. 2: Investing in Cultural Diversity and Intercultural Dialogue. Paris: UNESCO. Retrieved from http://www.unesco.org/en/world-reports/cultural-diversity

UNESCO. (2013). *Intercultural Competences. Conceptional and Operational Framework.* Paris, France: UNESCO. Retrieved from http://unesdoc.unesco.org/images/0021/002197/219768e.pdf

Wang, D., Freeman, S., & Zhu, C. J. (2013). Personality Traits and Cross-cultural Competence of Chinese Expatriate Managers: A Socio-analytic and Institutional Perspective. *The International Journal of Human Resource Management, 24*(20), 1–9.

Xing, Y., Liu, Y., Tarba, S. Y., & Cooper, C. L. (2016). Intercultural Influences on Managing African Employees of Chinese Firms in Africa: Chinese Managers' HRM Practices. *International Business Review, 25*(1 Part A), 28–41. https://doi.org/10.1016/j.ibusrev.2014.05.003

Yum, J. O. (1982). Communication Diversity and Information Acquisition among Korean Immigrants in Hawaii. *Human Communication Research, 8,* 154–169.

CHAPTER 2

Chinese Cultural Concepts and Their Influence on Management

Zhaoyi Liu

2.1 INTRODUCTION

Since the end of the 1990s, as part of economic globalisation and integration, the scale and scope of China's investment in Africa has continued to expand. Under the impetus of the Chinese government's "going-out" strategy and the China-Africa Cooperation Forum, economic and trade relations between China and Africa have developed rapidly.

China has invested as much as US$136 billion in Africa over the past 17 years (Reference news, 2018). China is Africa's largest investor and the largest trading partner of most African countries. The trade volume between China and Africa increased from US$765 million in 1978 to US$170 billion in 2017, an increase of more than 200 times (Liu & Huang, 2018). Approximately 3100 Chinese companies are investing in Africa, covering transportation, energy, telecommunications, industrial park construction, agricultural technology centres, water supply, schools and hospitals (Shen & Yu, 2019).

In particular, the projects involving Chinese enterprises have brought practical convenience to African countries by promoting local resource

Z. Liu (✉)
Department of Management, Rhodes University, Grahamstown, South Africa

© The Author(s) 2019
C.-H. Mayer et al. (eds.), *Managing Chinese-African Business Interactions*, Palgrave Studies in African Leadership,
https://doi.org/10.1007/978-3-030-25185-7_2

endowments and demographic dividends and accelerating the transformation of endogenous power. Take the Mombasa-Nairobi Railway as an example: it is the largest infrastructure project since Kenya's independence and is considered an engine for local economic development. Data show that the Kenyan railroad project undertaken by China Road and Bridge Corporation, including the Inner Mongolia Railway, has boosted Kenya's GDP growth by more than 1.5% (Guo, 2019).

For African countries, Chinese enterprises have provided funds and technology that are urgently needed by local communities and have made significant contributions to local economic and social development on the continent.

2.2 Origins of Chinese Culture

As a consequence of China's extensive global investment, Chinese culture has attracted the attention of the world as a cultural symbol with a wide influence. The nation's culture is well established, extensive and profound, having been shaped by China's unique geographical location, history, custom and traditions.

Chinese culture is based on Chinese civilisation and fully integrates the cultural elements of its varied regions, ideological traditions and conceptual forms. It refers to Confucius as its soul, but it has also adopted the theories of Tao, Buddhism, Law, Bing and Moh, and has finally formed a matured rule system (Zuo, 2015). Chinese traditional culture is closely related to people's lives and is deeply integrated into their daily behaviours.

Chinese culture is fostered by a natural agricultural economy. In ancient China, rulers used agriculture to establish the country, and it has become the foundation for maintaining the prosperity and stability of the entire society. Based on agriculture, China created a farming family system form that was unique in the world (Shi, 2007).

In the feudal society of China, the concept of patriarchal law evolved into a system of "three cardinal guides and five permanent members" as national governance guidelines (Shi, 2007). These guidelines also constituted the criterion for interpersonal relationship in the Chinese feudal era. Confucianism is at the core of Chinese traditional culture, and its development and evolution runs through the entire ancient Chinese culture (Jiang, 2007).

2.3 Application of Specific Concepts in Chinese-Style Management

Chinese-style management refers to a modern management science that is guided by Chinese philosophy, which fully considers Chinese cultural traditions, psychology, beliefs and behavioural characteristics (Jin & Jiang, 2008). Because Chinese culture has a profound influence on Chinese people's lives, it is also widely adopted in their management activities. The following are some specific concepts and terms from Chinese culture which are of great importance to researchers.

2.3.1 Confucianism

Stressing the importance of correct behaviour, loyalty and obedience to hierarchy, Confucianism is a system of ethics devised by the Chinese scholar K'ung Fu-tzu (latinised to "Confucius") in China of the sixth century BC (Goscha, 2017). Although transformed over time, it is still the substance of learning, the source of values and the social code of the Chinese (Tu, 2019). The main content of Confucianism is divided into two parts: *Ren* and *He* (Guo, 2007).

Ren (benevolence) is the core concept and highest category of Confucianism. In the Confucian view, benevolence is the ultimate value basis and psychological origin of all moral and ethical principles that guarantee social order (Jiang, 2007). Benevolence is a principle of behaviour derived from people. It requires people to love each other, which reflects people's awareness of themselves and an understanding of the essence of human beings (Guo, 2007). It contains a robust humanitarian spirit. When applied to management, *Ren* requires leaders to cultivate a higher moral standing, to be strict with themselves, to be patient with others and not to use powers indiscriminately. This concept is always able to encourage the enthusiasm and creativity of employees. Additionally, benevolence requires employees to be united, to help each other, to be friendly and to strive for progress together.

He (harmony) in Confucian philosophy is the criterion for dealing with interpersonal relationships (Chen, 2008). This principle requires people to support each other, to be tolerant and to be humble. Confucianism attaches great importance to harmony in terms of politics and society and regards it as one of the basic principles. In business management, *He* is the guarantee of corporate cohesion. It is believed that only when people can unite and work together can the business move forward. In a Chinese enterprise, it is commonly understood that the victory of the whole team is the only real victory. "*He*" reflects a high degree of collectivism in this aspect.

2.3.2 Guanxi

Guanxi (connections) plays a vital role in the social interaction of Chinese people and is also one of the most controversial topics in Chinese culture. Interpersonal interactions, whether in work or in private, are full of *Guanxi* elements. Sometimes people would even sacrifice their own interests to maintain or achieve valuable *Guanxi*.

Chinese society regards *Guanxi* as the foundation of economic and social organisations (Hwang, 1987). The essence of *Guanxi* is premised on reciprocal exchanges between "in-circle" members (Fei, 1992; Hwang, 1987). In China, it forms a unique social culture in which "who you know" is more important than "what you know" (Yeung & Tung, 1996). *Guanxi* is the social interaction between people in the interconnected network space. It can also be regarded as an infinitely cyclical game (Davies, 1995). *Guanxi* is a practice of conveying goodwill and benefits to each other, fully guaranteeing mutual trust and minimising external uncertainties and risky factors (Piao, 2006).

The Chinese are convinced that *Guanxi* can enhance the competitiveness of enterprises, make it easier to access scarce resources and achieve long-term survival and development (Luo, 1997; Pearce & Robinson, 2000; Tsang, 1998; Yeung & Tung, 1996). When compared with complex and rigid rules and regulations, the *Guanxi* network, based on mutual trust and mutual benefit, can better avoid risks and bring wealth to enterprises or individuals.

2.3.3 Mianzi

In Chinese culture, *Mianzi* (face) is reputation, and it is also the respect that people have earned in the process of continuous effort and progress. The basic principle of Chinese interpersonal communication is to maintain face. *Mianzi* is obtained in two ways: first, it is naturally obtained by a certain inherent identity or status; second, it is won by hard work (Wang, 2017). Chinese traditional society attaches great importance to family reputation. Fame and achievement belong not only to the person concerned but also to the whole family, including the ancestors and the offspring to come. This belief reinforces the stimulating effect of *Mianzi* on people's behaviour.

Mianzi is a non-institutional constraint mechanism in Chinese-style management, which has a very complicated impact on management. On the one hand, the intervention of *Mianzi* often weakens an enterprise's management system. Managers not only pursue the maximisation of company interests but also need to consider the involvement of *Mianzi* issues. On the other hand, *Mianzi* can work as a binding force. Enterprises need to bear more social ethical responsibilities and to gain a public appreciation for social recognition, which is also an aspect of *Mianzi* (Chen, 2018).

2.3.4 Industriousness, Righteousness and Integrity

The values of industriousness, righteousness and integrity in Chinese culture have always supported the Chinese in their darkest times.

China has a long history of practising industriousness as part of traditional culture, which is deeply embedded in the blood of the Chinese nation, and it has become the intrinsic quality and national spirit of the people (Zuo, 2015). The Chinese firmly believe that as long as they work hard, they will undoubtedly harvest successfully. Therefore, in Chinese companies, it appears that many employees and managers are delighted to work overtime in order to achieve sales goals or reach company targets.

Righteousness refers to ethics and corresponds to probability in business. Confucianists believe righteousness is essential to a person or a business, and they think profitability is less critical in comparison to righteousness (Feng, 2018). It is believed that profit obtained by using improper means will also be lost in illegal operations. Therefore righteousness is often a motto-like existence for Chinese business people.

Integrity is the essential requirement of a Chinese business person, and it is also a major reason for a company being widely respected. China's successful companies are all known for their loyalty and trustworthiness, and they rely on integrity to win in fierce market competition.

2.3.5 Collectivism

Chinese people are committed to teamwork and interdependence, often seeking recognition and belonging in the group. The Chinese feel comfortable being in the crowd, believing and relying on the power of the group, and tend to share or else evade responsibility. In real life, people believe that personal goals and interests will be sacrificed for the team when necessary, as the minority should obey the majority.

In Chinese enterprises, collectivism is manifested in a collective sense of honour and in "hiding personal existence" (Chen, 2008). The principle of a collective sense of honour opposes individual heroism. It emphasises the power of the group and encourages the honour that belongs to the team. Observing the principle of hiding personal existence makes people rather follow the crowd and be willing to keep silent when they encounter issues. The ancient teachings of "tall trees catch much wind" and "a famed person and a fattened pig are alike in danger" are still valued. The Chinese generally believe that following the tenet of "a man of great wisdom often appears slow-witted" is the best way to live (Huang, 2017).

2.3.6 Hierarchy

In China, the concept of hierarchy was formed with the emergence of feudal society, thousands of years ago. The hierarchies of ancient China were demonstrated in a formidable political system: all bureaucracies must obey the will of the emperor who has all powers and resources and the highest discretion.

Hierarchy is still a significant feature of Chinese-style management. It is a manifestation of the traditional Chinese leadership culture represented by class and patriarchy, and with autocratic rule at its core (Wei, 2003). For some leaders, authoritarianism may completely override Ren and He in the workplace. The authoritarian leadership style enables leaders to appoint people according to favouritism and to act in an arbitrary fashion, as there is no restriction on the leaders' behaviour. This indulgence severely limits the creativity and enthusiasm of the employees and affects the development of the enterprise. The authoritarian leadership style is further discussed under Sects. 2.4.3 and 2.5.3.

2.3.7 Patriarchy

As an extension of hierarchy culture, China's patriarchy is also worthy of attention. Patriarchy emphasises the male-centred form of power operation (Liu, 2005). In traditional Chinese society, all authoritative positions are reserved for men, and women are in a disadvantaged and obedient position (Li, 2003). Directly related to patriarchy is the concept of patriarchalism in China. According to Du (2001), daughters are considered useless from birth because a girl's future child is not allowed to carry her family name—whereas having a son is excellent because his family name will continue to be used.

In business, the patriarchal position is illustrated in the imbalance of the status of male and female employees. Usually, females have fewer opportunities for promotion, assignment and salary increases.

2.3.8 *Chinese* Baijiu *Culture and Tea Culture*

Baijiu is China's national liquor. This strong spirit-drinking culture dates back over 6000 years and holds a unique place in Chinese culture and history (GB Times, 2016, para. 1). In ancient times, alcohol was never absent from ceremonies honouring ancestors, holiday banquets or family celebrations (Shen, 2003).

Toasting is an essential ongoing ritual in China. The host or the eldest person is expected to make the first toast, and the honoured guests return the toast to the host or the eldest. Chinese people like to entertain guests with *Baijiu* to show their best wishes.

Tea-drinking is also an integral part of Chinese culture. China is an original tea producer and is known for its technology of growing and making tea. For centuries, tea has played an essential role as a significant beverage, therapeutic medicine and status symbol in China; this is why its theory of origin is often religious or royal.

The Chinese tea ceremony—drinking and appreciating tea—is regarded as a combination of philosophy and lifestyle. It contains the wisdom of oriental philosophy, which reflects the central idea of Taoism, Confucianism and Buddhism. Chinese people believe that the tea ceremony can enhance friendship, cultivate virtues and refresh the mind.

2.3.9 *Hukou*

Hu in Chinese is the family; *Kou* means the population. China's *Hukou* is a system in which the government registers and manages the population on a family basis, including name, age, birth, address, occupation, education level and marital status of each family member, all of which are registered in a small booklet called *Hukouben* (household registration booklet). Every family holds one of these booklets; it is an important family document.

Uneven development of politics and the economy in different regions of China has caused differences in the rights and opportunities that residents can receive. This difference has added value to the Hukou (Chen, 2005). In Chinese companies, the *Hukou* status of employees can sometimes determine whether they are eligible for a particular position. Many companies have strict restrictions concerning residents' *Hukou*, which can also lead to the loss of talent from a company, or unfair handling of employees' welfare.

2.3.10 Danwei

In the past, in Chinese urban communities, people were always affiliated with an individual *Danwei* (unit). In the *Danwei*, people live together, interact and depend on each other in their daily lives. Simultaneously, since the resources are mainly distributed by the unit monopoly, the relationship between individuals and units becomes abnormally close (Bo, 2014). The unit not only provides employment but also provides housing resettlement, organisational identity, childbirth management, education, training and other services to the urban population (Li, 2004). The unit has gradually evolved into the most effective means of socialist governance and has become a source of membership and social belonging (Li, 2008).

With China's ongoing development, the unit can no longer integrate everyone's work and life in the internal space; instead, increasingly more service functions are passed on to the market and society (Yang & Zhou, 1999). Today, the *Danwei* system still exists in China. The concept of the *Danwei* has trained the Chinese people's cohesiveness and living habits of unity. For Chinese enterprises, *Danwei* offers an ideal model for managers to create a collective spirit and a sense of belonging.

2.4 Questionable Value of Chinese-Style Management Behaviours

Because of the profound influence of traditional Chinese culture on business, some Chinese business management styles differ significantly from Western management styles. The value of some of these commonly used Chinese management approaches is therefore disputable in Western terms. The performance and possible consequences of these Chinese-style management behaviours in non-Chinese contexts are discussed in the following paragraphs.

2.4.1 Chinese-Style Decision-Making

For business leaders, corporate decision-making should be based on the company's goals and mission (Sun, 2005). However, in Chinese companies, achieving the company's goals and mission should not be the sole criterion for decision-making because everything is multifaceted. Any decision must be coordinated and balanced among various relevant factors. For example, the company may need to achieve the government's development goals, accomplish provincial tasks, meet the needs of the investors and grant *Mianzi* to some partners. Any decision-making process must be repeatedly considered and previewed, as it is not just to maximise corporate profitability. This opinion is a reappearance of the spirit of righteousness, collectivism and harmony in Chinese traditional culture. Obviously, such Chinese-style decision-making often delays the project and causes misunderstandings with Western partners.

2.4.2 Family-Based Management

The circle of Chinese interpersonal relationships spreads out from the family at the centre; the degree of trust and the affinity between people is progressively weakened in layers (Fei, 1998). In Chinese family-based companies, many business owners also wish to adopt a modern enterprise system to facilitate the company's growth. For this purpose, business owners may hire professional managers to take care of the company. However, for many important positions such as sales, finance, human resources and payroll, they still only employ their family members, in order to be able to monitor such non-family managers (Sun, 2005). In this situation, the actions of professional managers are highly constrained. As a consequence, the long-term development of the business will be affected.

2.4.3 Chinese Authoritarian Leadership

Authoritarian leadership stems from the cultural traditions of Confucianism and legalism (Farh & Cheng, 2000; Farh, Liang, Chou, & Cheng, 2008). Under the influence of the Confucian value system, a father has absolute authority and power over his children and other family members in a traditional Chinese family (Cheng & Wang, 2015). In traditional Chinese organisations, leaders often implement this value by establishing a centralised hierarchy and by assuming a father-like role with an authentic leadership style (Peng, Lu, Shenkar, & Wang, 2001). The leader controls all decisions, and little input from group members are needed (Cherry, 2010). Also, authoritarian leaders insist on adherence to high standards and punish employees for poor performance (Wang, Chiang, Tsai, Lin, & Cheng, 2013).

Authority which is based on hierarchical difference predicts adverse outcomes, including fear of the leader, work pressure and increased turnover intention (Farh & Cheng, 2000; Wang, Cheng, & Wang, 2016). Authoritarian leadership frequently results in the absence of creative solutions to issues, which could ultimately harm group performance (Chen & Farh, 2010). However, several recent studies have also identified positive consequences of authoritarian leadership on employee behaviours (Schaubroeck, Shen, & Chong, 2017). For example, when the organisational level is small, the structure is simple and information is transmitted directly and quickly within the company, which may save management costs and improve operational efficiency (Zhang & Zhang, 2005).

2.4.4 "Pushing, Dragging and Pulling" Crisis Management

From a traditional Chinese viewpoint, if a person has a successful career but is not proficient in using the golden mean to deal with interpersonal relationships, he has significant defects (Chen, 2003). Chinese people are trained to use the doctrine of the mean to handle various difficulties in their daily lives. Similarly, Chinese management is likely to utilise the doctrine of the mean to deal with conflict.

In a situation of conflict or crisis, Chinese managers advocate "pushing, dragging and pulling". This method comes from the Taoist culture, which instructs that one cannot solve a problem immediately; collect more information and approach it from other directions or else let the time change the problem, and then the problem will solve itself (Chen, 1996). As time goes on, many aspects of the problem will shift, which may lead to a transformation of the nature of the problem. Therefore, "pushing, dragging and pulling" method will return the initiative to the problem-solvers.

In Western management terms, however, this pushing, dragging and pulling approach generally becomes a form of repugnant bureaucratic behaviour and can be a manifestation of shirking responsibility.

2.4.5 Excessively Implicit Expression

The conservative traditions in Chinese culture prompt Chinese managers to express themselves indirectly by using euphemisms and implicit communication. They conceal the true meanings behind the words and require others to speculate on their real intentions from the context of speech at the time, using non-verbal clues such as tone, facial expressions and movements (Zeng, 2006).

In international business cooperation, Chinese managers often encounter problems and issues in cross-cultural communication, owing to the language barrier and cultural differences (Liu, 2018). Western employees or partners can either fail to discern the Chinese manager's real opinions or misunderstand the message and act according to incorrect assumptions.

2.5 Improvement Strategies and Recommendations for African Partners

Some of the Chinese management behaviours elaborated on in the previous section is now discussed in terms of the improvements required to make international collaborations succeed. Recommendations are also made to assist African managers and staff when dealing with these Chinese-style management approaches in Chinese-owned companies.

2.5.1 Chinese-Style Decision-Making

According to Janczak (2005), in some cases, when the future is uncertain and accurate information is limited, managers must rely on their past experience as well as their instincts to make decisions. However, in most decision-making, to avoid the influence of external factors, managers should comply with the company's existing core values to bring the company's goals and aspirations into the process (Richa & Tiwary, 2019).

In the case of Chinese-African business cooperation, if African managers meet a typical Chinese-style decision-maker, it is recommended that they urge the decision-maker to make comprehensive judgements, by following a standard procedure, based on the values and common interests of both parties.

2.5.2 Family-Based Management

Nordqvist, Sharma, and Chirico (2014) claim that family ownership percentage is a crucial variable that may influence family governance and business performance. O'Boyle, Pollack, and Rutherford (2012) also point out that a high proportion of kinship in business management will inevitably lead to the "ethicalisation" of interpersonal relationships in a corporation and eliminating the role of corporate rules and regulations. The goal of the business is to achieve competitiveness and sustainability. Therefore, the family business should craft strict policies on roles and responsibilities of key positions, to demonstrate the business's operation mechanism and the rule of integrity.

When encountering Chinese family-managed enterprises, African managers should respect the traditions of the family. In cooperation, the African management system should be gradually demonstrated and practised in work, to offset the constraints brought by their family governance.

2.5.3 Authoritarian Leadership

Studies reveal that leadership style, organisational performance and work satisfaction are closely interrelated (Bass, 1985; Bass & Avolio, 1993; Berson, 2003; Bogler, 2001). Therefore it is vital for leaders to intellectually stimulate their followers (Avolio, Bass, & Jung, 1999; Bass, Avolio, Jung, & Berson, 2003) and promote their efforts to be creative (Riggio & Reichard, 2008). New ideas and creative solutions to problems come from followers who challenge their traditions and beliefs; they should be encouraged (Jung, Chow, & Wu, 2003) so that the followers will express themselves openly without fear of negative interpersonal consequences (Kahn, 1990). Furthermore, a company must have clear rules and regulations. The power of the leader should not exceed the authority of these rules and regulations.

In the context of Chinese-managed companies in Africa, work efficiency will be of least concern to Chinese management. However, it is necessary for the company's team to adapt to transformational leadership. This is the form of leadership which will stimulate the potential, enthusiasm and individual initiative of the company's employees. It is recommended that a set of new company management regulations should be drafted to control the subjectivity and arbitrariness that existed in the previous authoritarian leadership style.

2.5.4 Moderate Crisis Management

The origin of the concepts of business management is different in Chinese and Western cultures; hence, one cannot judge which style is better than the other (Wei, 2003). Whether the Chinese style of pushing, dragging and pulling crisis management is useful depends on the way the methods are employed, the motivation for using them and the handler's quality.

When African and Chinese managers have different opinions facing a business crisis, both parties should first have open communication and discuss the nature of the issue, the pros and cons of each method, and time and cost consumption aspects. Sharing all the related information with all team members and using brainstorming to work out the possible solution options are recommended. Both parties must share the knowledge and responsibilities in this regard and work in a harmonious atmosphere.

2.5.5 Excessively Implicit Expression

Instead of utilising implicit expression, Chinese managers should try to express themselves in a straightforward manner to avoid misunderstanding, which may cause corporate losses and interpersonal relationship damage. Because the language barrier between Africans and the Chinese is already an issue for both parties, implicit expression will only make it worse. To solve this problem, managers need to establish a strict communication rule, which everyone must follow to avoid misunderstandings.

If African managers encounter implicit expressions during the communication, a request should be sent to Chinese management to explain their meaning and intention in a clear, unambiguous manner. If the Chinese managers find it difficult to express in simple words, the explanation can be requested in the form of an email, which will help to leave a written record for future reference.

2.6 CONCLUSION

Chinese culture is deeply imprinted in Chinese people's moral values, modes of perception, behavioural norms and even social psychology, and it has become the ascendant force shaping unique Chinese traits.

Chinese traditional management behaviours have both positive and negative aspects. In the process of establishing a modern enterprise system and management model, Chinese managers must adopt advanced Western management techniques and implement an organisational and scientific management system.

When Africans work in Chinese corporations, they need to respect the traditional culture and utilise various ways to eliminate the negative aspects of Chinese traditional management behaviours. African managers can employ positive and advanced management skills to seek efficiency in operation, understanding in communication and success in cooperation.

REFERENCES

Avolio, B. J., Bass, B. M., & Jung, D. I. (1999). Re-examining the Components of Transformational and Transactional Leadership using the Multifactor Leadership. *Journal of Occupational and Organizational Psychology, 72,* 461–462. https://doi.org/10.1348/096317999166789

Bass, B. M. (1985). *Leadership and Performance Beyond Expectations* (pp. 3–242). New York: Free Press.

Bass, B. M., & Avolio, B. J. (1993). Transformational Leadership and Organizational Culture. *Public Administration Quarterly, 12,* 113–121.

Bass, B. M., Avolio, B. J., Jung, D. I., & Berson, Y. (2003). Predicting Unit Performance by Assessing Transformational and Transactional Leadership. *Journal of Applied Psychology, 88,* 207–218.

Berson, J. L. (2003). An Examination of the Relationships between Leadership Style, Quality, and Employee Satisfaction in R&D versus Administrative Environments. *R & D Management, 35*(1), 51–60. https://doi.org/10.1109/IEMC.2003.1252304

Bo, D. W. (2014). *Social Space and Governance in Urban China: The Danwei System from Origins to Reform* (pp. 222–225). Nanjing: Southeast University Press.

Bogler, R. (2001). The Influence of Leadership Style on Teacher Job Satisfaction. *Educational Administration Quarterly, 37*(5), 662–683.

Chen, B. Y. (1996). Language Influence Cultural in Two Ways. *Philosophical Research, 2,* 8–11.

Chen, R. Y. (2003). *Entrepreneur's Outline* (pp. 259–587). Beijing: Science Press.

Chen, C. L. (2005, November 14). The Status Quo and Reform of China's "Hukou" System, CCTV News Interview. *China Law Network.* Retrieved from https://www.iolaw.org.cn/showArticle.aspx?id=1729

Chen, S. H. (2008). Research on the Construction of Enterprise Culture Based on Chinese Traditional Culture. *Changchun University of Science and Technology Researches, 8,* 20–21.

Chen, L. L. (2018). *Theories and Methods of Corporate Culture Shaping* (pp. 29–33). Chengdu: Southwestern University of Finance and Economics Press.

Chen, C. C., & Farh, J. L. (2010). Developments in Understanding Chinese Leadership: Paternalism and Its Elaborations, Moderations, and Alternatives. *Chinese Psychology, 29,* 599–622.

Cheng, M. Y., & Wang, L. (2015). The Mediating Effect of Ethical Climate on the Relationship between Paternalistic Leadership and Team Identification: A Team-level Analysis in the Chinese Context. *Ethics Journals, 129,* 639–654.

Cherry, K. (2010). *The Everything Psychology Book* (2nd ed., pp. 157–158). Avon, MA: Adams Media.

Davies, H. (1995). *China Business: Context and Issues.* Hong Kong: Longman Asia.

Du, F. Q. (2001). The Historical Context of Women's Studies: Patriarchy, Modernity and Gender Relations. *Zhejiang Academic Journal, 55*–59.

Farh, J. L., & Cheng, B. S. (2000). A Cultural Analysis of Paternalistic Leadership in Chinese Organizations. *Management and Organizations,* 84–127.

Farh, J. L., Liang, J., Chou, L. F., & Cheng, B. S. (2008). Paternalistic Leadership in Chinese Organizations: Research Progress and Future Research Directions. In *Leadership and Management in China: Philosophies, Theories, and Practices* (pp. 171–205). Cambridge: Cambridge University Press.

Fei, X. (1992). *From the Soil: The Foundations of Chinese Society.* Berkeley, CA: University of California Press.

Fei, X. T. (1998). *Native China Fertility System* (pp. 200–226). Beijing: Peking University Press.

Feng, F. (2018, September 5). Righteousness and Profitability, Choose the First One. *Guangming Daily.* Retrieved from https://www.rujiazg.com/article/14587

GB Times. (2016, November 2). The Spirit of Chinese Alcohol Drinking Culture. Retrieved from https://gbtimes.com/spirit-chinese-alcohol-drinking-culture

Goscha, C. (2017, March 9). What Is Confucianism? A Short Introduction to the Chinese Ethical System. *History Today.* Retrieved from https://www.history-today.com/history-matters/what-confucianism

Guo, X. D. (2007). A Modern Interpretation of Confucius's thought of "The Doctrine of the Mean". *China University of Petroleum Researches, 7,* 25–35.

Guo, J. (2019, March 11). Financial Observation: "One Belt, One Road" Boosts China-Africa Economic and Trade Cooperation towards High Quality Development. *Xinhua Net.* Retrieved from http://www.xinhuanet.com/2019-03/11/c_1210079151.htm

Huang, J. L. (2017). "Mianzi" and Human Order Function and Its Current Variation. *National Philosophy and Social Science Academic Journal, 1,* 14–56.

Hwang, K. (1987). Face and Favour: The Chinese Power Game. *American Journal of Sociology, 92*(4), 944–974.

Janczak, S. (2005). The Strategic Decision-Making Process in Organizations. *Problems & Perspectives in Management, 3,* 58–70.

Jiang, L. Y. (2007). *The Application of Confucian "Ren he Yi Xin" thought in Current Enterprise Management* (Vol. 7, pp. 13–14). Nanjing University of Science and Technology Researches.

Jin, S. Y., & Jiang, X. Z. (2008). Performance Evaluation of Chinese State-owned Enterprises: Status, Trends and Indicator Selection. *Journal of Management, 3,* 166–182.

Jung, D. I., Chow, C., & Wu, A. (2003). The Role of Transformational Leadership in Enhancing Organizational Innovation: Hypotheses and Some Preliminary Findings. *The Leadership Quarterly, 14,* 525–544.

Kahn, W. A. (1990). Psychological Conditions of Personal Engagement and Disengagement at Work. *Academy of Management Journal, 33*, 15–66.

Li, F. (2003). *The Evolution of Modern Patriarchal Theory* (pp. 20–28). Shanghai: Shanghai University Press.

Li, H. L. (2004). *Chinese Unit Society* (pp. 299–331). Shanghai: People's Publishing House.

Li, H. L. (2008). The 30 Years of Reform and the Change of China's Unit System-Analysis and Thinking. *Academic Dynamics, 18*, 25–29.

Liu, S. Q. (2005). About Matriarchy and Patriarchy. *Journal of Henan University (Social Science Edition), 11*, 25–26.

Liu, Z. (2018). Development Report on Chinese Private Enterprises in South Africa. In *China-South Africa Cultural Exchange Development Report 2017–2018* (pp. 30–45). Zhejiang: People's Publishing House.

Liu, A. L., & Huang, M. B. (2018). Analysis of the Impact of China's Direct Investment in Africa. *Xiamen University Forum on International Development, 2*, 50–55.

Luo, Y. (1997). Guanxi: Principles, Philosophies and Implications. *Human Systems Management, 16*(1), 43–52.

Nordqvist, M., Sharma, P., & Chirico, F. (2014). Family Firm Heterogeneity and Governance: A Configuration Approach. *Journal of Small Business Management, 52*, 192–209.

O'Boyle, E. H., Pollack, J. M., & Rutherford, M. W. (2012). Exploring the Relation between Family Involvement and Firms' Financial Performance: A Meta-analysis of Main and Moderator Effects. *Journal of Business Venturing, 27*, 1–18.

Pearce, J. A., & Robinson, R. B. (2000). Cultivating Guanxi as a Foreign Investor Strategy. *Business Horizons, 43*(1), 31–38.

Peng, M. W., Lu, Y., Shenkar, O., & Wang, D. Y. L. (2001). Treasures in the China House: A Review of Management and Organizational Research on Greater China. *Business Management, 52*, 95–110.

Piao, Y. C. (2006). The Guanxi Culture in Chinese Society. *Study View Journals, 5*, 1–5.

Reference News. (2018, September 18). China's Investment in Africa Has Brought Benefits to Both Sides, Making the West Unable to Match. Retrieved from http://mil.news.sina.com.cn/2018-09-18/doc-ifxeuwwr5497812.shtml

Richa, S., & Tiwary, M. L. S. (2019). *Decision Making* (pp. 1–2). Salem Press Encyclopedia.

Riggio, R. E., & Reichard, R. J. (2008). The Emotional and Social Intelligences of Effective Leadership: An Emotional and Social Skill Approach. *Journal of Managerial Psychology, 23*, 169–185.

Schaubroeck, J. M., Shen, Y., & Chong, S. (2017). A Dual-stage Moderated Mediation Model Linking Authoritarian Leadership to Follower Outcomes.

Journal of Applied Psychology, 102(2), 203–214. https://doi.org/10.1037/apl0000165

Shen, D. M. (2003). Spirits and Tea: A Comparative Study of Two Cultural Symbols. *China Economic History Forum, National History*. Retrieved from http://agri-history.ihns.ac.cn/scholars/sdm.htm

Shen, C., & Yu, J. X. (2019, June 4). China-Africa Trade Volume Reached US$204.2 Billion, up 20%. *Xinhua Net*. Retrieved from: http://www.xinhuanet.com/fortune/2019-06/04/c_1124583019.htm

Shi, J. L. (2007). China and the Harmonious Development of Our Society. *Shandong Normal University Researches, 47*, 57–58.

Sun, J. H. (2005). *Chinese Management Logic* (pp. 150–182). Beijing: Mechanical Industry Press.

Tsang, E. W. K. (1998). Can Guanxi Be a Source of Sustained Competitive Advantage for Doing Business in China? *Academy of Management Executive, 12*(2), 64–72.

Tu, W. M. (2019, March 8). Confucianism. *Encyclopaedia Britannica*. Retrieved from https://www.britannica.com/topic/Confucianism

Wang, R. M. (2017). The Differences between Chinese and Western Aspects and the Discussion of Pragmatic Strategies. *Journal of Culture Research (in Chinese), 6*, 42–43.

Wang, A. C., Chiang, J. T. J., Tsai, C. Y., Lin, T. T., & Cheng, B. S. (2013). Gender Makes the Difference: The Moderating Role of Leader Gender on the Relationship between Leadership Styles and Subordinate Performance. *Organizational Behaviour and Human Decision Processes, 122*, 101–113. https://doi.org/10.1016/j.obhdp.2013.06.001

Wang, L., Cheng, M. Y., & Wang, S. (2016). Carrot or Stick? The Role of In-group/Out-group on the Multilevel Relationship between Authoritarian and Differential Leadership and Employee Turnover Intention. *Ethics Journals, 10*, 1–16.

Wei, F. (2003). *Research on Chinese Enterprise Management Culture* (pp. 123–156). Northwest: A&F University Press.

Yang, X. M., & Zhou, Y. H. (1999). *Chinese Unit System* (pp. 202–209). China: Economic Publishing House.

Yeung, I. Y. M., & Tung, R. L. (1996). Achieving Success in Confucian Societies: The Importance of Guanxi (Connections). *Organizational Dynamics, 15*(2), 54–65.

Zeng, S. Q. (2006). *Chinese Management* (pp. 255–268). Beijing: China Social Science Press.

Zhang, J. J., & Zhang, Z. X. (2005). The Political Strategy of Chinese Private Enterprises. *World of Management (in Chinese), 7*, 22–23.

Zuo, W. S. (2015, February 03). Industriousness Is the Virtue of the Chinese Nation. *China Civilization Net*. Retrieved from http://www.wenming.cn/wmpl_pd/yczl/201502/t20150203_2435531.shtml

CHAPTER 3

African Cultural Concepts and Their Influence on Management

Samukele Hadebe and Dion Nkomo

3.1 INTRODUCING AFRICAN CULTURAL CONCEPTS

The growth in Chinese-African interactions, which have over the years seen China as Africa's biggest trade partner (Visser, McIntosh, & Middleton, 2017), necessitates an improved mutual cultural appreciation. Conducting business requires sensitivity to cultural nuances and effective intercultural communication skills as essential ingredients of business etiquette to avoid offensive behaviour. In the context of international trade, any offensive behaviour may have serious implications not only for business prosperity and sustainability but also, more significantly, for diplomatic relations.

S. Hadebe (✉)
Chris Hani Institute, Johannesburg, South Africa

Department of Sociology, Rhodes University, Grahamstown, South Africa
e-mail: samukele@chi.org.za; S.Hadebe@ru.ac.za

D. Nkomo
School of Languages & Literatures, Rhodes University,
Grahamstown, South Africa
e-mail: d.nkomo@ru.ac.za

© The Author(s) 2019
C.-H. Mayer et al. (eds.), *Managing Chinese-African Business Interactions*, Palgrave Studies in African Leadership,
https://doi.org/10.1007/978-3-030-25185-7_3

Culture may be defined as "a totality of traits and characters that are peculiar to a people to the extent that it marks them out from other peoples or societies" (Idang, 2015, p. 97). While the concept of culture is very broad, for the purpose of this chapter, two related concepts that elaborate on culture—values and world view (philosophical outlook)—are used. It is within the context of a value system that notions like *Ubuntu* (Etieyibo, 2016) are discussed later in the chapter, paying particular attention to social culture, kinship relationships, consensus in decision-making and deferment to responsible authority. We also discuss African Renaissance, together with its retrospective, current and prospective constituents, namely Afrotopia, Africentrism and Afrofuturism. However, first, we discuss some challenges regarding the title of this chapter and associated terminology.

3.2 Problematising African Cultural Concepts

Mudimbe (1988) aptly captures the paradox that Africa represents in terms of traditional thought systems in relation to normative epistemologies. He argues that "Western interpreters as well as African analysts have been using categories and conceptual systems which depend on a Western epistemological order" (Mudimbe, 1988, x). This makes it difficult to describe Africa in what may be considered original or collective terms. While we can comfortably refer to Chinese culture and, by extension, Chinese cultural concepts, the same cannot be said of African culture without courting controversy. Unlike China, Africa is not a country but an expansive continent with complex internal diversity.

The cultural landscape of Africa, just like its politics and political economy, has been shaped by colonial conquests whose vestiges remain very strong decades after the hoisting of post-colonial flags. Closely associated with political domination of Africa by outsiders is the crucial element of imported religions, mainly Christianity and Islam, that have become defining and sacrosanct features of many Africans. In terms of languages, Africa is now divided into Maghreb Africa, Francophone Africa, Lusophone Africa and Anglophone Africa. These descriptions define modern Africa in terms of exogenous official languages, which the majority citizens lack proficiency in (Kadenge & Nkomo, 2011; Wolff, 2016). The current geographical outlook of the continent is an enduring legacy of political, historical and cultural demarcations that would defy any idea of a collective African culture.

Furthermore, in the context of what Vertovec (2007) terms "superdiversity" (see also Foner, Duyvendak, & Kasinitz, 2019; Vertovec, 2019), culminating from globalisation, increased migration and digital technologies which have influenced various aspects of social, cultural, political and economic life, it is also difficult to say who or what is African. Citizenship is no longer a simple matter of birthright but is now an issue of complex, sometimes convenient, identity politics. Even corporate citizenship in Africa cannot afford to be insular to issues of culture, however defined. Owing to the growth of the former, the latter is in constant flux. Indeed, Africa needs to draw lessons from the past in order to chart pathways to future interactions (Visser et al., 2017) with the rest of the world, China included.

Also crucially important when it comes to intellectual engagement on issues related to African culture is a point made by Nussbaum (2003, p. 21): "Africa's traditional culture is inaccessible because most of it is oral rather than written and lived rather than formally communicated in books or journals; it is difficult to learn about from a distance".

Academics, for whom aspects of African culture constitute their lived experiences, sometimes struggle to have their experiences accepted in formal academic forums, since these experiences fail to conform to the established epistemological orders cited earlier. Nevertheless, there is still a reality out there faced by those interacting with Africans who will definitely feel the need to approach Africa differently from Europe, America or Asia. It is that peculiarly complex African experience that this chapter attempts to characterise, albeit in simplistic terms.

3.3 Impact of Africa's History on Intercultural Business and Intercultural Cooperation

As alluded to earlier, the indelible stamp of colonial history and slavery continues to influence Africa's intercultural business etiquette and intercultural cooperation. Europe's cultural imperialism, which was couched as a "civilising mission", tried to obliterate African institutions and thought systems that were perceived not only as primitive and backwards but also as heathen (Asante, 2001). Formal education and church teaching became vital instruments of Westernisation such that the emerging African elite identified culturally more with Europe than with Africa (Diop, 2012; Ranger, 1986; Ranger & Kimambo, 1976).

Consequently, the Western model of business practices was set as the yardstick of doing business generally. However, the colonists had no intention nor desire to teach the colonised any business acumen. Colonised

Africans were legally excluded from the commercial sphere, only involved as objects to further colonial interests. It is in this respect that the metaphor of robots and other technological inventions is evoked to caricature slaves and colonial labourers (Elia, 2014, pp. 85–90). After independence, the Africans had to concoct a business model imitating the former coloniser and book education. Yet the changing reality on the ground would force the Africans to "wake up" (Elia, 2014, p. 91). Needless to say, local and ethnic nuances would also loom large from the background, thereby creating conditions for leadership and management styles that could be loosely described as African (see 3.4). China is dealing with a different Africa from the one that Western colonisers dealt with.

With little research available in languages other than Chinese Mandarin on Chinese culture and hence work ethics, Africans tend to rely on Western notions of the Chinese, together with the associated stereotypes and distortions (see Geerts, Xinwa, & Rossouw, 2014). Similarly, the most likely information on Africa available to the Chinese came from European writings—which were ill-conceived, not only from ignorance but also from the arrogance of a perceived cultural superiority. China and Africa therefore need to heed Amadiume's warning (1997, p. 185) that

> [o]ne of the dangers of having our feet stuck in Western-produced literature is the tendency to use European terms and expressions uncritically when addressing non-European cultures and experiences. The history of European imperialism and racism means that the language which aided that project is loaded with generalized terms which do not necessarily have a general meaning, but serve a particularistic interest.

In order not to jeopardise her interests in Africa and the developing Chinese-African relations, China would be advised to take note of Africa's anti-colonial discourses such as the African Renaissance and defining philosophical foundations of *Ubuntu*. Likewise, Africa needs to learn about the Chinese, including the learning of Chinese language and culture. Convenient shortcuts of using the West as the middleman should be avoided. Increased cultural exchange and scholarship programmes between China and African countries over the past recent decades, as well as the establishment of Confucius institutes in Africa, have certainly increased cultural relations between China and Africa (Gillespie, 2014; Jiang, Li, Rønning, & Tjønneland, 2016; Meibo & Xie, 2012).

3.4 African Management and Leadership

Inasmuch as modern African management and leadership are heavily influenced by Western practices, there are discernible management and leadership styles and practices that could be loosely described as typically African (Bolden & Kirk, 2009; Nkomo, 2011; Van der Colff, 2003). While there is a general tendency to attribute such practices to culture (Van der Colff, 2003, p. 257), there are also structural features that partly explain these. For example, much of sub-Saharan Africa—with the exception of South Africa—remains largely rural, with sparse colonial infrastructure that hampers efficient communication, production and transportation. The situation continues to be dire despite patchy prospects ushered by the so-called industrial revolution (Murphy & Carmody, 2015). The issue of differentiating structural from cultural issues is aptly argued and exemplified by Simons (2012) in the following manner: If someone told you that it is cool for people to be late for meetings in Nigeria, as a random example, they are a joker. One of the qualities fast gaining universal credibility is punctuality. But the truth is that in Nigeria, as in many parts of the developing world, road transport looks like the Augean stables. Traffic is completely unpredictable, and there are rarely support systems when things go wrong.

It is often these structural factors that typify developing economies which reinforce prejudices against African business people in particular and Africans in general as less time-conscious (Simons, 2012). According to Nkomo (2011, p. 366), only "dangerous reductionism" will conveniently ignore the fact that "Africa's problems are rooted in her colonial past" and will associate African leadership and management with utter disregard for punctuality, attendance, performance output and all integral elements of business success and sustainability.

Generally African leadership, be it in business, sports or politics, is underpinned by consideration of the collective good rather than by individualism (Nkomo, 2011, p. 369). That does not mean that individuals do not desire personal glory and benefits. What it implies is that one can be individualistic in a leadership position, but most likely there will be resistance from rank and file in cases of deviance. Societal expectations tend to push for compliance with group rather than personal interests. Of course, invariably, the individualistic tendencies seem to override common interests. As is explained in the following sections, society expects those in authority not only to be magnanimous but to act in a manner that, according to Mbigi (1997, p. 2, in Nkomo, 2011, p. 376) captures "collective personhood and collective morality". However, various studies (such as Wanasika, Howell, Littrell, & Dorfman, 2011; Littrell et al., 2013) highlight some equally strong inherited individualistic and capitalist tendencies that are characteristic of colonial leadership. Inevitably, one must concede that some "African political leaders betrayed the philosophical and humanitarian principles on which African culture is based", thereby vindicating the generally negative views of many Western-orientated scholars (Nussbaum, 2003, p. 21) on the irrelevance or unhelpfulness of African cultural values in contemporary leadership and management.

The practice of leadership or management by consensus-building is definitely not peculiarly African (see Wodak, Kwon, & Clarke, 2011). However, it can be safely claimed that it is more pronounced in African societies and hence businesses. Africans generally detest rigidity; flexibility is consequently embedded in most African systems and processes. This flexibility manifests itself in disciplinary matters (Bolden & Kirk, 2009; Nkomo, 2011; Van der Colff, 2003). If a manager strictly adheres to agreed regulations and implements them mechanically at the expense of collegiality and humaneness, they might be met with hostility from colleagues and rank and file. So each case must be handled differently and should allow for the accused to explain themselves. Similarly, when one pleads for clemency, it is generally considered cruel not to concede. As demonstrated by Mqhayi, a legendary Xhosa writer in his classic drama text, *Ityala Lamawele* (the matter of twins), precolonial African societies had sophisticated legal and justice systems (Mqhayi, 1914), and some African leaders and managers continue to draw unconsciously and perhaps even consciously from such systems in modern business dealings. In politics, Mandela's reconciliatory approach to leadership post-apartheid South Africa is probably a fitting example (Lieberfeld, 2014).

Contemporary Africa has a number of challenges that business leaders have to factor into their management style. Generally, high levels of unemployment, increasing precariousness and dearth of special skills lead to intense competition in the job market in many African countries. Managers therefore tend to face challenges of income disparities: On the one hand, there is a need to retain the few skills available, and on the other, to keep the majority of workers on low wages, which demotivates workers. This is a colonial legacy issue, in that African economies have barely shifted from primarily extractive industries with relatively little value addition. While the colonial bosses could impose their will, contemporary managers no longer have that prerogative due to the changed political landscape and improved labour laws. African managers must be sensitive to workers' rights, and their Chinese partners ought to be mindful of that too. Most African countries recognise the eight-hour work day which is inclusive of tea and lunch breaks, and workers tend to be sensitive to violations of these rights, as was the case in the Zambian mineworkers' strike in Chinese-owned copper mines (Human Rights Watch, 2011).

3.5 Philosophical Backgrounds and Their Impact on African Management Culture

3.5.1 *Ubuntu*

The notion of *Ubuntu* has been subjected to many interpretations, and rightly so, considering that it does not mean exactly the same thing in the diverse languages, traditions and practices that constitute African culture (see Gade, 2012; Nkomo, 2011). The notion has often been taken at its literal level of meaning as "a person is a person through other persons" (*umuntu ngumuntu ngabantu* in Nguni languages like isiZulu, isiXhosa or isiNdebele). A closely related expression regarding leadership is: "a king is a king because of the people" (*inkosi yinkosi ngabantu* in Nguni languages). Both expressions denote what *Ubuntu* represents, but it is through the second expression that we may perhaps understand the deeper meaning of the first.

In attempts to use the notion of Ubuntu to derive African philosophical ethics, Metz came up with a principle which reads: "an action is right just insofar as it produces harmony and reduces discord; an act is wrong to the extent that it fails to develop community" (Metz, 2007a, p. 334). Unfortunately, the values encapsulated by *Ubuntu* have been taken superficially by writers like Metz (2007b, p. 2011), to create a binary that privileges the collective and, by implication, suppresses individual rights. The debates on *Ubuntu* by philosophers tend to be polarised between those who purportedly view African culture and philosophy through a Western lens and those said to be taking an Africentric view. In the latter group, the African scholars Appiah (1992), Eze (2010a, 2010b), Oyowe (2013) and Etieyibo (2015) are the leading proponents, who see the Metz notion of *Ubuntu* as a perpetuation of cultural imperialism.

We mention these polemics around *Ubuntu* to show that the concept is not a given; it is part of the ideological contestation that typifies characterisation of most things African, be they history, music, religion or philosophy. Nevertheless, there are positives to be derived from *Ubuntu* that could help shed light on intercultural communication and doing business in the African context. Far from promoting the community at the expense of the individual, *Ubuntu* promotes respect of human dignity and its priority ahead of preoccupation, for example, with profits and most systems and processes. This flexibility perhaps manifests itself in disciplinary matters (Nkomo, 2011; Van der Colff, 2003). If the concept of *Ubuntu* were to be adhered to in business, surely, the high levels of poverty, environmental degradation and pollution of rivers would be contained. But, as many would agree, the dog-eat-dog competitive spirit of capitalism has eroded most of these cultural values in business.

Ubuntu carries within it values of sharing as opposed to greed, and honesty as opposed to dishonesty (Nkomo, 2011; Van der Colff, 2003). The basis of African sharing, especially in traditional and communal societies, was the sharing of labour as well as the fruits of that labour. Villagers could be invited by one household to spend a day cultivating the fields, or fencing or any other activity requiring intensive labour (Wanyama, Develtere, & Pollet, 2009). Similarly, during difficult times like funerals, all adults in the surrounding community were, and still are, expected to attend and participate in the burial. The same spirit of cooperation would extend to happy events like weddings and celebrations where all community members are welcome. No formal, selective invitations to or payments for participation would be required, as has become the case among the African elite. To say "a person is a person because of other persons" implies that whatever you do or have succeeded in, one must acknowledge the sacrificial participation and contribution of others directly or indirectly (Nussabaum, 2003). This may include them foregoing their own welfare, including work, in solidarity and support of their fellow community members. African business leaders and managers would need no reminder as to the significance of this communal spirit, but their Chinese counterparts and business partners might struggle to be convinced.

Respect and appropriate decorum among Africans could also be explained within the broad notion of *Ubuntu* (Gade, 2012, p. 485). Most often the issue of respect is misconstrued to imply that it is only to be directed to the elderly. In essence, the young should respect the elders, and they in return are obliged to respect the young. The same would apply in the context of professional or administrative seniority in workplace environment.

Respect is usually interlinked with many taboos (Mawere & Kadenge, 2010). For example, a father may not normally enter his daughter's bedroom, particularly when the daughter is adolescent and older. That is part of respect inasmuch as the daughter might kneel when giving her father food. It is considered disrespectful for men to wear hats in a house, but not for women. Unfortunately, some such forms of expressing respect may be deemed backwards and incompatible with the requirements of modern-day business etiquette. More so given that very little is written about them from an African perspective. As Nkomo (2011, p. 366) avers, African leadership and management is now characterised by tensions and contradictions.

Generally, the way one conducts oneself in dress, greetings, eye contact and voice projection in particular contexts could be interpreted as good or bad behaviour. Certain expectations are associated with age, gender, marital status, occupation and social standing. Even jokes could be considered inappropriate depending on who is in that audience and the nature of the joke. One of the sources of discontent against colonialists by African workers was the feeling that they were treated like children (Dei, 2013), as captured by Ferdinand Oyono's (1990) novel *Houseboy*. Because of the way they interacted with Africans, colonialists were perceived as lacking *Ubuntu*. Africans are generally receptive and accommodative of foreigners who show respect and willingness to learn some basics of the host society. Indeed, Chinese managers or workers should avoid being perceived in the same way as colonial whites (see Geerts et al., 2014; Jauch, 2011; Lumumba-Kasongo, 2011).

3.5.2   African Renaissance

A cultural appreciation of contemporary Africa, as well as its political and economic aspirations, would be incomplete without reference to the African Renaissance. Without even dwelling on the contestations around this concept—or even the appropriateness of "renaissance" to describe an African condition, it is helpful to place the concept into a background, at least in its current application in Africa. Reference to more dedicated and comprehensive works, such as, among others, Bongmba (2004), Mangu (2006), Patterson and Winston (2017) is advised.

The point of departure in understanding the notion of the African Renaissance is Africa's history of conquest, subjugation and oppression at the hands of the West. Asante (2001, p. 226) reckons that slavery and colonialism in Africa are "real times in which Africans were brutalised physically, psychologically and historically". The legacy of colonialism continues to haunt Africa and her prospects of economic, political, technological and cultural progress. According to Bell (2002), "the slave trade, introduction of new diseases, forced colonisation, foreign language and religious impositions, and new administration threw most of the continent into social, religious, political, and cultural confusion".

The net effect of that cultural confusion is what Kodjo describes about the African as "the deformed image of others" (Ravindran, 2016, p. 1). This unfolding tragedy has manifested itself in post-colonial Africa's apparent penchant for political violence such as civil wars, coups, ethnic cleansing and xenophobia. Buri Mboup (2008) and Ebegbulem (2012), for instance, characterise African leadership in terms of bad governance, corruption and human rights abuses, as well as erosion of constitutionalism and rule of law. In the midst of all this unethical leadership, African wealth is siphoned out of the continent through business deals, most often with complicit of government leaders, resulting in unrelenting poverty levels, hunger and citizens perishing from otherwise curable diseases. It is against this background that Buri Mboup (2008, p. 94) echoes the clarion call for an African Renaissance.

Far from being a "re-traditionalisation" of Africa—to use Chabal's (1996) terminology to describe a misconception among many Western-orientated scholars that "to Africans time is a matter of past and present" (Winston, 2017, p. 185)—African Renaissance should be seen as "a revival of an Africa of hope and prosperity" (Louw, 2000, p. 4). We consider it to be a composite concept of perspectives that are historical (i.e. Afrotopia), current (i.e. Africentrism) and futuristic (i.e. Afrofuturism). Thus the Renaissance should be a futuristic re-imagining of an African society to redress the current social, cultural, economic and political distortions inflicted upon it by centuries of foreign domination. It is partly informed by and resonates with Aime Cesaire's *Return to the Native Land* and Amilca Cabral's *Return to the Source*, which both give primacy to African dignity. Understandably, the African Renaissance has also been described as "an expression of the quest for African self-pride, identity and dignity" (More, 2002, p. 64). While the issue of the politics of identity is paramount in the concept of an African Renaissance, following Thabo Mbeki's 1996 speech, "I am an African", it is nevertheless not the only defining feature, let alone thrust of an African Renaissance.

Asante (2001) rejects hypocritical and superficial interests in Africa as definitive of whatever political or intellectual allegiance to Africa one may claim. This is especially relevant for outsiders with vested interests in Africa projecting themselves as having a messianic role in saving Africa from herself. Instead, emphasis must be placed on "African agency, centeredness, psychic integrity, and cultural fidelity as the vital tenets of Africentrism" (Asante, 2001, p. 228) and, by implication, Afrotopia and Afrofuturism. "The African is no longer a loser" (Elia, 2014, p. 94) nor a victim. Africans are survivors who are determined to reclaim themselves from a position of equal potential, despite their disadvantaged past. The futuristic conception of African Renaissance, therefore,

> still looks back at the past in order to re-evaluate it, but it primarily seeks to overcome this demoralising future scenario by showing a positive outlook on the potential of Africa and of the people of the African diaspora in the world. (Elia, 2014, p. 85)

The renewal and reinvention of an African dream is as economic as it is political and cultural. Writing on this matter, Moeletsi Mbeki says: "This renewal should, however, be built on a growing and sustainable economy capable of assimilating the best characteristics, contribute to and take advantage of the real flows of the economic activities around the world" (Mbeki, 1999, pp. 210–211). Thabo Mbeki, a recent proponent of African Renaissance, called upon African intellectuals residing in the West to return and

> add to the African pool of brain power, to enquire into and find solutions for Africa's problems and challenges, to open the African door to the world of knowledge [and] to elevate Africa's place within the universe of research, the formation of new knowledge, education and information. (Mbeki, 1998, p. 299)

For example, the Economic Freedom Fighters' implicit evocation of the African Renaissance has contributed to their fortunes—despite being described as "a paradox" (Nieftagodien, 2015, p. 446) and a party whose rapid rise in South African politics presents a case of the world's turn towards the politics of populism (Mbete, 2015).

How then does African Renaissance relate to understanding of intercultural communication and doing business in Africa? First, it is important to appreciate that African Renaissance as articulated by Thabo Mbeki did not just remain as a slogan. An economic plan accompanied its implementation in the form of *the New African Initiative* as adopted by the African Union in 2001. Second, it is necessary to consider the new thinking by African political leaders, at least concerning Africa's economic trajectory or its aspirations. Africans have realised that economic development and prosperity for Africa's citizens would require, as a matter of urgency, peace and political stability. With varying degrees of success, Africa has tried to arrest civil wars and coups and promote peaceful transfer of power. Non-interference in Africa's internal affairs is a principle advanced within the broader African Renaissance. Hence, Mbeki (1999, p. 212) speaks of: "the mobilisation of the people of Africa to take their destiny in their own hands and thus preventing the continent being seen as a place for the attainment of the geo-political and strategic interests of the world's most powerful countries". Peace-building and political stability are inseparable from economic development.

With South Africa setting the tone of opening up the economy to competition and efforts to "increase the proportion of exports that consisted of competitive, value-added manufactured goods as opposed to commodities" (Barrell, 2000, p. 88), Africa's business priorities include attracting foreign direct investments, technology transfer and infrastructure development. Other priorities include "investment in people and improvement of the quality of life of Africans" (Nkuhlu, 2001, p. 1). Perhaps the New African Initiative's focus was aptly described by Fabricius as: "a human resource development initiative, a diversification of production and exports initiative, a rehabilitation of infrastructure initiative, a market access (for African products) initiative, a capital flow initiative and an environmental (protection) initiative" (Louw, 2000, p. 15).

Therefore, apart from identity issues of Africans' self-assertion and dignity, the African Renaissance articulates Africa's economic development aspirations and trajectory in addition to political and governance matters. An appreciation of African management and leadership in business interactions is a necessity for long-term business relations and mutual benefits. It is positive to note that already China has played a significant role in Africa in both energy and infrastructure development. Of course, the African Renaissance faces a number of challenges whose discussion would be beyond the scope and purpose of this chapter.

3.6 Culture-Specific Concepts in Intercultural Management

3.6.1 Social Culture: Socialising and Greetings

Initial contact tends to create lasting impressions. In most African communities, the first contact would normally be initiated with a greeting and the common greeting is "How are you?" or *Bonjour, Jambo* or in the country's local language *Unjani? Makadini? Ukae?* (Ravindran, 2016). Greetings play an important role in communities and may give good or bad impressions about the interlocutors (Sibadela, 2002). Africans greet strangers and friends alike. In a typical African city when one boards a commuter taxi, one greets those who are already inside, otherwise they would find your behaviour unbecoming. Similarly, when you walk approaching a person from the other direction, both of you give space and greet as you pass.

In a home environment and even in workplaces, the greetings could be more formalised; the time taken to greet varies according to ethnic and linguistic groups. Based on a study conducted in Nigeria, Chiluwa (2010, p. 126) observes that Nigerians generally devote considerable time to greeting, making "particular references to the family, where 'family' (in the traditional sense) represents the nuclear and the extended family, the ancestors and the children yet unborn". Most often, unless otherwise stated, the greetings are accompanied by handshakes and even hugging. To reiterate, Yorubas are considered social greeters, even in formal business interactions (Chiluwa, 2010, p. 117). Doing so may be considered as an expression of *Ubuntu* in many African contexts, since, as Waldvogel (2007, p. 747) proffers, "[t]he importance of greetings … as a linguistic resource lies in the affective role they play". Waldvogel (2007, p. 471) considers lack of affectionate greetings as a suggestion of a "business-first, people-second culture" in typically Western workplace environments such as in Sweden.

Robinson (2014) extends the courtesies even to the wording of email: It often boils down to an understanding of how cultural standpoints differ between Western rule–based and African relations–based communication, so how you word an email can make or break a nascent business relationship. A Western direct approach in writing with minimal greetings and an emphasis on rules and deadlines is not necessarily acceptable in many

African cultures. You will get better results with indirect communication with emphasis on polite greeting and perhaps enquiries about the person's health and family (Robinson, 2014, p. 1).

Nussbaum (2003, p. 22) observes that those who are unfamiliar with the African values that underpin social practices such as greetings may fail to see their value and associate the practices with the lack of a sense of urgency and timeliness. Socialising is not a waste of time among Africans, and in planning meetings and events, it would be wise to allocate reasonable time for greetings, which are part of the agenda. Building and nurturing a relationship begins in the greetings and pleasantries accompanying it, and this helps build trust, which is important in doing business in Africa (Nussbaum, 2003, p. 22). Therefore, closely linked to the social practices associated with greeting is establishing lasting relationships as if they were kinship ties.

3.6.2　*Building Kinship-Type Relationships*

There is a belief that people do business with those they know. To an extent, that is true. Most African communities still value kinship, even urbanised communities. However, what has not been carefully interrogated is how these kinship ties are created, sustained and utilised beyond seeing them as blood ties—which is often not the case. Undoubtedly in traditional societies, kinship ties could have correlated to blood ties but not necessarily so in contemporary Africa. One's circle of kinship relations would include school mates, church mates, work mates, neighbours and perhaps even WhatsApp group associations.

There is a tendency drawn from traditional practices to create apparently familial relations with people in general. Hence, when one refers to the other as sister, uncle, grandmother or nephew, it does not always mean these are relatives at all. It is an extension of kinship relationships to facilitate the friendships that would have developed. In a similar way, outsiders should endeavour to be part of this familial relationship which Africans tend to be comfortable with. Making business links and contacts would be a lot easier should one, for instance, say, "So-and-so is my uncle, so-and-so's friend". Rarely do people concern themselves about even the authenticity of the claimed kinship, yet it plays an important role in cultivating relationships and also in doing business. It builds business confidence and trust (Luke & Munshi, 2006; Nussbaum, 2003), although, without sufficient care, it may be linked with nepotistic business and leadership tendencies that have not spared Africa.

3.6.3 Consensus in Decision-Making

Those not familiar with the consultative approach to decision-making based on a consensus have often felt that African business leaders and managers were either slow in decision-making or indecisive (Bolden & Kirk, 2009; Nkomo, 2011; Van der Colff, 2003). Far from it, making hasty decisions is frowned upon among Africans. Apart from the need to consult widely on an issue, it is also a common practice to sleep over the matter before a final decision is communicated. As observed by Ravindran (2016), it is "the cultural significance of consensus and consultation, which tend to guide the decision-making process in Africa's group-oriented cultures". The values and practices bequeathed from communalism seem to have permeated contemporary African societies as well as management practices.

Generally, Africans do not like vacillation, and when they give you their word, they normally feel obliged to stick to it. It is considered bad behaviour and being untrustworthy to make a promise and fail to fulfil it. Therefore, decision-making tends to be a protracted process, in that all angles to the matter are considered and weighed. Besides, any decision is not just for an individual but for the common good (Handley & Louw, 2016).

What also should be appreciated is that in most African communities, once relationships are established, they are expected to last long. Building trust and confidence are essential in any business interface, and hence decision-making is of necessity built on consensus (Luke & Munshi, 2006). The African value system as enunciated by *Ubuntu* demands honesty, trustworthiness and truthfulness (Bolden & Kirk, 2009; Nkomo, 2011; Van der Colff, 2003). By consulting before making a decision, the leader would be drawing in witnesses to an agreement. Actually, "successful African leadership is thus not about holding a position of power in the organisational hierarchy, but concerns personal power that enables individuals to create their own future and quality of life" (Handley & Louw, 2016, p. 139). Consensus in decision-making is essential in promoting collective participation in the affairs of an organisation.

3.6.4 Deferment to Responsible Authority

Most traditional societies, African included, were patriarchal, with males wielding relatively more but not absolute power. In fact, power tended to reside in elderly males as head of families and hence controlling household wealth. The vestiges of traditional culture survive and permeate business leadership too, as generally a disproportionate number of males are in business leadership positions compared to females. Instead of referring to deference to elders, which is the case anyway, we opted to refer to deference to responsible authority. So much distortion has been done to African traditions, practices and value systems that caution should always be taken to avoid perpetuating negative stereotypes (Asante, 2001).

Our position here is that, generally, age is a distinguishing feature in African societies, and one is expected to show respect to those older than oneself. Normally, the elder person cannot be addressed by the younger using a first name. Similarly, those in authority are treated with respect reserved for that status and even addressed accordingly. A manager in a company, whether young or female, will be respected because of the authority associated with that position. This respect for authority has been misconstrued and even abused as dictatorship on the part of leaders or docility on the part of subordinates. Normally in many communities you would not speak back to your superior, especially when that person is admonishing you.

When certain decisions are left to the leadership to decide, the subordinates would actually be expecting a decision that is fair and that takes into account their own interests. A good leader would first ask for the opinion of subordinates before making a final ruling so that the decision taken resonates with the general mood. By deferring to authority, the intention would not be to create dictators but to honour the leader. Even at a domestic level, the wife would normally defer to the husband as head of the family, but only a reckless man would make a decision without the consent of his wife. Of course, deference to authority has been open to abuse as leaders have manipulated their authority for personal gain. Therefore, in a business interaction, certain information can only be released by the most senior manager, even if known by everyone in the organisation. It is important to know what to expect and even to ask from people in an organisation, depending on their hierarchy in the organisational structure. Respect of authority is not necessarily fear of authority, but it is based on an assumption and belief that those in authority would reciprocate respect to subordinates (Handley & Louw, 2016).

3.7 Conclusion

There is a need to understand the dynamics of Chinese-African intercultural engagement (Handley & Louw, 2016, p. 139), considering the growing presence of Chinese companies in Africa. This chapter outlined what we consider salient African cultural features that are likely to impact on business and management practices. In any case, variation in managerial practices, approaches and conceptualisations occurs across countries (Bird & Fang, 2009; Bräutigam, 2009). As already discussed, there is much diversity in African culture inasmuch as there is barely consensus on what constitutes "African". Nonetheless, there are trends and practices that are peculiarly associated with Africa. Besides, the growing presence of the Chinese in Africa necessitates the understanding of Africa from African perspectives and not from the Western viewpoint with perceived colonial bias.

While Africa still carries the burden of a colonial legacy that has left imprints on business practices, it is noteworthy that the world of business is rapidly changing with globalisation. Africa too is undergoing change, and African culture, whichever way it is defined, is not static. Increased Chinese-African cultural and business contact would, in the long run, create shared cultural and business practices, considering that in any cultural contact, blending is unavoidable. Cross-cultural and intercultural awareness largely depends on attitudes of the interlocutors. Since most of what is publicly known about Africa comes through a Western lens, African and Chinese people need to create their own knowledge of one another, not tainted by Western perspectives.

Considering the vast size of Africa and the cultural diversity within it, what we have presented here of necessity, are generalisations, largely drawn from the Zulu, Ndebele, Shona, Tswana and Bemba cultures. Therefore, it is imperative for Chinese business people and workers in Africa to pay particular attention to local cultures wherever they are. Coming to Africa with preconceived ideas and generalised understandings could actually complicate relations, as Africa is as culturally diverse as is complex. Similarly, it should be in the interests of Africans to help the Chinese—and any foreigners for that matter—to understand them from their own standpoint. With enhanced intercultural awareness, the mutual benefits to Africans and Chinese could be great, especially for both groups to learn to reciprocate respect and make conscious efforts to understand and appreciate local cultures.

REFERENCES

Amadiume, I. (1997). *Re-inventing Africa: Matriarchy, Religion and Culture*. London: Zed Books.
Appiah, K. A. (1992). *In My Father's House: African in the Philosophy of Culture*. London: Methuen.
Asante, M. K. (2001). Afrotopia: The Roots of African American Popular History (Review). *Journal of World History, 12*(1), 226–230.
Barrell, H. (2000). Africa Watch – Back to the Future: Renaissance and South African Domestic Policy. *African Security Review, 9*(2), 82–91.
Bell, R. H. (2002). *Understanding African Philosophy: A Cross-cultural Approach to Classical and Contemporary Issues*. New York: Routledge.
Bird, A., & Fang, T. (2009). Editorial: Cross Cultural Management in the Age of Globalisation. *International Journal of Cross Cultural Management, 9*(2), 139–143.
Bolden, R., & Kirk, P. (2009). African Leadership: Surfacing New Understandings through Leadership Development. *International Journal of Cross Cultural Management, 9*(1), 69–86.
Bongmba, E. K. (2004). Reflections on Thabo Mbeki's African Renaissance. *Journal of Southern African Studies, 30*(2), 291–316.
Bräutigam, D. (2009). *The Dragon's Gift: The Real Story of China in Africa*. New York: Oxford.
Buri Mboup, S. (2008). Conflicting Leadership Paradigms in Africa: A Need for an African Renaissance Perspective. *International Journal of African Renaissance Studies, 3*(1), 94–112.
Chabal, P. (1996). The African crisis: context and interpretation. Postcolonial identities in Africa, 29, 54.
Chiluwa, I. (2010). Discursive Practice and the Nigerian Identity in Personal Emails. In R. Taiwo (Ed.), *Handbook of Research on Discourse Behavior and Digital Communication: Language Structures and Social Interaction* (pp. 112–129). IGI Global: Hershey.
Dei, G. J. S. (2013). Reflections on "African Development": Situating Indigeneity and Indigenous Knowledges. In E. Shizha & A. A. Abdi (Eds.), *Indigenous Discourses on Knowledge and Development in Africa* (pp. 27–42). London: Routledge.
Diop, S. (2012). African Elites and Their Post-colonial Legacy: Cultural, Political and Economic Discontent – by Way of Literature. *Africa Development/Afrique Et Développement, 37*(4), 221–235.
Ebegbulem, J. C. (2012). Corruption and Leadership Crisis in Africa: Nigeria in Focus. *International Journal of Business and Social Science, 3*(11), 221–227.
Elia, A. (2014). The languages of Afrofuturism. *Lingue e Linguaggi, 12,* 83–96.
Etieyibo, E. (2015). The Question of Cultural Imperialism in African Philosophy. In J. O. Chimakonam (Ed.), *Atuolu Omalu: Some Unanswered Questions in*

Contemporary African Philosophy (pp. 147–170). Lanham, MD: University Press of America.
Etieyibo, E. (2016). *African Philosophy in the Eyes of the West*. Retrieved March 12, 2019, from https://upjournals.co.za/index.php/Phronimon/
Eze, M. O. (2010a). *The Politics of History in Contemporary Africa*. New York: Palgrave Macmillan.
Eze, M. O. (2010b). *Intellectual History in Contemporary South Africa*. New York: Palgrave Macmillan.
Foner, F., Duyvendak, J. W., & Kasinitz, P. (2019). Introduction: Super-diversity in Everyday Life. *Ethnic and Racial Studies, 42*(1), 1–16.
Gade, C. B. (2012). What Is Ubuntu? Different Interpretations among South Africans of African Descent. *South African Journal of Philosophy, 31*(3), 484–503.
Geerts, S., Xinwa, N., & Rossouw, D. (2014). *Africans' Perceptions of Chinese Business in Africa, A Survey*. Geneva: Globethics.net/Hatfield: Ethics Institute of South Africa. Retrieved from https://www.globethics.net/
Gillespie, S. (2014). *South-South Transfer: A Study of Sino-African Exchanges*. Routledge.
Handley, R. C., & Louw, M. J. (2016). The Similarities and Differences between South African and Chinese Definitions and Descriptions of Leadership Style: A Mining Joint Venture Case Study. Retrieved from https://www.up.ac.za/media/shared/643/ZP_Files/2016/
Human Rights Watch. (2011). 'You Will Be Fired If You Refuse' Labour Abuses in Zambia's Chinese State-Owned Copper Mines. Retrieved from http://www.hrg.org/
Idang, G. E. (2015). African Culture and Values. *UNISA Phronimon, 16*(2), 97–111. Retrieved from www.scielo.org.za/pdf/phronimon/v16n2/06.pdf
Jauch, H. (2011, June). Chinese Investments in Africa: Twenty-first Century Colonialism? *In New Labor Forum, 20*(2), 49–55.
Jiang, F., Li, S., Rønning, H., & Tjønneland, E. (2016). The Voice of China in Africa: Media, Communication Technologies and Image-Building. *Chinese Journal of Communication, 9*(1), 1–7.
Kadenge, M., & Nkomo, D. (2011). The Politics of the English Language in Zimbabwe. *Language Matters, 42*(2), 248–263.
Lieberfeld, D. (2014). Nelson Mandela: Personal Characteristics and Reconciliation-Oriented Leadership. In B. Jallow (Ed.), *Leadership in Postcolonial Africa: Trends Transformed by Independence* (pp. 143–167). Palgrave Macmillan.
Littrell, R. F., Wu, N. H., Nkomo, S., Wanasika, I., Howell, J., & Dorfman, P. (2013). Pan-Sub-Saharan African Managerial Leadership and the Values of Ubuntu. *Management in Africa: Macro and Micro Perspectives*, 232–248.
Louw, A. H. (2000). *The Concept of the African Renaissance as a Force Multiplier to Enhance Lasting Peace and Stability in Sub-Saharan Africa*. Research Paper,

Executive National Security Programme 02/2000, South African National Defence College, October 17, 2000.

Luke, N., & Munshi, K. (2006). New Roles for Marriage in Urban Africa: Kinship Networks and the Labor Market in Kenya. *The Review of Economics and Statistics, 88*(2), 264–282.

Lumumba-Kasongo, T. (2011). China-Africa Relations: A Neo-imperialism or a Neocolonialism? A Reflection. *African and Asian Studies, 10*(2–3), 234–266.

Mangu, A. M. B. (2006). Democracy, African Intellectuals and African Renaissance. *International Journal of African Renaissance Studies - Multi-, Inter- and Transdisciplinarity, 1*(1), 147–163.

Mawere, M., & Kadenge, M. (2010). Zvierwa as African IKS: Epistemological and Ethical Implications of Selected Shona Taboos. *Indilinga African Journal of Indigenous Knowledge Systems, 9*(1), 29–44.

Mbeki, M. (1999). The African Renaissance. *South African Yearbook of International Affairs*. Johannesburg: South African Institute of International Affairs.

Mbeki, T. (1998). *Africa – The Time Has Come*. Cape Town: Tafelberg.

Mbete, S. (2015). The Economic Freedom Fighters-South Africa's Turn towards Populism? *Journal of African elections, 14*(1), 35–59.

Meibo, H., & Xie, Q. I. (2012). Forum on China-Africa Cooperation: Development and Prospects. *African East-Asian Affairs, 74*, 10–20.

Metz, T. (2007a). Toward an African Moral Theory. *Journal of Political Philosophy, 15*(3), 321–341.

Metz, T. (2007b). Ubuntu as a Moral Theory: Reply to Four Critics. *South African Journal of Philosophy, 26*(4), 369–387.

More, M. P. (2002). African Renaissance: The Politics of Return. *African Journal of Political Science, 7*(2), 62–80. Retrieved from http://digital.lib.msu.edu/projects/africanjournals

Mqhayi, S. E. K. (1914). *Ityala lamawele*. Alice: Lovedale Press.

Mudimbe, V. Y. (1988). *The Invention of Africa: Gnosis, Philosophy, and the Order of Knowledge*. Bloomington: Indiana University Press.

Murphy, J. T., & Carmody, P. (2015). *Africa's Information Revolution: Technical Regimes and Production Networks in South Africa and Tanzania*. John Wiley & Sons.

Nieftagodien, N. (2015). The Economic Freedom Fighters and the Politics of Memory and Forgetting. *South Atlantic Quarterly, 114*(2), 446–456.

Nkomo, S. M. (2011). A Postcolonial and Anti-colonial Reading of 'African' Leadership and Management in Organization Studies: Tensions, Contradictions and Possibilities. *Organization, 18*(3), 365–386.

Nkuhlu, M. (2001). *Millennium Partnership for the African Recovery Programme*. Bua, April/May 2001.

Nussbaum, B. (2003). Ubuntu: Reflections of a South African on Our Common Humanity. *Reflections: The SoL Journal, 4*(4), 21–26.

Oyono, F. L. (1990). *Houseboy*. London: Heinemann.
Oyowe, A. (2013). Strange Bedfellows: Rethinking Ubuntu and Human Rights in South Africa. *African Human Rights Law Journal, 13*, 103–124.
Patterson, K., & Winston, B. E. (Eds.). (2017). *Leading an African Renaissance Opportunities and Challenges*. Palgrave Macmillan.
Ranger, T. O. (1986). Religious Movements and Politics in Sub-Saharan Africa. *African Studies Review, 29*(2), 1–70.
Ranger, T. O., & Kimambo, I. N. (Eds.). (1976). *The Historical Study of African Religion*. California: University of California Press.
Ravindran, N. (2016). The Role of Culture in Doing Business in Africa. Retrieved from http://africabusiness.com/2016/06/23/the-role-of-culture-in-doing-business-in-africa/
Robinson, L. (2014). The Cultural Differences and Doing Business in Africa. Retrieved from https://www.bizcommunity.com/Article/196/610/120256.html
Sibadela, J. M. (2002). *The Speech Act of Greetings in Tshivenda*. Doctoral dissertation, Stellenbosch University, Stellenbosch.
Simons, B. (2012). Five Business Culture Tips from an African Perspective. *African Arguments.*. Retrieved from https://africanarguments.org/
Van der Colff, L. (2003). Leadership Lessons from the African Tree. *Management Decision, 41*(3), 257–261.
Vertovec, S. (2007). Super-diversity and its implications. *Ethnic and racial studies, 30*(6), 1024–1054.
Vertovec, S. (2019). Talking Around Super-Diversity. *Ethnic and Racial Studies, 42*(1), 125–139.
Visser, W., McIntosh, M., & Middleton, C. (2017). Corporate Citizenship in Africa: Lessons from the Past; Paths to the Future. In *Corporate Citizenship in Africa* (pp. 10–17). Routledge.
Waldvogel, J. (2007). Greetings and Closings in Workplace Email. *Journal of Computer Mediated Communication, 12*(2), 456–477.
Wanasika, I., Howell, J. P., Littrell, R., & Dorfman, P. (2011). Managerial leadership and culture in Sub-Saharan Africa. *Journal of World Business, 46*(2), 234–241.
Wanyama, F. O., Develtere, P., & Pollet, I. (2009). Reinventing the Wheel? African Cooperatives in a Liberalized Economic Environment. *Annals of Public and Cooperative Economics, 80*(3), 361–392.
Winston, B. E. (2017). The Stage Is Set for African Renaissance. In *Leading an African Renaissance* (pp. 185–187). Palgrave Macmillan, Cham.
Wodak, R., Kwon, W., & Clarke, I. (2011). 'Getting People on Board': Discursive Leadership for Consensus Building in Team Meetings. *Discourse & Society, 22*(5), 592–644.
Wolff, H. E. (2016). *Language and Development in Africa: Perceptions, Ideologies and Challenges*. Cambridge University Press.

PART II

Intercultural Training Cases: Dealing with International Communication, Cooperation and Negotiation

CHAPTER 4

Case 1: Dealing with Organisational Strategies in the Tanzanian-Chinese Chalinze Water Project

Christian Martin Boness

4.1 CASE NARRATIVE

Shortly after the former Tanganyika Territories gained their independence, the Foreign Aid department of China's Ministry of Railways helped to build links between Tanzania, Zambia and the southern African regional transport network through launching the project known as TAZARA (1968–1976) (Tanzania-Zambia Authority, 2018). This project has been followed by other similar projects in East Africa, as reported by the economic and commercial counsellor of the Chinese Embassy to South Africa, Ron Yansong (Pretoria News, 2016, p. 12). An example provided is the continent's first electrified railway linking Addis Ababa in Ethiopia and Djibouti in Somalia (Pretoria News, 2016, p. 12).

Sub-Saharan African countries have benefitted from various Chinese infrastructure investments, especially in terms of African integration (Schiere & Rugamba, 2011). Chinese enterprises in Tanzania support Goal 6 of the United Nations Agenda 2021, which aims to provide universal clean water and sanitation (United Nations Report of the Secretary-

---

C. M. Boness (✉)
Department of Management, Rhodes University, Grahamstown, South Africa

© The Author(s) 2019
C.-H. Mayer et al. (eds.), *Managing Chinese-African Business Interactions*, Palgrave Studies in African Leadership,
https://doi.org/10.1007/978-3-030-25185-7_4

General, 2017). The country benefits from a sound freshwater ecosystem that contributes to essential human health and environmental sustainability and economic prosperity. Not only access to basic sanitation and freshwater systems, but also effective water and sanitation management relies on the participation of a range of stakeholders, including local communities (United Nations, 2017).

The Tanga Province in North-East Tanzania is characterised by a humid coastline and dry upcountry areas. The Chalinze district within the province is semi-arid, the groundwater is not potable and its water level falls below an accessible depth during the dry season. The Chalinze Water Project is a showcase project of the Chinese government. The official newspaper, *The People's Daily*, writes on 20 October 2001 about the commencement of the works:

> The 10.4 billion Tanzanian shilling (about 11.73 million U.S. dollars) worth project, a grant by the Chinese government, will assure the availability of 7,200 tons of safe and clean water a day to 105,000 residents in the Chalinze area of the region upon its completion in two years. (*People's Daily Online*, 2001)

The entire water pipeline that was built from the Chalinze Water Treatment Centre towards the surrounding villages spans approximately 126 kilometres, and the distribution pipe is 34 kilometres long. Water delivered through this project has standpipes monitored by village members who collect funds for each litre of delivery.

The China Hainan Company has been involved with the Chalinze project since 2001 by employing 50 Chinese and approximately 500 local Tanzanian workers. In the company, anti-corruption strategies are outlined visibly as part of the basic organisational principles (Mabeya, 2017, p. 28): "RUSHWA NI ADUI WA HAKI, MKANDARASI PIGA VITA RUSHWA. EPUKA KUSHAWISHI, KUSHAWISHIWA, KUTOA AU KOPOKEA RUSHWA"[1].

Despite this politically correct strategy of the China Hainan Company, Mr Ndugu Kirefu, a Tanzanian human resource manager in the organisation, raises concerns and questions about the Tanzanian-Chinese cooperation regarding the Chalinze project. He states critically:

> Although the official goal of the China Hainan Company Corporation is the upgrading of water supply and sanitation infrastructure – and we appreciate

this goal very much – the majority of the Tanzanian local workers do not believe in the strategy of the project and the international cooperation across the different departments of the organisation. (Hainan International Ltd, 2018)

Tanzanian employees understand that a part of the organisational strategy is to strive to become the best water supply provider in the country. However, the strategy to become a top player in this sector is not explicitly stated, and this lack of information creates a sense of insecurity for the Tanzanian employees. Aside from external factors such as a lack of cooperation with the municipality and a deteriorating transport infrastructure, internal hierarchical factors seem to limit communication of company strategies within the organisation. Employees, particularly the local Tanzanian employees, are not expected to participate in decision-making of the organisation and are therefore not informed about the strategies. From the Tanzanian perspective, the organisation's major aim should be to distribute clean water to the households living in the district, but the Tanzanian employees believe that the organisation does not want to invest into Tanzania, and it aims to use Tanzanian resources for its own Chinese benefit.

Mr Kirefu, the Tanzanian human resource officer, emphasises that finding a solution to care for all the interests involved in the project is not easy. So, he has begun a campaign to involve the employees to collect ideas of improvement of the internal organisational communication structure and the aims of the organisation, including responses to the question of how to deal with the aim to produce accessible public water supply for the locals, while maintaining Chinese interests. The challenge for Mr Kirefu is then how to submit the ideas of the employees to the Chinese managers who make up the majority of the organisational management as well as the local authorities who are mainly responsible for the water tariffs.

4.2 Questions and Points of Discussion

- Which classical and new Chinese business strategies impact on the Chalinze water supply project?
- Discuss aspects of the Chinese official policy of aid and trade with reference to the Chinese water distribution in the Chalinze district.
- Consider Tanzanian survival values such as sharing the water supply through the Chalinze project.

- If you see Tanzania scoring much higher in culture-specific uncertainty avoidance than China, what do you think Tanzanians want to make sure of?
- Develop short- and long-term solutions for this case from each of the Chinese and the African points of view.

4.3 Chinese Perspectives

After the cultural revolution (1966–1976), China became interested in building a South-South trading cooperation with African countries, since China had experienced itself as a developing country for many decades with similar structures to those found in African countries (Bräutigam, 2009). Early experiences in economic cooperation projects with Japan supported the Chinese idea to act similarly and intensify cooperation with African countries, and provide aid:

> In Mali, China was to rescue a leather producing factory. Spare parts and other hardware were needed to upgrade the equipment. A loan was given by Chinese agreeing the barter arrangement 'leather for loan'… Tanzania bought spare parts … by exporting cashew nuts. Sierra Leone exported coffee and cocoa to make some of its loan payments. (Bräutigam, 2009, p. 56)

Summarising, important strategic principles that affect organisational strategies comprise:

- flexible bartering—no money-for-money policies,
- long-term orientation—no quick profit-thinking and
- no interference in national politics—ethical or human rights standards are not guidelines for economic investments.

Chinese enterprises try to translate the strategic goals of aid and trade from the macro-level into meso-level strategic goals on organisational levels of Chinese-Tanzanian projects. This is particularly true for governmental organisations (as used in the Chalinze project), while private organisations are less bound by strategies defined by the Chinese government. Government-supported investors are convinced that Tanzania can gain mutual benefit from China's plans to provide drinking water for the population, while Chinese fulfil their own interests and needs within African countries (Dingding, 2017).

However, the Chalinze Water Project is weakened by a lack of interaction and intercommunication with the Tanzanian staff, with communal organs such as Water Management Chalinze (WAMACHA), the villagers and with the communal authorities. For the Chinese management of the Chalinze Water Project, it appears that non-commitment of their African counterparts makes it difficult to implement the project within the proposed time frame.

4.4 African Perspectives

The organisational atmosphere in the Chalinze project has become tense from the perspective of the Tanzanian employees. The Chinese management, who sees rising tension within the Tanzanian employees, is worried that this increasing tension and dissatisfaction may cause problems and delay the project's progress. Therefore, the Chinese management is willing to listen and cooperate with local Tanzanian employees and the communal authorities to achieve a win-win situation and see positive results of the project as soon as possible.

Despite the positive aspects of the project, there are several serious problems with local administration, especially with WAMACHA (Shayo, 2013). WAMACHA is an organ installed by the local government. The local administration is supposed to give guidance, training, technical and financial support, whereas the main function of WAMACHA is to actively be involved in decision-making, contributions and management (Shayo, 2013, p. 24).

From the perspective of the Tanzanian workforce, there are many open questions concerning cooperation between the communal authorities, WAMACHA and the Chinese management. The employees are unsure of the organisational as well as the project structure and want the organisation to be transparent about the aims and detailed plans of the stakeholders. The employees wish to avoid uncertainties and risks with the local water supply and strive for mutual beneficial cooperation and a quickly established access to drinking water for the local communities. They want to ensure that the water project will help local communities through international aid rather than being an "economic trade project" in which, in the end, the Chinese organisation will define the water market of the local communities and will go with the highest benefit, while the "weak" local communities continue to suffer from lack of water and/or an exaggerated water price policy defined by an international organisation.

Following a recent international study on culture-specific "uncertainty avoidance" (Hofstede, 2018), Tanzania as a country scores 50 out of 100 points. In terms of international comparisons, this indicates a relatively balanced preference regarding uncertainty avoidance and a high ability to take risks. China, however, scores only 30 out of 100 points in the same study, significantly lower in uncertainty avoidance than Tanzania (Hofstede, 2018). In this context, the uncertainty of the Tanzanian employees is understandable, since there may not be the needed measures in place to build certainty and trust coming from the Chinese management of the organisation so that mutual benefits will be derived from this project. Since water is a basic requirement for life in the semi-arid area of Chalinze, and the Tanzanians are not assured that their water supply needs will be met, tension arises within the organisation.

4.5 Culture-Specific Solutions

4.5.1 Short-Term Solutions from Chinese Perspectives

The Chinese management wishes to implement the Chalinze Water Project timeously. The managers in charge fear obstacles and try to overcome them by improving the intercultural communication between Chinese management and Tanzanian employees. Accordingly, Chinese management is trying to arrange meetings to exchange information about the project. The managers provide guidelines of the organisation policies, the short- and long-term strategic plan, the aims and the benefits for all parties involved. They can further inform the employees and local communities openly about their water distribution and sale price policy with the communal government. A public exposition of the history, present and future of the project with aims, plans and implications involved can support the de-escalation of tension and fulfil the Tanzanian employees' need of certainty with regard to essential survival.

4.5.2 Long-Term Solutions from Chinese Perspectives

A new international and intercultural project awareness can be achieved through information sharing, not only within the organisation but also in the district or even in the province. This would affect the Chinese aid and trade strategy and their organisational strategy at different levels. The interactions at communal level (i.e. with the WAMACHA and local government interactions) and decision-making, for example, on water tariffs, would be affected.

The Chinese management should ensure that they meet the priorities of the employees and local communities to encourage cooperation and willingness to work for the organisation. The management should declare the plans for water supply and pricing estimates for the local communities. The local employees and communities should not be treated as from top-down, but on an equal basis to ensure cooperation. Mutual trust should be developed in a long-term perspective by implementing social responsibility projects and goals, which are in the interest of the local Tanzanian employees and communities. Openness and transparency and beneficial mutual relationships should be defined and adhered to from the Chinese side, to create trust and cooperation.

4.5.3 Short-Term Solutions from African Perspectives

One major option to ameliorate tensions is to improve the working and living conditions of Tanzanian employees and their families in the district. Therefore, the intercultural communication between Chinese management and Tanzanian employees should be improved, and an open-door policy and cooperation across hierarchical levels could support the building of trustful, beneficial relationships. Besides formal "suggestion boxes", as often implemented in organisations, the Chinese organisation could implement weekly meetings, known in Kiswahili as *mikutano* (gatherings) or *shauri* (counselling), to ensure successful intercultural communication and cooperation throughout the project and sustainable success afterwards.

The Tanzanian employees could choose a representative to negotiate and discuss with the Chinese management and receive information on a regular basis to pass on to the employees.

4.5.4 Long-Term Solutions from African Perspectives

Chinese management and employees should learn about basic Tanzanian values, especially the value of sharing (translated in Kiswahili as *kushirikiana*, or *kugawana*), and provide clean and safe sanitation systems and improved healthcare facilities. Chinese management should become aware that values and actions that are successful in China cannot be transferred exactly into Tanzanian or even African contexts. It would be helpful if the Chinese management was aware of the heterogeneity of cultural influences in the region of Chalinze and of their implications in the rural context. In terms of decision-making, Chinese managers should understand the need of the local employees and communities to secure the water supply for their families and communities, and therefore their need for certainty without a heightened risk. The introduction of Tanzanian labour trade unions could be considered, to provide Tanzanian employees with a sense of being represented by a larger organisation and to know that their needs were being heard and dealt with in terms of labour laws and working conditions. Managers and employers need to provide plans to improve the working conditions in their organisations and increase the participation of employees, not only in normal organisational functions but also in creating socially responsible organisations.

The WAMACHA organ should be bolstered with experts in water management and financially supported by the communal government. Social media projects could also be involved in the long term to show the mutual benefits of the Chinese-Tanzanian projects across districts and provinces in the country.

4.6 Recommendations for Chinese-African Intercultural Cooperation

The main aim to improve cooperation between the Chinese management and the Tanzanian employees can be met through the application of transparent, open channels of communication across hierarchical and cultural divides. Strategic organisational and cultural goals should be communicated, and mutual interests and needs should be defined and tackled. By improving communication strategies, the chances strengthen to make the Chalinze project a nationally known pioneer project in local water supply systems, which are built on mutual benefits and social responsibility values rather than being a one-way exploitation project. This could contribute positively to the image of Chinese organisations in Tanzania.

A major recommendation could be to launch a public, intercultural information campaign to further ensure the mutual beneficial cooperation on governmental, organisational, community and individual levels. At a communal level, the local communities should be educated on community participation in the Chalinze Water Project through seminars, explaining topics such as environmental preservation, supervising design and construction of water projects (Shayo, 2013).

The water management organ WAMACHA should be strengthened and project management skills be taught to enable the organ to participate and interact appropriately. A village fund should be installed for minor maintenance of water infrastructure. Additionally, it is recommended to install "water user committees" taking full responsibility and being accountable for water issues in the region (Shayo, 2013).

References

Bräutigam, D. (2009). *The Dragon's Gift: The Real Story of China in Africa.* Oxford: Oxford University Press.
Dingding, C. (2017). *China Has a New Grand Strategy and the West Should Be Ready.* Retrieved from https://thediplomat.com/2017/10/china-has-a-new-grand-strategy-and-the-west-should-be-ready
Hainan International Ltd. (2018). Retrieved from http://crb.go.tz/hainan-international-limited-2
Hofstede, G. (2018). *Hofstede Insights. The Six Dimensions of National Culture.* Retrieved from https://www.hofstede-insights.com/product/compare-countries
Mabeya, C. (2017). China Encourages Further Investment in Tanzania. *China Daily Africa.* Retrieved August 25, 2017, from http://www.chinadaily.com.cn/a/201708/25/WS5a2926eca310fcb6fafd40e7.html
People's Daily Online. (2001, October 20). China-Aided Water Project Begins Construction in Tanzania. *People's Daily Online.* Retrieved from http://en.people.cn/200110/20/eng20011020_82736.html
Pretoria News. (2016, October 10). China Injects Positivity for Africa's Social, Economic Benefit. *Pretoria News*, p. 12.
Schiere, R., & Rugamba, A. (2011). *Chinese Infrastructure Investments and African Integration.* African Development Bank Group. Retrieved from https://www.afdb.org/fileadmin/uploads/afdb/Documents/Publications/WPS%20No%20127%20Chinese%20Infrastructure%20Investments%20.pdf
Shayo, D. (2013). *Community Participation and Sustainability of National Water Projects: Case Study of Chalinze Water Supply Project in Bagamoyo District.* MPA dissertation, Mzumbe University, Daressalaam, Tanzania.
Tanzania-Zambia Authority. (2018). Tanzania-Zambia Railway. About Tazara. Retrieved from https://tazarasite.com/15.11.2018
United Nations Report of the Secretary-General. (2017). *Progress towards the Sustainable Development Goals.* E/2017/66. Distribution: General. 11 May 2017.

CHAPTER 5

Case 2: "Not who I am, not what I mean": Intercultural Communication in Chinese-South African Interactions

Fungai B. Chigwendere

5.1 Case Narrative

In Chinese-African organisational contexts, there have been reports of intercultural communication (IC) challenges such as ineffectiveness, inappropriateness and, at times, misunderstandings (see Anedo, 2012; Arsene, 2014; Men, 2014; Westropp, 2012). Chinese and African perspectives on each other's communication behaviour in sub-Saharan and South Africa may provide insights into the prevailing IC challenges. For example, there are reports of loud African people simply talking for enjoyment, not necessarily to reach a particular conclusion (Matondo, 2012), and of Chinese people being quiet and rude (Fan, 2015). These views could be either reflections of a lack of IC awareness or deeply held prejudices on the part of either culture. China's Ambassador to South Africa, Zhong Jianhua (2007–2012), asserts that IC challenges between Chinese and African people arise from the gap between Chinese culture and the varied cultures of Africa's diverse population (Von Schirach, 2012). This cultural diversity is also evident within individual countries such as South Africa.

F. B. Chigwendere (✉)
Department of Management, Rhodes University, Grahamstown, South Africa

© The Author(s) 2019
C.-H. Mayer et al. (eds.), *Managing Chinese-African Business Interactions*, Palgrave Studies in African Leadership,
https://doi.org/10.1007/978-3-030-25185-7_5

There is little in-depth research of IC in Chinese-African interactions, making it impossible for the Chinese to avoid potential cultural complications when they enter African markets (Von Schirach, 2012). Dietz, Orr, and Xing (2008) concur, stating that successfully combining Chinese and foreign forms of communication and cultural norms is one of the biggest challenges facing Chinese organisations going abroad. Given the business and interaction complexities resulting from cultural differences, it is imperative that interactants engage in IC continually to improve the way they communicate, by seeking ways to reduce barriers and challenges.

In a project exploring IC experiences of Chinese and African organisational colleagues in South Africa during 2016, several Chinese and African experts were interviewed. Purposive and snowball sampling is engaged in this study to identify experts where an "expert" is defined as being a practising Chinese or African manager or staff member, born and socialised in the Chinese society or any of the African countries south of the Sahara, and with experience working in a Chinese-African organisational context. In this case study, which arises from the project, excerpts from conversations with Chinese and African experts bring to the fore some of the issues and challenges faced in the IC encounter. For the sake of confidentiality, pseudonyms are used in this narration.

5.2 Chinese Perspectives on Intercultural Communication

Mr Ping is a 50-year-old Chinese businessman who has spent over 20 years interacting with South Africans in mining and other industry sectors. He highlights the diversity and complexity of the South African context by making reference to differences between communication behaviours of the different racial groups. He describes White South African Afrikaans-speaking people as "very straightforward, very frank", while the Black[1] South Africans are seen as "curious and eager to get along with the Chinese people". This view suggests greater cultural proximity between the Black African people and Chinese people. Mr Ping comments further:

---

[1] According to the South African Employment Equity Act (Act 55 of 1998), the term "Black" is a generic term used in reference to Africans, Coloured and Indian people. However, for the purpose of this case study "Black" refers to Black Africans, in the sense of the indigenous Black African people.

5 CASE 2: "NOT WHO I AM, NOT WHAT I MEAN": INTERCULTURAL... 73

It's a problem to the Chinese people and to the Western and African people. For Western and African people when you are working for a Chinese organisation or you go to China and you behave in such a way. There are always wars between you and the people because they don't like to accept your manner. Sometimes they say you are good but you not educated. These people don't treat you fairly and nicely. That's one challenge. Then on the other side for Chinese people like me myself, there are many who come to work in other places such as Africa, America, Europe, and everywhere, who also suffer because they were brought up in a Chinese environment. So, they are used to behaving the Chinese way and when they come to the Western and other worlds, they try and behave the same way but, as I said, in the Western world if you don't speak out then the people just interpret that you don't know. You don't need to say anything but in your heart you want to say something. They cannot just work everything out straightforward, then they suffer. For instance, if they see something wrong in the office then they don't like to speak out, or if they see some decisions from the leaders which aren't correct then they won't speak out. Then people ask later why did not say anything? So here in the Western organisation, the Chinese has to take the blame.

Providing another example, Mr Ping continues:

The other thing is that in Chinese culture if you are working together as a team, if your boss is Chinese and he says, 'We need to buy this property for x amount of dollars as it can produce fifty million dollars next year'. And you are the team leader who has more technical background and think that this is impossible, you can't say that. You will probably be fired if you say that. You are basically saying he is weaker and that's an insult to the Chinese boss. You could have said, 'Yes, you are right, that's wonderful, maybe we need to do more work and investigate further, let me help you gain more information'. So, in this way you did not say you agree with him but also you did not say he is wrong.

Another Chinese expert, Mr Lan, is a 46-year-old Chinese entrepreneur who has been operating a manufacturing company in South Africa for over 15 years. He paints a picture of lazy and dishonest Africans who are proud and more concerned with words than with actions:

South African locals say lies too easily and their business relations are dishonest. They have a sweet mouth with a multitude of fine words, but they seldom do what they say.

More of Mr Lan's perspectives, quoted below, appear to question the sincerity and humility of some of his African counterparts:

> In my experience, many South Africans believe themselves to be exceptionally smart. They are boastful and lack credibility, so I couldn't take their words too seriously and couldn't keep their company, let alone have deep fellowship with them.
> You find the South Africans saying, 'Hi, how are you? I am good'—too much hypocritical. And then they laugh and hug and each other—oh my goodness wasting time! If you are too friendly, Chinese people have doubt.

In summary, the perspectives above suggest that IC challenges are largely centred on a lack of knowledge and understanding of others' culture, on prejudice, and on stereotyping.

5.3 South African Perspectives on Intercultural Communication

Mr Muz is a 37-year-old Black African senior engineer working in the IT and telecom industry in South Africa. Mr Muz is originally from one of the Southern African Development Community (SADC) countries and has four years' experience working in a Chinese organisation and interacting with Chinese people. His view of his Chinese counterparts is that:

> They are very impersonal in their relations with other people—even amongst themselves... They defer mostly to rank. So, if someone is high ranked they interact with them in a different way and then if they are on the same level they also interact with them differently... It is like a military type of setup, you know, where you have a major and a colonel and a sergeant and that sort of thing—that is how they relate.

Mr Muz finds that his Chinese counterparts seem to have expectations of how their African colleagues should relate to them:

> [W]hen they interact with us ... they expect you to defer in a specific way, acknowledging those ranks that they defer to amongst themselves. But then you find that we don't operate like [that] ... we don't call each other 'Mr' in South Africa; if it is Thabo, it is Thabo.

5 CASE 2: "NOT WHO I AM, NOT WHAT I MEAN": INTERCULTURAL... 75

According to Mr Muz, certain behaviours and ways of doing things will ensure success in Chinese-African interactions:

So, if I want a raise from the manager ... I need to go to the big, big boss: I need someone to take me to the big, big boss. He is going to say, 'Okay, this is X, he is the one who is doing this and this and this'—he will explain. And then the boss is like, 'Oh yeah, yes, yes, that one'. And he will say, 'X is a very good chap, he does his job very well, blah, blah and he deserves a raise'. Then I will get a raise. If I just go directly to the boss, you will not get anything. So, you need to learn those things. ... when you are speaking to them, if you stand with your hands behind your back looking very firm and strong, it shows you are very stable. But if you just fidget in front of them, you are weak. ... Chinese you don't necessarily have to look a boss in their eyes, it shows that maybe you undermine his authority or something. So, you learn those things so that you also don't offend the other people.

Another African expert, Ms Sue, is a 40-year-old senior manager working in the finance department of a Chinese-owned manufacturing company in South Africa, who illuminates day-to-day intricacies of Chinese-African interactions in her organisation. A number of telling perspectives from Ms Sue are quoted below:

The Chinese don't seem to believe in greeting and when they angry with you, they won't speak to you. Whereas in African culture, it is a complete 'no, no'.
  The Chinese just think they are bigger. We have to prove to them we have competence because they just don't trust.
  It's not a good thing when you are dealing with them, to be so confrontational. I think in a way they do find it disrespectful and think that you are being unnecessarily resistant in working with them to achieve their objectives.
  When he speaks [Chinese manager], it doesn't sound like it is very harsh but when she [Chinese translator] tells us, it sounds harsh. They so calm, but those words are so sharp, when you leave there you go out and you cry. You won't cry in the boardroom but you will cry.
  They didn't have to say much, or they did say it in Chinese, but you could see in the body language (no eye contact) that it's a no.
  The Chinese will never say no... They don't offend, but it's no. They don't come back to you, they just simply ignore you and do their own thing anyway.

These statements are open to diverse interpretations, hence giving credence to the view that without IC awareness, erroneous conclusions may be reached. In summary, the perspectives shared by African experts as with the Chinese experts similarly suggest IC challenges are largely centred on a lack of knowledge and understanding of others' culture, prejudice and stereotyping.

5.4 Questions and Points of Discussion

- Identify and explore the issues impacting IC from the perspectives of the Chinese and African experts.
- Identify which values play a role in each of the culture-specific viewpoints of Chinese and African colleagues (What Chinese or African values are implied? How do these values differ from traditional Chinese and African values as commonly described in literature?)
- Develop short- and long-term solutions for this case from each of the Chinese and African points of view.

5.5 Chinese Perspectives

From Mr Ping's perspective, it appears that IC in Chinese-African interactions is punctuated with conflict arising from prejudice, ethnocentrism and differences in cultural values, which influence the manner in which people communicate. There are also challenges of failure to follow protocol and adapt to others' manner of communication as necessary. When a cultural group is ethnocentric, it typically holds the view that everything should be rated with reference to its own way, which represents the only legitimate way of doing things (Neuliep, 2012; Washington, 2013), and this often results in misunderstandings and misinterpretations in IC (Hilton & Kameda, 1999; Victor, 1992). For example, Mr Ping suggests that people belonging to some cultural groups refuse to accept the manner of communication of another because they see them as inferior or "not educated". This narrative illustrates the existence of ethnocentric beliefs in some individuals during Chinese-African interactions.

Just as with ethnocentrism, stereotyping or judging people based on assumptions and generalisations can result in unmet expectations (Martin & Nakayama, 2010; Samovar & Porter, 1995), which present a barrier to enhanced IC. Furthermore, people can hold general negative or positive stereotyped ideas of those from other cultural groups, based on little or no experience (Martin & Nakayama, 2010; Phatak, Bhagat, & Kashlak, 2005; Verderber & Verderber, 2008), resulting in problematic "us and them" behaviour (Alberts, Nakayama, & Martin, 2010, p. 97). Mr Lan's experience of interacting with African people leads him to conclude that they are dishonest, arrogant, talk too much and do not follow through on their word. Such judgements, where one cultural group views itself as superior to another, may obscure the necessity of communicating with the other, hence ignoring any legitimate issues that may arise resulting in poor IC.

Communication behaviours and perspectives expressed by Chinese experts could be explained in reference to traditional Chinese culture, values and Confucianism, which is a Chinese philosophy of human nature, relating to principles of benevolence and humanness, the family system, insider versus outsider relationships, hierarchy and role relationships, filial piety, reciprocity, *Guanxi* (relationships) and *Mianzi* (face) (Gan, 2014; Gao & Ting-Toomey, 1998). There is an expectation that virtuous qualities such as righteousness, faithfulness and justice are maintained in social interaction (Chen & Chung, 1994; Gan, 2014; Yum, 1988). People interact respectfully in a proper manner and are guided by a code of ethics, forming an underlying structure of what constitutes appropriate behaviour in different contexts and relationships, thus ensuring maintenance of the social order, stability, peace, prosperity and harmony (Gan, 2014, pp. 110–112).

Guanxi, which best translates as relationships or connections (Fang & Faure, 2011; Lockett, 1988, p. 489), is regarded as the most influential principle in communication (Huang, 2010). With *Guanxi*, people exist through and are defined by honouring requirements of their roles in their hierarchically structured relationships (Huang, 2010; Ma, 2011), suggesting the importance of appropriateness. Reportedly in the business context, building and maintaining relationships are placed ahead of actual business transactions and speed (Yum, 1988, p. 381). Because of this, *guan-xing* (concern talk), such as enquiry after the family and other personal matters, is an expected norm (Yum, 1988). Interestingly, this may not be appropriate in the Chinese-African organisational context where, early in the relationship, the insider versus outsider aspect of Chinese relationships may limit the extent of interaction with non-Chinese colleagues, as they may be treated as outsiders. This cultural nuance is something African colleagues should be aware of, not to be seen as alienation.

Apart from *Guanxi*, the earlier-mentioned concept of *Mianzi* (face) plays a pivotal role in communication in Chinese culture. In this case study, the perspective that Chinese subordinates are neither confrontational nor direct in conversations with their superiors can be explained in terms of the emphasis of hierarchy, roles, relationships and *Mianzi*. For example, in an organisational setting rather than saying outright to a superior, "I do not agree", Mr Ping explains that a subordinate would likely say, "Yes, you are right, that's wonderful; maybe we need to do more work and investigate further. Let me help you gain more information". By being diplomatic in approach, the subordinate will not have embarrassed their superior. They will have maintained their superior's *Mianzi*, as their reputation and honour are maintained.

Chinese experts view their African counterparts as insincere. In particular, they see African people as overly affectionate in their greetings. Mr Lan comments that when African people greet, laugh and hug each other every day, it does not seem genuine, and it makes the Chinese people suspicious. What Mr Lan probably does not comprehend is that African behaviour is to a large extent guided by the African humanist philosophy of *Ubuntu*, which emphasises values of caring, reciprocity, sharing, compassion, hospitality, cohabitation, cooperation and tolerance (see Bell & Metz, 2011; Praeg & Magadla, 2014; Van den Heuvel, 2008). Greeting and showing affection is very much a part of African culture, given that "I am because you are, and you are, because we are" (Khoza, 2005). Whatever happens to the individual happens to the whole group (Briggs, 1996, cited in Waneless, 2007, p. 117).

Furthermore, *Ubuntu* is about the display of ethical behaviour or "being human", where failure to display ethical human behaviour leads to being labelled an animal (Metz, 2015, p. 85). For instance, the Shona people of Zimbabwe say *Haazi munhu, imhuka* if someone displays unethical behaviour, which translates as: he is not a person; he is an animal. An imperative, therefore, exists for individuals to behave appropriately and ethically as they are under the constant assessment of their communities.

5.6 African Perspectives

From an African point of view, Mr Muz touches on differences in culture, ways of communicating and general way of life, essentially contributing to IC awareness of Chinese and African culture in the organisational context. Cultural patriotism appears to be strong for both Chinese and African employees and colleagues who maintain their own cultural nuances in the way they communicate, this despite being in a multicultural context. For example, Mr Muz states that even though he was educated in England, he remains "a modest African man" true to his core value system, which neither changed contexts nor modified working environments. This, he says, holds equally true for his Chinese colleagues, who continue in most instances to behave in what he calls a Chinese way. "Culture is communication and communication is culture" (Hall, 1959, p. 159), and values do not simply change over time. Because of the enduring nature of culture, Chinese and African colleagues in the Chinese-African context may unwittingly present their way of doing things as the legitimate way, without due consideration of the other party. "This is not necessarily the way that we do things around here" is an approach depicting a level of ethnocentrism and a lack of appreciation of a different cultural environment from one's own.

Mr Muz observes that the Chinese manner of communication is impersonal, hierarchical, protocol-driven and rule-bound, and it does not completely align with African culture, though there are some overlaps. Reference to a military-style setup, deference to rank as well as having the correct posture and following the correct procedure in asking for a raise are examples of the perceived importance of rules and protocol in interacting with Chinese people. In addition to good performance, the difference between getting a raise and not getting a raise in a Chinese-African organisational context can also depend on the manner of communication, including the subtle messages projected through non-verbal communication. By not standing at attention when being addressed by the manager, an African person may project an image of weakness and therefore might not be taken seriously.

From another perspective, Ms Sue depicts Chinese colleagues as not showing emotion, unfriendly and lacking in transparency. She says, "The Chinese don't seem to believe in greeting and when they angry with you, they won't speak to you. Whereas in African culture, it is a complete no-no". To the observer, this could be interpreted as such, or seen as a complete misunderstanding, each of the other. However, when traditional Chinese culture is revisited, the behaviour of the Chinese could be explained in terms of gravitating towards their in-group and not being prone to greeting everyone they meet. In addition, their quest for harmony, avoiding conflict and not showing emotions could be reasons why Chinese people do not speak when angry. On the other hand, the idea of ethnocentrism can also not be entirely discarded, likely driven by a view that certain colleagues are inferior and therefore not worthy to be spoken to. These are however speculations that could arise from a lack of IC awareness.

5.7 Culture-Specific Solutions

5.7.1 Short-Term Solutions from Chinese Perspectives

When interacting with those from a different culture, it is important to avoid stereotyping and, instead, adopt an open-minded approach. It is also wise to acknowledge, understand and respect the differences in others' culture. For example, on speaking of his Chinese counterparts, Mr Ping says, "I think that is one key issue about what they need to do. They must be prepared to open, accept and even to appreciate difference". The Chinese experts are also of the view that any positive change must start at the individual level. The key is not to be judgemental and, instead, seek to understand why things are done the way they are done by others. Being mindful is also important as expressed by Mr Ping: "Don't try to just apply your own framework and enforce them onto other people ... so you need to teach yourself to be prepared to learn new things, to accommodate and listen too". People in the interaction encounter must each individually take responsibility to enhance IC by committing to learn about others. Mr Ping says: "For myself, when I decided to come to South Africa, I made the commitment to learn".

5.7.2 Long-Term Solutions from Chinese Perspectives

Mr Ping mentions that at both the organisational and individual level, "there is a necessity for training in each other's culture and to develop each other's good cultural points so that we have a fusion of the two cultures. Also, when you communicate there is a need to keep others' values in mind so you can get harmony". Thereafter, research should be conducted and strategies crafted to reconcile any conflicting communication cultures and disseminated to Chinese and African counterparts alike through training. As Mr Ping comments, "If we understand more of each other, we will enjoy more benefits. More Chinese investors are going to come to Africa and we are going to enjoy more opportunities". Thus, in the long term, with greater IC awareness, Chinese and African colleagues will come closer to reaching IC congruence, the point at which communication is mutually effective and appropriate.

5.7.3 Short-Term Solutions from African Perspectives

As a short-term solution, African experts, like their Chinese counterparts, should seek to learn about and understand communication in their counterparts' culture, and then they should "guide each other accordingly, until you come up with something reasonable". Mr Muz contends that open communication and the creation of an environment where Chinese and African colleagues "can actually interact, exchange words and have dialogue or commune in a certain way" will go a long way towards enhancing IC. "It takes two to tango" and neither party should be taken for granted as both seek to learn from the other to achieve enhanced IC. The same ideas of open-mindedness and mindfulness as raised in the Chinese perspectives on enhancing IC also apply. As such, it would be desirable for Chinese and African colleagues to work towards collectively developing and building a welcoming greeting culture in organisations that could lead to mutual respect and acknowledgement.

5.7.4 Long-Term Solutions from African Perspectives

As hosts, African experts underscore the importance of their Chinese counterparts understanding *Ubuntu* and what it means for interaction and business success. This is seen in Mr Muz's statement:

> *In business you don't get what you deserve, you get what you negotiate, right? So, if people come to do business, and then they say, 'Ah I am just coming here to do business because I am motivated by profit', then we are actually neglecting the essence of our humanism, or Ubuntu, and this can have consequences within the organisation.*

To facilitate cross-cultural learning, organisations must implement cultural exchange programmes and hold sessions that will help colleagues understand others' culture and the reasons why they do the things they do. This could include appointing cultural exchange champions in the organisation. These champions, with the aid of the organisation, actively seek to learn about own and others' culture, and then informally and formally impart this knowledge to others. In the end, equipped with IC awareness, it is plausible that many IC challenges will gradually be overcome and a state of IC congruence achieved. In such a scenario, communicating parties are both understood and accepted for who they are, and their messages are received as intended.

5.8 Recommendations for Chinese-African Intercultural Cooperation

The perspective shared by Chinese and African experts highlights that a lack of IC awareness perpetuates the IC challenges in Chinese-African interactions. As such, in view of the long-term outlook of China-Africa engagement, government-level cultural exchange initiatives with the support of business are encouraged from as early as primary school level. Furthermore, intercultural trainings within organisations must be conducted for employees to learn about their own and the other's cultures and how this could affect communication with others. It is imagined that adopting a proactive and long-term outlook in cultural exchange initiatives will allow Chinese and African counterparts destined for interaction in diverse contexts to learn about and get to understand each other's culture before, during and after the interaction. In addition, issues, considerations and suggestions unearthed through research should be taken into cognisance at the highest levels, while simultaneously feeding into interventions for enhancing IC at the micro- and meso-levels. For example, preliminary insights suggest that African colleagues are human-orientated, while their Chinese colleagues are more in-group harmony-orientated. This has implications for how they communicate and perhaps how they expect others to communicate. Where Chinese colleagues appear to be indirect in their communication, African colleagues appear comfortable with a blended manner of communication, comprising a mix of direct and indirect messaging. These examples, however, merely scratch the surface of the dynamics and complexities of Chinese-African communication. Indeed, based on a comprehensive review of the experiences and perspectives of those in interaction, a handbook for IC in Chinese-African interactions with country-specific focus would be a worthy investment.

References

Alberts, J. K., Nakayama, T. K., & Martin, J. N. (2010). *Human Communication in Society* (2nd ed.). Hoboken, NJ: Pearson Education.

Anedo, O. (2012). China-Africa Culture Differences in Business Relations. *African Journal of Political Science and International Relations*, 6(4), 92–96.

Arsene, C. (2014). Chinese Employers and Their Ugandan Workers: Tensions, Frictions and Cooperation in an African City. *Journal of Current Chinese Affairs*, 43(1), 139–176.

Bell, D. A. A., & Metz, T. (2011). Confucianism and Ubuntu: Reflections and a Dialogue between Chinese and African Traditions. *Journal of Chinese Philosophy, 38*, 78–95.

Chen, G. M., & Chung, J. (1994). The Impact of Confucianism on Organisational Communication. *Communication Quarterly, 42*(2), 93–105.

Dietz, M. C., Orr, G., & Xing, J. (2008). *How Chinese Companies Can Succeed Abroad*. [Pdf] McKinsey on Finance. Retrieved from https://www.whatsonweibo.com/too-loud-too-rude-switzerland-introduces-separate-trains-for-chinese-tourists/

Fan, Y. (2015). *"Too Loud, Too Rude": Switzerland Introduces Separate Trains for Chinese Tourists*. Retrieved from https://www.whatsonweibo.com/too-loud-too-rude-switzerland-introduces-separate-trains-for-chinese-tourists/

Fang, T., & Faure, G. O. (2011). Chinese Communication Characteristics: A Yin Yang Perspective. *International Journal of Intercultural Relations, 5*, 320–333.

Gan, S. (2014). *How to Do Business with China: An Inside View on Chinese Culture and Etiquette*. Milton Keynes: AuthorHouse.

Gao, G., & Ting-Toomey, S. (1998). *Communicating Effectively with the Chinese*. Thousand Oaks, CA: Sage.

Hall, E. T. (1959). *The Silent Language*. Garden City, NY: Doubleday.

Hilton, C., & Kameda, N. (1999). Email and the Internet as International Business Communication Teaching and Research Tools: A Case Study. *Journal of Education for Business, 35*(4), 181–185.

Huang, Y. H. (2010). Theorising Chinese Communication Research: A Holistic Framework for Comparative Studies. *Chinese Journal of Communication. 3*(1), 95–113.

Khoza, R. J. (2005). *Let Africa Lead: African Transformational Leadership for the 21st Century Business*. Sunninghill: Vezubuntu Publishers.

Lockett, M. (1988). Culture and the Problems of Chinese Management. *Organisational Studies, 9*(4), 475–496.

Ma, R. (2011). Social Relations (Guanxi): A Chinese Approach to Interpersonal Communication. *China Media Research, 7*(4), 25–33.

Martin, J. N., & Nakayama, T. K. (2010). *Intercultural Communication in Contexts*. New York: McGraw Hill.

Matondo, M. J. P. (2012). Cross-cultural Value Comparisons between Chinese and Sub-Saharan Africans. *International Journal of Business and Social Science, 3*(11), 38–45.

Men, T. (2014). Place-Based and Place-Bound Realities: A Chinese Firm's Embeddedness in Tanzania. *Journal of Current Chinese Affairs, 43*(1), 103–138.

Metz, T. (2015). Values in China as Compared to Africa. In H. Du Plessis, T. Metz, G. Raza, R. Poplak, D. Cisse, M. Davies, Y. Zhao, G. Le Pere, A. Ross,

& M. Lauzon-Lacroix (Eds.), *The Rise and Decline and Rise of China: Searching for an Organizing Philosophy*. Johannesburg: Real African Publishers.

Neuliep, J. W. (2012). The Relationship among Intercultural Communication Apprehension, Ethnocentrism, Uncertainty Reduction, and Communication Satisfaction during Initial Intercultural Interaction: An Extension of Anxiety and Uncertainty Management (AUM) Theory. *Journal of Intercultural Communication Research*, 41(1), 1–16.

Phatak, A. V., Bhagat, R. S., & Kashlak, R. J. (2005). *International Management: Managing in a Diverse and Dynamic Global Environment*. New York: McGraw Hill.

Praeg, S. L., & Magadla, S. (2014). *Ubuntu: Curating the Archive*. Scottsville: UKZN Press.

Samovar, L. A., & Porter, R. E. (1995). *Communication between Cultures* (2nd ed.). Belmont, CA: Wadsworth.

Van Den Heuvel, H. (2008). 'Hidden Messages' Emerging from Afrocentric Management Perspectives. *Acta Commercii*, 8, 41–54.

Verderber, K. S., & Verderber, R. F. (2008). *Communicate* (12th ed.). Belmont, CA: Wadsworth.

Victor, D. (1992). *International Business Communication*. New York: Harper Collins.

Von Schirach, P. M. (2012). *China's Point Man for Africa in an Interview Admits that Chinese Companies Operating in the Continent Follow Unorthodox Practices to Get Business – "Bags of Money on the Table, and Bribes"*. Schirach Reports. Retrieved from http://schirachreport.com/index.php/2012/04/07/chinas-point-man-for-africa-in-an-interview-admits-that-chinese-companies-operating-in-the-continent-follow-unorthodox-practices-to-get-business-bags-of-money-on-the-table-and-bribes

Waneless, D. (2007). Ubuntu: We All Belong to Each Other. *International Congregational Journal*, 7(1), 117–119.

Washington, M. C. (2013). Intercultural Business Communication: An Analysis of Ethnocentrism in a Globalized Business Environment. *Journal of Business and Management*, 1(1), 20–27.

Westropp, S. (2012). Cultural Comparison of China and Sub-Saharan Africa. *Otago Management Graduate Review*, 10, 67–87.

Yum, J. O. (1988). The Impact of Confucianism on Interpersonal Relationships and Communication Patterns in East Asia. *Communication Monographs*, 55, 374–388.

CHAPTER 6

Case 3: Dealing with Organisational Structures, Decision-Making and Participation in the Zambian Textile Industry

Christian Martin Boness, Naiming Wei, and Claude-Hélène Mayer

6.1 CASE NARRATIVE

The Republic of Zambia is a landlocked country bordering Angola in the west, the Republic of Congo and Tanzania in the north, Malawi in the east, Mozambique, Zimbabwe, Botswana and the Namibian Caprivi strip in the south. Zambia covers an area half the size of Europe. The 16 million Zambian citizens belong to more than 70 ethnic groups and live on a high savannah plateau. Zambia gained its independence from the UK in 1964

C. M. Boness (✉) • C.-H. Mayer
Department of Management, Rhodes University, Grahamstown, South Africa

N. Wei
Department of Business Administration, University of Applied Science, Nuremberg, Germany
e-mail: Naiming.wei@th-nuernberg.de

© The Author(s) 2019
C.-H. Mayer et al. (eds.), *Managing Chinese-African Business Interactions*, Palgrave Studies in African Leadership,
https://Doi.org/10.1007/978-3-030-25185-7_6

and since then keeps on developing without major violent disruptions. The climate is dry, temperate and subtropical (Embassy of the Republic of Zambia, 2018).

Zambia has important natural resources like copper, cobalt, zinc, lead, coal, gold, silver, uranium and, in particular, hydropower, which is exported to neighbouring countries. Zambian industries combine copper mining and processing, chemicals, textiles and fertilisers. Zambia is one of the rising countries in Africa in terms of economy. From 2005 to 2010 the gross domestic product (GDP) grew from US$8332 million to US$20,265 million and, thereafter, at a slower pace to US$21,255 million in 2017 (UN Statistics, 2018; Zambia Business Times, 2018). The most important export partners (2017) are China (25%), the Democratic Republic of the Congo (13%) and South Africa (6.4%), whereas the main import partners are South Africa (34.5%), the Democratic Republic of the Congo (18.2%) and Kenya (9.7%) (Embassy of the Republic of Zambia, 2018).

Contemporarily, Chinese-Zambian relations and investments are among the most important on the African continent (Bwalya, 2016). Investments are diversified to several sectors of Zambia's economy, not only to copper mines, agriculture and infrastructural constructions but also to the textile industry (Bwalya, 2016). This case focuses on the textile industry, and on a specific organisation under international cooperation.

The joint venture between the Chinese and the Zambian government is an organisation called Mulungushi Textiles Limited (MTB), one of the biggest textile producers in Zambia. Research (Munoni, 2017) shows that after one decade of standstill of the factory, the organisation was reopened by the Zambian President Chagwa Lungu in August 2016, who explained that the organisation was now a new, prosperous and successful Chinese-Zambian enterprise (Munoni, 2017).

From 1997 onwards, MTB had already been a joint venture built by a Chinese corporation holding 66% of the shares, while the Zambian government held only 34% of the organisation's shares (Business & Human Rights Resource Centre, 2018). The organisation had closed down, but China recently invested in revamping MTB as a joint project of cooperation between the two countries. The Chinese proclaim the success of the organisation, in providing expertise in running a successful textile industry and bringing the company up to become the largest textile mill in the country, manufacturing 17 million metres of fabric per year and 100,000 pieces of clothing. The organisation also won international awards for the high quality of its products (Hare, 2007).

Beneath these external successes, however, lie internal organisational factors, which lead to a suboptimal performance of MTB staff, such as the disparity in salaries between Chinese and Zambian employees. The Chinese assistant manager, for example, is paid five times more than the higher-positioned Zambian deputy general manager (Munoni, 2017, p. 55). This creates dissatisfaction and conflict within the organisation. Additionally, there are external factors, which impact negatively on the performance and success of the organisation, such as US and European non-governmental organisation (NGO) donations of clothing, as well as cheap Chinese textile imports. These factors affected competition and led to the closing down of the company.

Apart from MTB's undercapitalisation, the high operational costs, conditions of servicing of machinery and poor governmental support from China and Zambia contribute to the low performance of the factory. Finally, one major factor in the situation is underestimated: human work power and its impact on the efficiency and success of the company.

The majority of Zambian employees in MTB feel disrespected in terms of decision-making processes and participation structures in the Chinese-Zambian MTB plant. The wages paid to the local Zambian employees are extremely low and strictly bound to the minimum wage regulations imposed by the Zambian government. Apart from the minimum wage implications, no further negotiations are happening in either of the governments to support the employees. Therefore, the employees of MTB, particularly the local ones, become highly dissatisfied.

Since the reopening of the organisation in 2016 and the confidence of the Zambian president, many of the previous problems remain unaddressed, although a new management approach has been launched. To avoid a second closure of the organisation, resulting in thousands of Zambian employees being left without work or payment, many employees of the Zambian workforce are now uniting to create new textile designs. By coming up with their own design ideas, these employees aim to create participation in decision-making and innovation in responding to the clothing needs of the Zambian and African market.

Mrs Kabelo is an assistant designer in middle management at MTB. As part of the management, she receives a 20% discount when she buys clothes directly from the organisation. Mrs Kabelo is the mother of four children and is happy with her position in the company, since she studied design at a local university. She has already developed her own design ideas, which she believes would appeal to the local market. She therefore asks herself: although I am only an assistant designer, why not introduce an innovative local design concept to the MTB management? Mrs Kabelo is convinced that a new Africanised design of the products would enhance employee engagement and organisational commitment as well, since employees could identify with their cultural patterns, idioms and colours of the products and expand the product portfolio.

Mrs Kabelo, in her position as an assistant design manager, is very concerned about her influence on the design of patterns and use of colours and believes that, through developing this designed product, she could gain influence and accreditation. Therefore, during the past months, she has tried repeatedly to approach the top managers in design and production to discuss her ideas. However, top management does not show interest and declines her requests for discussing her ideas.

The conclusion she draws from this failing intercultural interaction is that Zambian employees do not have a say, that there is no proper meeting structure in place and that the management does not take Zambian employees seriously. Although she holds a master's degree in textile design, she has come to believe that her professionalism is not in demand. She is angry about the top-down decision-making approaches, the disregard of her work input and the highly bureaucratic and centralised management structures. Out of frustration, she develops a plan to implement employee-based decision-making structures by mobilising her fellow Zambian employees.

Mrs Kabelo calls upon her fellow employees, who share her perceptions of being disregarded by the management, to attend a consensus-orientated meeting. At the meeting, other Zambian middle-management employees complain about the rigid organisational structure of MTB, of being unengaged, and frustrated by the limited impact they have in the organisation. A senior employee points out that not even older, experienced employees at MTB are invited to consult on any decision-making issues, and that he has lost his trust in and commitment to the organisation. The meeting's members decide to proactively write a letter to MTB's Chinese top management. A young Zambian employee recommends that the letter should be written using Chinese communication patterns, including a well-known Chinese idiom as a door-opener for further communication. He is aware, so he says, that Chinese employees will be more open to read letters that refer to their own cultural patterns than to letters without any connection to Chinese culture. The meeting then studies a list of Chinese idioms that Mrs Kabelo provides. The young Zambian employee suggests beginning the letter with the following words:

Bù wén bù ruò wén zhī, wén zhī bù ruò jiàn zhī, jiàn zhī bù ruò zhīzhī, zhīzhī bù ruò xíng zhī; xué zhìyú xíng zhī ér zhǐ yǐ.

不闻不若闻之, 闻之不若见之, 见之不若知之, 知之不若行之。学至于行之而止矣出自《荀子·儒效》

A translation by the authors:

> Listening is advantageous by learning, but seeing is more advantageous than listening, and understanding is even more advantageous than seeing. Finally, acting is more advantageous than understanding and reaches the last station of learning.

The employees in the meeting agree to include this idiom as an access point to encourage further negotiations with the Chinese top management. The Zambian employees are convinced that this will demonstrate their respect for and interest in the Chinese culture and language, and their willingness to cooperate interculturally, leading to an improved communication and mutual understanding between Zambian employees and Chinese managers. This is also viewed as a first step towards an increased influence in decision-making and participation.

6.2 Questions and Points of Discussion

- How should an African middle-management employee, such as Mrs Kabelo, approach the Chinese top management in a culture-appropriate manner?
- What do you think: which meanings do colours have in Zambian and in Chinese cultural contexts?
- Discuss which procedures and strategies Zambian employees and Chinese top management can develop to improve their intercultural decision-making processes within the organisation.

6.3 Chinese Perspectives

Chinese organisations usually are structured in a top-down, bureaucratic and centralised way with strict hierarchies in decision-making processes (Thomas & Schenk, 2014) because the Chinese culture has been influenced by the rule of the dynasties for more than 5000 years of their existence. In the

Chinese tradition, the centralised decision-making process has mainly positive impacts: a clearly defined process, minimisation of responsibilities on different hierarchical levels and efficiency and quality of the decision-making process.

These phenomena result in a minimal involvement of Zambian managers in decision-making because traditional Chinese management methods emphasise hierarchy, efficiency and centralised decision-making. Having broad employee involvement is not considered a "mainstream" style. There is no focus on formal process structure, but rather on flexible working practice, which has strength and weakness at the same time.

It is not surprising that many Chinese companies pay low salaries whenever they can because the market defines the salaries, and they find enough labour in the market. Chinese companies also will only fulfil a minimum of legal requirements. These points result in both cost efficiency and timeous implementation of projects. In a situation similar to the case study, in the coastal region of China 20 years ago, salaries were found to increase as soon as markets could develop positively in the long term. However, the issue of salaries is a general problem for global companies investing in less-developed countries, such as Western companies investing in China. Western companies operating in Africa face the same difficulties with salary gaps. It is widely observed that Western managers seem to gain more understanding of these inequities from African managers than Chinese managers gain from their African counterparts.

MTB needs to take its competition seriously. The economic success of a joint venture does not automatically enrich its reputation in comparison to other competing international companies, and this appears to be the case regarding MTB.

Generally, in Chinese communication, idioms are used to illuminate, substitute for and strengthen ideas to improve business and communication. Therefore, it seems an appropriate suggestion to have a Chinese idiom in the proposed letter in this case study.

In China, colours have different cultural meanings, and the preference of colours depends strongly on cultural preferences as well as individual preferences. China uses colours as symbols in nearly every ceremony or celebration. Especially in clothing, colours play a huge role. For example, the colour red (fire) expresses joy and happiness, while white (metal) expresses sorrow (Olesen, 2018). Yellow (earth) represents royalty and power, prosperity—but also pornographic expressions (Olesen, 2018). The colour black (water) is associated with destruction, cruelty, sadness and profundity. If displaying the colour of blue (wood), associations of spring, immortality and advancement may arise. The Chinese will express wealth and riches using the colour of gold, while the colour green might indicate pure, organic or toxin free, but it is also the symbol of an unfaithful wife. Purple might be translated to represent love and romance but also divinity and immortality. So, in the case of MTB, colours have been used for the design of fashionable products that reflect more Chinese colour meanings than Zambian preferences. Chinese colours are colours to be shown publicly—they can be displayed in the design of MTB textiles that are sold on the Zambian markets.

It will not be necessary to have long discussions about colour and design concepts if the Zambians have a clearly defined plan to influence and change management's ideas about design and colours.

6.4 Zambian Perspectives

Of course, Zambian employees and customers of MTB are eager to see their colours, patterns and cultural symbols being printed on the textiles. They want to find a way to push their preferences through the channels of decision-making and participation in the organisation. In MTB, Zambian employees complain about decision-making processes regarding patterns and colours of the designed textile products. They miss out on meetings and feel excluded by the top-down structure of the organisation.

The majority of Zambian employees at MTB belong to the Bemba ethnic group. Bemba traditionally uses the word *mulesangwa* for a scheduled consensus-orientated meeting and the word *balekumana* for meetings to resolve conflict or problems. Elders usually invite and conduct these meetings (Bemba Dictionary Online, 2018). In an organisational context, the employees with extended experience or aged senior employees usually call the meetings. In a *mulesangwa*, the participants would agree on their way forward to resolve their problems and concerns on a collective level. Thereby, they would try to change the perspective, not only taking their own views into account but also the views of the other person or group involved, as expressed symbolically by using a Chinese idiom in the letter.

The major aim of a *mulesangwa* is to reach a peaceful decision-making on the basis of *Ubuntu*, a pan-African philosophy for social network management (Tutu, 2000). *Ubuntu* describes an African lifestyle that is practised in daily life, referring to the concept "I am because you are"

(Mayer & Boness, 2003). The concept of *Ubuntu* underlines the collective thought of the group-based decision-making processes in many African societies and describes a kind of collective consciousness, a general spiritual approach, including ethics, political and ideological impacts on life and social relationships (Gade, 2012; Tutu, 2000). *Ubuntu* defines social relationships and how people should behave, speak, express themselves and live and work in the spirit of brotherhood in sharing, in reciprocity and in giving and taking on equal basis. South African Anglican Archbishop Tutu explains *Ubuntu* as "My humanity is caught up, is inextricably bound up, in what is yours" (Tutu, 2000).

While *Ubuntu* is understood as a soul force that connects people with each other, it also underlies the purpose of the Truth and Reconciliation Commission (Tutu, 2000; Metz & Gaie, 2010) in encompassing a healing force for people who were separated and fighting against each other. Bateman (2018) reports on Barak Obama's plea made during a speech in South Africa to mark Nelson Mandela's legacy, to return to a global *Ubuntu*. That makes *Ubuntu* —originally derived from a local Nguni word meaning "proper behaviour towards the community" (Thompsell, 2018)—into a multinational, worldwide ethical approach to govern all countries in a humanistic and caring way.

In terms of culture in Zambian ethnic groups, the concepts of *mulesangwa* and *balekumana* are essential because they are based on *Ubuntu* and encompass participation and consensus in decision-making processes. These processes have to follow certain traditional principles to be successful:

- The *mulesangwa* is scheduled properly and conducted by recognised elders of the Bemba community.
- Consensus has to be developed through discussion and exchange of ideas.
- Decisions taken should give a "good feeling" to the people involved.
- Decisions have to be group based on collective, not individual principles.
- Basic principles should be outlined for the decision-making. Details might be designed and discussed at later stages and other meetings.

Unfortunately, Mrs Kabelo's design is rejected by the Chinese management. However, it appears that the Chinese do not yet have an appropriate alternative design concept, nor a professional explanation of the reasons for the rejection. Mrs Kabelo believes that there is no clear market strategy defined. She would like to support the Chinese management with her ideas on colours in the Zambian cultural context.

Zambian employees do not experience a respectful treatment by the Chinese management. They seem not to be regarded as people who have a rich cultural background of art and design. It is assumed that Zambian employees do not mind receiving second-class treatment by Chinese. Often, the attitude of cultural superiority of Chinese managers is responsible for such treatment. Therefore, proposals of Zambian manager, Mrs Kabelo, are not considered seriously. Mrs Kabelo is convinced that she and her fellow employees pay respect to the Chinese managers as far as they deserve it, but there is no mutual and balanced respect of cultures and persons.

It is in the interests of the Zambian employees to demonstrate that in Zambia, colours bear other meanings than those understood in China. Black can mean power, evil, death and mystery, while white is mostly associated with hope and purity, coolness and light. Purple is regarded similarly to Western colour concepts, as being connected to royalty, luxury and wisdom. Yellow is a colour that expresses joy, energy and warmth, while red will warn of danger and urgency. The colour of blue bears the meaning of peace and calmness, confidence and affection. Green communicates life, growth, freshness and healing (African Art Symbolism, 2018). Many designed patterns in Zambia mix and interconnect colour with crops, indicating the basis of survival. Very often, there are idiomatic expressions incorporated into the design of clothing, showing issues of love and uncertainty, of life and perishability.

Additionally, patterns on cloth prints show typical African symbols of strength, adaptability, peace, transformation and supremacy of God among other symbols (African Art Symbolism, 2018). The colours of Zambia's national flag have particular meanings:

> The background of the national flag is green, symbol of the country's natural beauty, with three vertical stripes in the lower right corner. The three stripes are: red, symbol of the country's struggle for freedom; black, representing the racial makeup of the majority population; and orange, representing the country's copper riches and other mineral wealth. A copper-colored eagle in the upper right corner symbolizes the country's ability to rise above its problems. (Everyculture.com, 2018)

6.5 Culture-Specific Solutions

In the following paragraphs, culture-specific insights with regard to solutions are presented.

There are obviously serious issues in three areas of the company: strategy, process/structure and attitude (organisational culture). It is usually time-consuming to change personal attitudes and organisational culture. In order to reduce the actual business risk of a second shutdown and to reach "quick wins" within a reasonable time frame, the company should start with a clarificatoin or reorientation (if needed) of the strategy, following by related alignment and optimisation of relevant business processes. Here, the use of the "Balanced Score Card" as developed by Kaplan and Norton (1992, 1996) as a strategic controlling tool could be helpful. From the company's strategy, the management team designs a balanced performance measurement system, considering four different perspectives: financial perspective (final result), customer and market perspective (as enabler for the financial result), business process perspective (as enabler for customer satisfaction and market acceptance) as well as learning and organisational development perspective (as enabler for a solid business process). For each perspective, a focused set of key performance indicators have to be defined, which are reviewed and eventually adapted on a regular basis (for instance, quarterly). The Chinese and the Zambian middle management should work together in order to develop such a new strategic programme.

Regarding the process and structures in the company, it is important to introduce monthly formal joint venture management meetings and that the Zambian joint venture partner should have a visibly proactive role. Additionally, Zambian managers should be assigned partial responsibilities in the in-house decision chain. In the long term, attitudes should be altered through defining a code of conduct for all management members in compliance with other international guidelines of code of conduct in large-scale companies. The second-class treatment of Zambian employees must be addressed regularly.

6.5.1 Short-Term Solutions from Chinese Perspectives

Management should study the letter forwarded by Mrs Kabelo carefully and refer to it by taking Zambian cultural concepts into account. Managers should conduct discussions on the issue of participation and decision-making structures, first, within their own groups, and, second, by reaching out to Zambian employee representatives at management level.

Chinese managers should become familiar with the concepts of traditional African consensus in terms of *mulesangwa* and *balekumana* to increase their understanding of the local cultures involved in the success of the organisation. It should be discussed how and to what extent decisions based on traditional consensus-building could be incorporated into the company.

The Chinese management could identify and acknowledge the lack of proper meeting structures for opinion exchange within MTB.

6.5.2 Long-Term Solutions from Chinese Perspectives

The management of MTB could offer design competitions and reward the winners for innovative and original ideas for the African textile market, to improve MTB's market position and create advantages regarding the competitors. Further, Chinese managers should involve Zambian employees more actively in the design of the products. Thereafter, they can analyse the increase in work satisfaction, feelings of respect and well-being of Zambian employees. Local fashion designers could also be involved and thus enhance cooperation with universities and local communities, by including local knowledge on an expert level.

Chinese-Zambian communication should increase in transparency to meet the expectations of the Zambian employees. This would increase participation and engagement and thereby create sustainability and success on the local markets. Chinese management needs to discuss Chinese values in compliance with African traditions and value sets. Organisational values and cultural values should be outlined clearly, and core values of the organisation should be developed, incorporating values of all cultures involved.

This can be implemented if MTB takes cognisance of the "share value" concept. This concept can be used in order to develop policies and operating practices that enhance the competitiveness of MTB. Additionally, the Chinese management must cooperate in depth with local government and with the employees of MTB to improve the economic, cultural and social conditions in the communities in which the company operates. The intersection of social values of the region and its communities and the business values of MTB is defined as "share value". This is the realm where investments simultaneously meet Chinese business interests and Zambian social, economic and cultural interests. Strengthening the "share value" concept would give a boost to satisfying the expectations of the employees and would also improve the market position of MTB in offering products that are attractive to a wide range of consumers.

6.5.3   Short-Term Solutions from Zambian Perspectives

One of the major complaints of the Zambians in the company is the lack of opportunity to attend and take part in decision processes in MTB. Zambian employees should use their traditional, consensus-building *mulesangwa* and *balekumana* strategies and make these known to the Chinese managers. Cultural perspectives should be taken into account and discussed, to be used to build an intercultural base.

Zambian employees should elect representatives to meet with the Chinese management and present their ideas regarding participation, decision-making, engagement and sustainable business cultures within their local context. Zambian envoys especially should be given the opportunity to propose designs in colour and idioms that can promote the demand for MTB products on the markets. These ideas, including a proposal for better involvement in the decision-making process at MTB, should be in written form. A letter including an idiom and an endorsed concrete proposal can reduce the risk of rejection by the Chinese management.

6.5.4   Long-Term Solutions from Zambian Perspectives

Zambian employees could set up an employee committee with representatives to give advice to the Chinese management with regard to local knowledge to improve design, marketing, market strategy and product decisions. Zambian employees should be further trained in cultural knowledge of the Chinese management, with traditional Chinese cultural concepts and views on business culture and business strategies. They could also suggest local social responsibility strategies, such as including local designers or universities to produce local expertise that can support the market expansion. Finally, the involvement of trade unions and the Zambian government as shareholder could help to strengthen the position of Zambian employees in the organisation.

6.6 Recommendations for Chinese-Zambian Intercultural Cooperation

On the macro-level of national and intercultural cooperation of Chinese-Zambian society, interests of the stakeholders in MTB should be made transparent, discussed openly and defined on a short- and long-term basis. Cooperation with academic universities for applied design sciences could be strengthened and national as well as regional competitions for fashion design could be established, including awards for best practice in design. This could result in higher self-esteem for those designing with patterns from their own culture, and it may curb the feeling of being dominated by Chinese art and design. Open-day academic discussions can be conducted on relevant topics such as the culturally bound meanings of colour in design. Zambian and Chinese idioms can be displayed and the importance of the power of idioms in daily communication can be emphasised. These measures can help to improve the home market position in textiles, which currently faces strong competition in cheaper imports from India and China.

At the meso-level of the company, the management is urgently recommended to open the way for growing participation of the employees in clothing design, using the skills and expertise of the local workforce and communal designers. It is highly recommended to acknowledge the importance of local structures like *mulesangwa* and the philosophy of *Ubuntu*, in order to achieve compliance of organisational goals and strategies with regional preferences in participation and decision-making procedures. Introducing the balanced scorecard as a measurement tool for MTB can help to make the company's goals for the near future much more transparent.

The Zambian government, in holding more than one-third of the joint venture shares, should proactively help to introduce the balanced scorecard and support its own citizens in the region, especially the employees of MTB in their expectation and desire to participate actively in the process of making culturally sound decisions.

Identifying major characteristics of an MTB strategy and creating a vision for future goals and activities are needs that must urgently be addressed by the management. The balanced scorecard must be published in the organisation to show the sustainable perspectives of its textile plant. The Chinese management should be particularly flexible when it comes to designing new perspectives. It has to be supported by outstanding Zambian employees and managers, as well as by government bodies. The balanced scorecard focuses also on implementation: it advocates a strong involvement of employees.

In conclusion, the balanced scorecard approach can help to reposition the company. The development process of the MTB will be improved as soon as there are monthly formal joint venture meetings in place. Zambian MTB managers must be given partial responsibilities in the fields of product design and decision-making. The need to publicly establish a code of conduct is widespread and acknowledged in many international companies. These recommendations could benefit both parties in preventing a second shutdown of the company, with all the negative consequences that this would entail.

REFERENCES

African Art Symbolism. (2018). Retrieved from https://africanartsymbolism.weebly.com/color-meanings.htm

Bateman, C. (2018, July 18). Barack Obama's Plea for a Return to Global Ubuntu Locally Pertinent. *Biznews*. Retrieved from https://www.biznews.com/leadership/2018/07/18/barack-obama-speech-ubuntu

Bemba English Dictionary Online. (2018). Retrieved from https://glosbe.com/en/bem/

Business & Human Rights Resource Centre. (2018). *Zambia-China Mulungushi Textiles (Joint Venture Qingdao Textile & Zambia Ministry of Defence)*. Retrieved from https://www.business-humanrights.org/en/zambia-china-mulungushi-textiles-joint-venture-qingdao-textile-zambia-ministry-of-defence

Bwalya, E. (2016). China-Zambia Relations. In S. Adem (Ed.), *China's Diplomacy in Eastern and Southern Africa*. London and New York: Routledge.

Embassy of the Republic of Zambia. (2018). *About Zambia*. Washington, DC. Retrieved from http://www.zambiaembassy.org/page/about-zambia

Everyculture.com. (2018). Countries and Their Cultures Forum. *Zambia. Symbolism*. Retrieved from https://www.everyculture.com/To-Z/Zambia.html#ixzz5ZJMOKXt1

Gade, C. (2012). What Is Ubuntu? Different Interpretations among South Africans of African Descent. *South African Journal of Philosophy, 31*(3), 487.

Hare, P. (2007). *China and Zambia: The All-Weather Friendship Hits Stormy Weather* Association for Asian Research. Retrieved from http://www.asianresearch.org/articles/3009.html

Kaplan, R. S., & Norton, D. P. (1992, January/February). The Balanced Scorecard – Measures that Drive Performance. *Harvard Business Review*.

Kaplan, R. S., & Norton, D. P. (1996, January/February). Using the Balanced Scorecard as a Strategic Management System. *Harvard Business Review*.

Mayer, C., & Boness, C. (2003). Südafrikanische Kulturstandards. Handlungsrelevantes Wissen für Fach- und Führungskräfte (South African Cultural Standards). *Africa Spectrum, 38*(2), 173–196.

Metz, T., & Gaie, J. (2010). The African Ethic of Ubuntu/Botho: Implications for Research on Morality. *Journal of Moral Education, 39*(3), 273–290.

Munoni, C. M. (2017). *Cotton Textile Industry in Zambia: The Economic Viability of Revamping Mulungushi Textiles Limited*. Dissertation, University of Cape Town, p. 56. Retrieved from https://open.uct.ac.za/bitstream/handle/11427/25081/thesis_com_2017_munoni_chiluba_mercy.pdf?sequence=1

Olesen, J. (2018). Color Symbolism in Chinese Culture: What do Traditional Chinese Colors Mean? https://www.color-meanings.com/

Thomas, A., & Schenk, E. (2014). *Beruflich in China. Trainingsprogramm für Manger, Fach-und Führungskräfte* (5th ed.). Göttingen: Vandenhoeck & Ruprecht.

Thompsell, A. (2018). *Get the Definition of Ubuntu, a Nguni Word with Several Meanings*. ThoughtCo. Retrieved from https://www.thoughtco.com/the-meaning-of-ubuntu-43307

Tutu, D. (2000). *No Future Without Forgiveness: A Personal Overview of South Africa's Truth and Reconciliation Commission*. Retrieved from https://www.penguinrandomhouse.com/books/181253/no-future-without-forgiveness-by-desmond-tutu/9780385496902

United Nations Statistics. (2018). *Zambia*. General Information. Economic Indicators. Retrieved from http://data.un.org/en/iso/zm.html

Zambia Business Times. (2018, July 19). *Zambia's 2018 Half Year Economic Performance Highlights*. Retrieved from https://zambiabusinesstimes.com/2018/07/19/zambias-2018-half-year-economic-performance-highlights-mof/

CHAPTER 7

Case 4: A Negotiation Between Chinese and Namibian Organisations in Namibia

Haiyan Zhang, Chen Ni, and Liusheng Wang

7.1 INTRODUCTION TO THE CASE

In the twenty-first century, China has become one of Africa's most important economic partners. During this period, China-Africa trade has grown at a rate of about 20% per year (Sun, Jayaram, & Kassiri, 2017). In the past decade, China's foreign direct investment in Africa has grown at an average annual rate of 40% (Sun et al., 2017). If the flow of funds from unofficial channels is taken into account, funds flowing from China to Africa are estimated to be about 15% higher than official statistics (Sun et al., 2017). Currently, with the development and implementation of the "One Belt One Road" policy, China has become one of the important providers in African countries, especially regarding infrastructure projects.

H. Zhang (✉) • C. Ni
College of Foreign Studies, Nantong University,
Nantong, People's Republic of China
e-mail: hldhaiyan@ntu.edu.cn

L. Wang
Department of Psychology, Nantong University,
Nantong, People's Republic of China

© The Author(s) 2019
C.-H. Mayer et al. (eds.), *Managing Chinese-African Business Interactions*, Palgrave Studies in African Leadership,
https://doi.org/10.1007/978-3-030-25185-7_7

As a consequence of long-term colonial rule, African cultural communication is not only influenced by local traditional culture but also by the culture of some European countries, such as Germany (Moctar, 2009). By contrast, in China's high-context culture, most of the cultural information is already within the person, while very little information is in the coded, explicitly transmitted part of the message being communicated (Hall, 1976; Hu, 2018). Words are used by Chinese people in a more euphemistic manner than is apparently understood (Zhou, 2016). More dependence on the context in which communication takes place makes Chinese people say less, but imply more. Alternatively, they express meaning indirectly so as to explore the other's opinion or to avoid losing face. Such differences between the two countries' cultures can potentially harm the cooperation between them and cause economic losses.

This study takes place in Namibia, in 2004. Namibia is located in the southwest region of Africa. After its independence in 1990, Namibia's stable political transition allowed its economy to develop continuously. The current population is about 2.1 million. Namibia's three traditional economic pillars are mining, fisheries and agriculture, but the industrial base is weak and agricultural production is backward. It is a typical export-orientated economy and is affected by external factors such as climate, ocean conditions and international markets. Although bilateral trade between China and Namibia began late, it has developed rapidly, and the trade volume has grown steadily, especially in recent years. However, Chinese cooperation with local organisations in Namibia has been somewhat problematic for both countries as a result of cultural differences (Zhang, 2010).

The manager of a Chinese organisation in Namibia wants to personally negotiate with the manager of a local Namibian organisation (Yang, 2003). The Chinese manager is in his 50s and holds a senior position in a government institution, whereas the manager of the local organisation is in his early 30s and is of European descent. After exchanging business cards, the negotiations officially begin. The Chinese manager explains the intentions of his visit, at first, and then mentions the quantity and quality requirements of the materials they need. Finally, he expresses hope that the Namibian organisation can give him an ideal price which would be lower than the previous price or the market price. The Namibian manager responds quickly and explains the price in detail to the Chinese manager.

The Chinese manager finds the price is higher than expected. He says that he travels a long distance to do this business, which is enough to show his sincerity and expectation of successfully completing the business. He also mentions that the two organisations have had good business relationships before, so he hopes that the Namibian organisation can lower the current price to show their sincerity, which is the best way to show their respect to the Chinese manager. The Namibian manager replies: "Our prices will not be reduced. If you lose less, it means that we will lose more. Who will be responsible for our losses?" At the time, the Chinese manager feels uncomfortable and embarrassed and leaves the negotiation.

During another meeting, the Namibian manager says, "Well, I agree to reduce by nought-point-five per cent. If you accept, we can draft and sign the contract; otherwise, no more negotiation on this. I have my own principles for doing business". The Chinese manager cannot accept the price, nor the Namibian manager's attitude. He signals his colleagues, who accompanied him to Namibia, to leave the meeting. Later, on the way back to their hotel, the Chinese manager complains to his colleagues that the Namibian manager is too proud and arrogant. He feels embarrassed by the Namibian manager's words.

7.2 Questions and Points of Discussion

- Explore the reasons for the failure of the negotiation.
- Discuss the cultural background of the two managers and the collision between Chinese and African cultures.
- Develop short- and long-term solutions for this case from each of the Chinese and African points of view.

7.3 Chinese Perspectives

China is a high-context culture (Hall, 1976), in that much of people's communication depends on context. When the Chinese talk, they like to "beat around the bush"; they seldom directly verbalise their intentions because they think they share a context in which everything is widely known and internalised (Zhou, 2016).

Confucianism is a Chinese philosophy with ancient roots, which has a profound impact on Chinese culture. Thousands of years ago, in the feudal society, people were deeply influenced by the "Four Books" (四书, namely *The Great Learning*《大学》; *The Doctrine of the Mean*《中庸》; *The Analects of Confucius*《论语》; *Mencius*《孟子》) and "Five Classics" (五经, namely *The Book of Songs*《诗经》; *The Book of History*《书经》; *The Book of Changes*《易经》; *The Book of Rites*《礼记》; and *The Spring and Autumn Annals*《春秋》). Confucianism is not only a unique and traditional spiritual product of China but also a value principle gradually formed in the long-term historical development of the Chinese nation. Its importance in Chinese civilisation history is self-evident. The codes of conduct that people follow in daily life are all from Confucianism, such as "be kind to others", "respect teachers and emphasise education", "be honest and trustworthy", "advocate etiquette" and so on. All these norms and behaviours are closely related to Confucianism (Li, 2013).

The traditional Chinese responsibilities of gratitude, temperance, loyalty and filial piety are also the result of a combination of Confucianism and feudal rites. Confucianism remains the mainstream thinking of the contemporary era, and it still has a huge potential impact on China's politics and economies.

Age is an important element of China's high-context culture; respect for the elderly is a virtue (Jiang, 2003), and it is impolite for the young to directly refuse those older than themselves. In this study, the Chinese manager is older than the Namibian manager and, in Chinese culture, should be respected accordingly by the younger manager. However, the words of the Namibian manager make the Chinese manager uncomfortable and embarrassed, which is an offence to him.

Another important aspect of Chinese culture is that China is a "personal" society. In the *Dream of Red Mansions* (the most famous classic work in China, which is said to be written by Cao Xueqin more than 200 years ago), there is a saying: "A grasp of mundane affairs is genuine knowledge, understanding of worldly wisdom is true learning" (世事洞明皆学问，人情练达即文章). So, the Chinese attach great importance to interpersonal relationships in their daily life, including when doing business. They tend to work with those organisations they have worked with before or with organisations in which they have acquaintances.

The Chinese manager is a 50-year-old man. Based on his background, he is a highly respected and respectable leader. In China, people will give him full respect and his viewpoints should be usually accepted. People will listen to his requests and complete the tasks he orders without any hesitation or complaint. When cooperating with other Chinese organisations, he usually dominates the whole working process.

Because the Chinese manager's experiences of dealing with this Namibian organisation in the past have been positive, he considers members of this organisation not only as business partners but also as friends. Therefore, when "friends" are involved in the business and refuse him directly, the Chinese manager feels hurt.

7.4 African Perspectives

The total population of Namibia is nearly 2.5 million, including the Ovambo, Herero, Kaprivi, Nama and Bushman (Xue & Wu, 2018). The customs and habits of the local people in Namibia share the prominent characteristics of both African Indigenous people and the Europeans. The cultural habits of Europeans have a considerable impact on local people (Xue & Wu, 2018).

In this case, the Namibian manager is of European descent (Yang, 2003). His thinking style could be described as "Western", in that he has a strong sense of personal independence and believes that his business decisions should not be affected by factors such as his counterpart's age, position or gender. This is distinctly different from the Chinese perspective and value set, which emphasises obedience in the young who must respect and follow the old, and in which the lower level is subordinate to the higher level. In Western cultures, one's personal independence and individual rights are supreme, which make the "self" the central point of reference.

Another factor to consider is that the African people have formed their own communicative style, specifically that "[you should] say what you mean and mean what you say" (Yang, 2003). The Namibian top manager says what he wants to say, without considering the face of the Chinese manager, which leads to failure of the conversation. "Face" refers to the psychology and behaviour that can be seen by others in terms of the type of image that the individual expresses (Zhai, 2004). In Chinese, there are many expressions of "face", which stands for a person's social position and relationship with others (Gong, 2016). For example, if you have a high social position, other people must give you face to show respect, which is the same if you have a close relationship with them.

In business cooperation, Chinese people always consider meaningful contextual factors such as identity, attitude, interpersonal relationships, location of negotiations and the environment (Yang, 2003). But Namibians prefer to talk about things and focus on the subject of negotiations. Interpersonal relationships do not affect business cooperation. Therefore, the Namibian manager does not understand the significance of the previous interaction with the Chinese manager (Yang, 2003).

7.5 Short-Term Solutions from Chinese Perspectives

First, the Chinese manager needs to discuss matters and increase the awareness of the subject of negotiation. He needs to reduce Chinese contextual elements in negotiations because Chinese contextual elements cannot have an influence on the Namibian manager. Second, he needs to negotiate in a simple and clear language to express his own purposes; otherwise, the Namibian manager cannot understand his ideas beyond his words.

7.6 Long-Term Solutions from Chinese Perspectives

The Chinese manager should learn more about the Namibians, especially concerning their cultural values, thinking styles and history. Only in this way can the Chinese manager truly understand the ideas of the Namibian manager, which will improve their future cooperation and development. When he negotiates with businessmen from African cultures, he needs to slowly change the Chinese business mode which emphasises the interpersonal relationship and hierarchy of rights. He cannot simply relate the problems to identity and face. In China, if the businessmen have a close relationship with one another, business would be smoothly and successfully completed. Therefore, relationship is the most important factor in Chinese business field.

The Chinese manager should also understand and accept the Namibian manager's thinking style and change his mindset if he wants the collaboration to be successful. He needs to treat himself and the Namibian manager on equal terms, and he cannot place himself in a higher position just because he is older than his counterpart.

Finally, Chinese management need to train their employees to have an improved understanding of African history and the cultural differences, as a good foundation to prepare for future cooperation and development.

7.7 Short-Term Solutions from Namibian Perspectives

First of all, the Namibian manager should learn about Chinese traditional culture, especially the Chinese values, such as "stress piety more, than your lore" (首孝悌, 次见闻) in the *Three-Character Scriptures* (《三字经》).

The Namibian manager should respect the Chinese manager's seniority in terms of age.

Second, for the Chinese manager, the Namibian manager's words do not sound friendly; therefore, the Namibian manager needs to express his attitude and meaning in an understated, careful and indirect manner. China's high-context culture makes Chinese people exchange information subtly. They do not like to express their own ideas directly; instead, they like to show their ideas to others in a gently polite and inoffensive way.

Finally, the Namibian manager should not only focus on the negotiating theme but also on the need to enhance the close relationship with the Chinese manager, by writing emails or greeting him on Chinese holidays. For example, during the Spring Festival, the Namibian manager can send an email to the Chinese manager to express his best wishes. If they are in the same place at that time, they should have dinner together to improve their relationship. The Namibian manager should understand that the business relationship is based primarily on their interpersonal relationship, this being an inseparable aspect of the other for Chinese people.

7.8 Long-Term Solutions from Namibian Perspectives

The Namibian manager needs to learn about Chinese culture and history to understand Chinese people's values. Through mutual understanding of each other's cultures, the cooperative relationship overall between China and Africa can become closer and closer. Learning about Chinese culture can help the Namibian manager understand the Chinese people's thinking styles and allow him to better cooperate with the Chinese in the future.

Second, he should change his way of speaking, namely, not to express his ideas too directly which may inadvertently hurt the feelings of people from Eastern cultures and make them feel embarrassed.

Ultimately, he would benefit from paying more attention to his personal exchanges with Chinese people. China is a human-orientated society, and people pay great attention to their mutual feelings. Therefore, he needs to communicate with the Chinese manager occasionally to enhance their relationship. This will make both sides more aware of each other and improve their cooperation.

7.9 Recommendations for Chinese-Namibian Intercultural Cooperation

Both the Chinese manager and the Namibian manager are responsible for the failure of this interaction. Cultural differences are the main reasons for their communication failure. There is an old saying in the famous Chinese military book, *The Art of War* (《孙子兵法》) that "If you know the enemy and know yourself, you need not to fear the result of a hundred battles" (知己知彼百战百胜). This saying can also be applied to Chinese-Namibian economic and commercial cooperation.

The administrative personnel in Namibia pay less attention to interpersonal relationships than do the Chinese. So in order to solve the problems caused by cultural misunderstandings, they should learn the similarities and differences between Chinese and African cultures and accept the differences. In future interaction, they need to consider these differences both in personal characteristics and in culture. This will increase the chances of success.

Cross-cultural training needs to be a prerequisite for the employees in Chinese and African organisations. After the manager made the decision, many specific matters were completed by the employees. Therefore, it is very important to train the employees of both parties to have a better understanding of each other's culture. Only when employees understand bipartisan culture, can they complete the tasks efficiently and successfully.

References

Gong, S. (2016). The Face Perspective Between the Chinese and American Business Culture. *Journal of Ningbo University, 29*(3), 118–122.

Hall, E. T. (1976). *Beyond Culture*. New York: Anchor Books.

Hu, Q. (2018). Cultural and Stylistic Differences Between Chinese and American Business English Negotiations from the Perspective of High and Low Context Culture. *Journal of Hunan University of Technology, 23*(6), 116–119.

Jiang, X. (2003). Social Background for and Characteristics of Chinese Tradition of Respecting the Elderly. *Journal of Southeast University, 5*(6), 34–38.

Li, F. (2013). *Research on the Influence of Confucianism on Chinese Culture*. Forward Position.

Moctar, A. A. (2009). *The Research on Trade Between Africa and China*. Dalian Maritime University.

Sun, Y., Jayaram, K., & Kassiri, O. (2017, July). *What Is the Current Situation of China-Africa Economic Cooperation? How Will the Future Develop?* McKinsey & Company. Retrieved from www.mckinsey.com

Xue, H., & Wu, W. (2018). China's Investment in the Namibian Tourist Hotels: Opportunities, Environmental Factors and the Challenge. *Reformation & Strategy, 34*(10), 106–110.

Yang, G. (2003, March 28). *Cultural Elements of Contradictions and Disputes in China-Africa Economic and Trade Exchanges.* Retrieved from http://cm.mofcom.gov.cn/article/ddgk/zwfengsu/201205/20120508144469.shtml

Zhai, X. (2004). Reproduction of Human Favor, Face and Power – The Social Exchange Way in a Reasonable Society. *Sociological Research, 5,* 48–57.

Zhang, J. (2010). China-Namibia Economic Cooperation: Progress and Perspective. *Journal of Shanghai Business School, 11*(5), 1–7.

Zhou, H. (2016). Chinese Cultural Transmission of Euphemism. *Journal of Chifeng University, 37*(9), 135–136.

CHAPTER 8

Case 5: How to Make Friends in Rwanda: A Chinese Tea Ceremony

Christian Martin Boness

8.1 CASE NARRATIVE

Rwanda is a landlocked country in East Africa. Its population is approximately 12 million inhabitants. Rwanda is one of the most densely populated countries in the whole of sub-Saharan Africa (CIA, 2018). Its grassy uplands and hills offer space and opportunities for agricultural land use (74.5%). The population consists of Tutsi, Hutu and Twa-Pygmys (CIA, 2018). In Rwanda, Kinyarwanda and Kisuaheli are the main African languages spoken. Besides that, French and English, as colonial languages, are spoken across the country (Expert Africa, 2018). The main African ethnic groups are the Hutu (85%) and the Tutsi (15% of the population) (CIA, 2018).

Historically, the government of Rwanda (2017) views the systematic killing of members of the ethnic group of the Tutsi and of the moderate Hutu ethnic group as the most threatening event in recent times in the country's history. The genocide of almost one million people changed the society fundamentally.

C. M. Boness (✉)
Department of Management, Rhodes University, Grahamstown, South Africa

© The Author(s) 2019
C.-H. Mayer et al. (eds.), *Managing Chinese-African Business Interactions*, Palgrave Studies in African Leadership,
https://doi.org/10.1007/978-3-030-25185-7_8

After the collapse of the economy in 1994 following the civil war, Rwanda worked on several five-year economic development and poverty reduction strategies. The consequent work towards a strategic management and rebuilding of the country led to a sustainable growth of the economy (World Bank, 2018). The more recent National Strategy for Transformation in Rwanda focuses primarily on the economic, social and governance transformation until 2050 (World Bank, 2018).

The latest development in the national strategic economic plan is the strong engagement of China in Rwanda's economy. The Chinese economy placed itself at the centre of the Rwanda Economic Zone in Kigali. The Chinese President Xi Jinping, who regularly comments on China's involvement on the African continent, is convinced that a new page of cooperation between China and Rwanda has opened: 272 hectares of the Special Economic Zone in Kigali are hosting 160 plots for industries and services mainly for Chinese companies but also for other national and international companies. (KT Press Staff Writer, 2017).

Mr Sung, as a prominent Chinese entrepreneur, has invested in a plot close to this special area and expects business and huge spillover effects from the fast-growing business zone. For several years, he has held a business permit in Rwanda and has advanced to become one of the leading flower retailers in Kigali, with his enterprise having a growing six-digit turnover. He is now the leading flower provider for celebrations in the city's hub, serving celebrations, marriages, funerals and businesses across the different ethnic and cultural groups. Mr Sung is not only a great entrepreneur and investor, but he is also a witty communicator who knows how to deal with the wishes and desires of his customers.

One day, Mr Sung invites his long-time friend Mr Nyara—who is a leading manager of a well-maintained and successful tin smelting plant near Kigali—to a Chinese tea ceremony and explains:

> *Tea culture in China differs from the culture in Europe, Britain or Japan insofar that it uses different preparation methods and tasting rituals. Further on, the occasion at which tea ceremonies take place in China and how tea is consumed differs from other cultures. Even at present date, Chinese usually consume tea in both formal and informal situations on a regular basis. But Chinese tea is not only a common beverage—it is also understood and used as a medicine and it is used in the Chinese cuisine.*

Mr Nyara enjoys listening to Mr Sung's narrations on Chinese culture and learns that the tea ceremony even includes spiritual aspects. In former times, tea was cultivated as herbal medicine and used by monks for its peaceful and calming effects. The philosophies of Confucianism, Taoism and Buddhism gave birth to the magical Chinese tea ceremony. In recent times, tea ceremonies shifted from originally religious manifestations to social, cultural and economic settings, marking different important meetings (Rotaru, 2013).

Mr Nyara starts feeling comfortable and enjoys the open-minded atmosphere between them. Therefore, he starts discussing Chinese-Rwandan communication practices and relationship-building in Kigali, which he has witnessed over the past years. Mr Nyara expresses his appreciation of Chinese culture, their work ethic and of Chinese organisations running social responsibility projects in Rwanda. He is impressed by the way Chinese investors and organisations aim to build relationships with local communities to support schools, build up school libraries, run various social projects and implement different socio-economic initiatives within the Rwandan communities. Mr Nyara highlights that the Chinese investors are viewed as interacting well with local businesses and entrepreneurs, as they purchase goods and services from local organisations, thereby supporting the local industries.

The increasing presence of Chinese organisations in Kigali is largely beneficial for the local community in the perspective of Mr Nyara, not least because it increases new employment and investment opportunities. Mr Nyara emphasises that Rwandans in general see Chinese organisations playing an important role in helping local entrepreneurs in gaining increasing experience in managing work-related matters and even organisations.

During the tea ceremony, Mr Sung grows enthusiastic about Mr Nyara's feedback and perceptions, and he invites Mr Nyara into the Casino Kigali Hotel, just 15 minutes' drive from Kigali's international airport, for a round of poker. Mr Nyara knows the place very well, but he has not played any game at the casino. His religious community does not allow the playing of games of chance or gambling. He hesitates to accept Mr Sung's suggestion, thinking, "They play poker, but in Rwanda people actually like to play soccer together. Why does he want me to play against him?"

Poker, in Mr Nyara's opinion, is a game for adversaries or even enemies, and this offer might be a Chinese stratagem, an "artifice of war," a strategy of his Chinese friend to seize control over Mr Nyara. Mr Nyara once read a book on Chinese business strategies, and he begins to wonder whether Mr Sung is a real friend and business partner and if he really can be trusted.

While the talking continues, Mr Nyara's trust in Mr Sung decreases, and the tea ceremony seems to become a real burden. Mr Nyara imagines that Mr Sung and his Chinese friends and business partners might be aiming to buy stakes in his tin smelting company, searching for a weakness in the company's system to get a grip on the precious metal resources. Maybe the friendship between China and Rwanda is not actually as trusting, fair and just as it is made out to be in governmental and organisational top management meetings.

Reflecting on the relationship with Mr Sung, Mr Nyara remembers the words of the two political leaders who met in Beijing in 2017: Kagame, the Rwandan president, and Xi Jingping, the Chinese president. They spoke of enhancing future Chinese-Rwandan cooperation for mutual benefit of the nations—something similar to what he has just heard from Mr Sung during the tea ceremony.

Now, Mr Nyara suddenly remembers that he read a Cameroon survey (Cerutti & Tacconi, 2006) reporting on experiences with radical Chinese policies and strategies that are aiming to gain natural resources, like forestry. In the report (Cerutti & Tacconi, 2006), it is assumed that Chinese policies are focused on exploiting resources in African countries rather than on benefitting both sides in a win-win situation. The survey (Cerutti & Tacconi, 2006) emphasises that Cameroonians generally believe they lack information about Chinese investments and interests in their countries. According to the survey (Cerutti & Tacconi, 2006), a limited Chinese forestry concession allows a large number of smaller Chinese private and independent enterprises to operate informally and largely invisibly as loggers, lumber producers or timber buyers in a type of established "parallel market." But he is also reminded of a Chinese official spokesperson in Cameroon reporting that the survey was incorrect and might—with its wrong accusations—destabilise the extraordinarily good relationship between Cameroon and China.

Mr Nyara now brings all this knowledge and information together and interprets it with regard to the tea ceremony. Mr Sung might have certain interests that are invisible and incomprehensible to Mr Nyara. Is the tea ceremony just a strategy of implementing hidden and unfair business strategies? What interests may Mr Sung have? Which interests might Mr Nyara and Mr Sung have in common; what interests may separate them?

8.2 Questions

- What does Mr Sung intend by inviting Mr Nyara to the tea ceremony?
- What does friendship, in Chinese cultural concepts often associated with the concept of *Guanxi*, mean and how does it work from a Chinese perspective? To what extent does bribery or gifts fuel the friendship?
- From an African point of view, how is the natural environment viewed and how should you treat it?
- What does Mr Nyara need to learn about Chinese long-term orientation, its impacts on investments and the maintenance of environmental and social standards? Please include reflections on recent Chinese environmental policies.

8.3 Chinese Perspectives

The tea ceremony concept is based on Chinese philosophy. Elements of the Chinese tea ceremony include predominant value concepts which are strongly connected to the idea of creating harmony between nature and humanity, self-cultivation and enjoying tea in a formal or informal setting. When tea becomes more than a beverage and the tea ceremony is understood and practised to foster self-cultivation and discipline of the mind, quietening of the heart and attaining the purity of enlightenment, then the art of the tea ceremony becomes "Teaism" (Richardson, 2010).

The tea ceremony is often a tool to exchange ideas in a peaceful and formal situation, following a specific ceremonial ritual that allows the attendants to talk about relevant issues. The Chinese partner might, for example, use a tea ceremony to make friends in China through concepts such as *Guanxi*, which are expressed during the ceremony (Goh & Sullivan, 2011).

In Chinese culture, the concept of *Guanxi* is commonly applied to relationship-building and communication. It can be used within the broader society, in organisational settings or on an individual, interpersonal relationship-building level. A Chinese idiom emphasises: "If you have Guanxi, you have no problems. If you have no Guanxi, you have problems" (Goh & Sullivan, 2011).

The practice of friendship is based on *Guanxi* and if people disrespect the concept in daily life activities, they may have to deal with the consequences. Consequences could be that they do not experience support from their supporting systems such as family and friends in daily activities, which could lead to less success in their activities, businesses, organisations and enterprises.

According to Steidlmeier (1999), *Guanxi* refers to mutual relationships that are built on favours that permit the parties to make almost unconditional requests of one another. The concept requires mutual trust and obligation. However, the boundaries of favours and gifts on the one side and bribery and corruption on the other are not easily detected. *Guanxi* as a concept of mutual favours is an essential tool of ethical management of business relationships in Chinese cultures (Steidlmeier, 1999).

The following paragraphs offer various perspectives on Chinese understanding of Confucius and on corruption in today's China. Rothlin (2004), a Swiss researcher, emphasises China's own philosophical traditions when he talks about Chinese business ethics. He sees the problem of corruption often including favouring family and friends. He argues that Chinese are encouraged in such reciprocity of favours by their traditions. Confucius is seen as a paramount philosopher who puts the focus on responsibilities towards the family, admonishing that a person who sees his father steal a sheep should not turn his father over to the authorities (Rothlin, 2004).

However, other ancient Chinese philosophers address the principles and values of *Guanxi* in a different way. For instance, Mozi (fifth century BC) shifts the accent from family favours to a more universal caring. Both philosophers impact on contemporary business ethic discussions about Chinese culture traditions (Rothlin, 2004). Current results of the corruption perception index (CPI), published annually by Transparency International (2019), are discussed in Chinese management and political circles. The CPI ranks countries like Cameroon and Rwanda, China, USA and Germany among 180 surveyed countries. The higher the scores of CPI approaching 100%, the more the transparency in private and public businesses and services is maintained. From 2012 to 2017, Chinese CPI improved slightly by 2%, suggesting that the Chinese perceive a slight improvement of corruption in business and service.

Chinese business people usually expect gifts and favours to be offered by foreign business partners (Price, 2018). These gifts usually reflect the wealth of a person or a country. However, *Guanxi* might also be judged as implying an "under-the-table system of gifts and favours" or even a gloss for corruption and back-door dealing if the difference between a gift and a bribe is not transparent for all partners (Price, 2018). Additionally, maintaining face or reputation among people within one's own network is an important characteristic of Chinese culture and is also included in the concept of *Guanxi*. *Guanxi* is further connected to Chinese stratagems and built on management philosophy (Goh & Sullivan, 2011).

The behaviour of Chinese business has been studied by a variety of strategic management scholars (Gao, 1991; Hafsi & Yan, 2007). Although very little attention has been paid to Chinese history as a determinant of strategic behaviour, it has been proposed that the cognitive orientation of Chinese managers is dominated by their knowledge and understanding of Chinese history.

An understanding of the philosophy of *The Thirty Six Stratagems* of ancient China is essential for interpreting Chinese management approaches, which are deeply embedded in Chinese history and culture. Hafsi and Yan (2007, p. 146) explain that stratagems

> are not unique to China, being commonly found in low-trust societies and relationships ... low trust is longstanding because of the size of the country and its ancient political structure in which hundreds of independent states fought many wars against one another. Stratagems have been an important part of Chinese culture and everyday life for more than 2500 years.

Hafsi and Yan (2007, p. 172) point out that the aim of applying the stratagems in Chinese culture is to take initiative and to "put the other party on the defensive. But they can also be used diplomatically to avoid causing the other party to lose face." In this context, many Chinese people see the postmodern capitalist markets as "battlefields" (Hafsi & Yan, 2007, p. 145) and argue that there "can never be too much deception in war" (Hafsi & Yan, 2007, p. 146).

In research and literature on international business in China (Hafsi & Yan, 2007), it has been discovered that the following four stratagems are most frequently used (Hafsi & Yan, 2007, pp. 148–152):

1. Murder with a borrowed knife: A "company playing its competitors off against each other; people taking detailed notes of what others say to possibly trick them later with their own words; and holding back of approval ... until foreign investors accept additional requirements."
2. Leisurely await the exhausted enemy: "When the enemy (i.e. a foreign party) has come from afar in high spirits and seeks a quick

battle, we should stay on the defensive behind deep trenches and high bulwarks and ignore their challenge, waiting for it to wane. If the enemy challenges us by creating incidents, we must not move. The principle is: when secure, remain immobile."
3. To catch the bandits, first catch their ringleader: "The Chinese regard the leader of a group of bandits as the cohesive element and decision maker of the entire posse. Once the leader has been captured, the group will disintegrate and join its captors. This stratagem is often applied to business situations in China."
4. Beauty trap: "Chinese history has many stories of beautiful women causing the downfall of a kingdom on the basis of an underlying principle—the strong can be subdued by the 'weak'." In modern-day language, the weak include women, wining and dining, gifts and travel.

Related to these four stratagems, Chinese management philosophy essentially deals with a vivid ancient myth: that of *the Three Kingdoms*, attributed to Luo Guanzhong. This fourteenth-century historical epic offers basic behavioural norms and values with implications for business behaviour in Chinese business and management contexts (Hafsi & Yan, 2007, p. 1). According to the story, Chinese civilisation centres on the emperor, the so-called son of heaven (Encyclopedia Britannica, 2018). The message of the myth has not really been affected by either the proclamation of the Republic or the great communist transformation. The Chinese civilisations built a profound base and important cultural, political and economic pillars that gave shape to the emperor's powers (Encyclopedia Britannica, 2018), such as:

- The bureaucracy, designed from the very beginning about 2000 years ago to be meritocratic, which manages operations and actions that are the results of the Centre's decisions;
- An elaborate system of laws, rules and procedures, which reinforces the Centre's legitimacy;
- A set of values and norms of behaviour, which provides shape to the elites' education.

These civilising characteristics have been amazingly similar in all the periods of Chinese history (Encyclopedia Britannica, 2018).

It is assumed that these characteristics similarly influence the behaviour of contemporary Chinese elites, most notably managers and business people. Accordingly, decoding business and management cultures and behaviours needs to be anchored in understanding Chinese history. *The Three Kingdoms* might still be viewed as one of the main guiding historical directions of the elite groups in China, and almost every Chinese citizen is taught the story. Chinese leaders in the political, economic or cultural realm usually make reference to the Three Kingdoms in one way or another. It is no surprise that rulers would make interpretations of this epic that favoured their own goals and projects.

8.4 African Perspectives

Chinese managers and organisations usually focus on investments in natural resources in African contexts. However, African civil societies, individuals and organisations feel that they are not well informed about the ongoing investments of Chinese organisations in Africa and that they hardly understand the strategic movements and long-term goals behind the plans and actions.

A survey provides evidence that there is a lack of basic figures on Chinese forest commissions that are of interest to the public. Chinese companies do not operate informally and invisibly, although African employees and individuals often develop this perception. On the contrary, however, Chinese organisations are usually open to respond to every question arising in connection with forestry investments and activities. Chinese investors and entrepreneurs are very long-term orientated in their activities (Hofstede, 2018), while sub-Saharan countries often seem to be more normative and short-term orientated (Hofstede, 2018). These conditions lead many Africans to develop a strong desire to explain as much as possible. Rwandans also expect explanations of thoughts, plans and actions in order to improve their understanding of what is happening.

In the case presented, Mr Nyara has learnt that Cameroon, like Rwanda, is an African country with a comparatively low focus on projects far in the future. It does not cultivate a prospective plan of what will happen over the next 25 years in African-Chinese businesses. According to Hofstede (2018), Rwanda, South Africa and Cameroon score low on long-term orientation. These countries exhibit great respect for traditions, a relatively small propensity to save for the future, and a focus on achieving quick results, making them normative, short-term-orientated cultures.

China scores highly in this dimension, which means that the Chinese are long-term orientated to a large extent. In societies with long-term orientation, people believe that truth is relative. In the Chinese culture, the expectation of having explanations of business interactions and relationships is fairly low; individuals and organisations do not have a need to explain everything in detail, as they believe that it is impossible to fully understand the complexity of life (Hofstede, 2018). From a Chinese perspective, the challenge in life is not to know the truth, but rather to live a virtuous life. The Chinese show an ability to easily adapt traditions to changing conditions, and they have a strong propensity to save and invest, demonstrating thriftiness and perseverance in achieving results (Hofstede, Hofstede, & Minkov, 2010).

Mr Nyara also considers the way in which the Chinese deal with the natural environment. From his point of view, they do not worry about nature and wildlife in Cameroon. Nature, for them, is mainly a matter of resources that can be exploited. By contrast, for Cameroonians and Rwandans, nature is largely an environment that is inhabited by living beings, also spirits and ancestors. However, environment protection laws in both countries are relatively weak and not well enforced, therefore making it easier to exploit the natural resources. Additionally, it is in the interest of Cameroon society to see benefits deriving from international business interactions, entrepreneurship and foreign investments, as well as from social responsibility projects in education, health and infrastructure. But an increasing number of Cameroonians and Rwandans are worried about the environmental issues. Increasing income from the international tourism sector indicates that a protected environment, nature, national parks and wild animals are pivotal for the economy of Cameroon and Rwanda. Both countries have developed a new awareness, deriving from the problems of pollution of the environment through reckless exploitation.

At the same time, the development of social and environmental standards is a core topic of change in China's policymaking. China itself suffers from the effects of low environmental standards and strives for a change in political and economic attitudes. As Bräutigam (2009, pp. 299–300) emphasises, Chinese international cooperation still lacks:

> [adequate] social and environmental conditions. The Chinese are notoriously lax about labor standards ... Hydropower dams, concessions for tropical hardwood and large rainforest plantations, roads, and large-scale mining

all pose risks for the environment in Africa. They also all require that people affected by the project be consulted, compensated, and properly resettled ... China's investors are way behind the curve on all of this. So are many African governments.

Mr Nyara is also very aware of the fact that in Cameroon, the issue of commissions for forest investment is a pending hazard. Emerging parallel markets are often linked to deals that are made between communal partners and Chinese businessmen. But Mr Nyara knows there are also causes of corruption in Cameroon and even Rwanda. Causes may vary depending on economic, political and cultural circumstances (Lumumba, 2014). Research shows that, apart from the colonial legacy, various factors are likely to foster bribery between persons and also organisations (Lumumba, 2014). Some of these are poor leadership, an omnipotent state, weak government institutions, an absence of political will and general insecurity and conflict.

From a Rwandan perspective, it can be emphasised that the country makes progress on the issue of graft. A new sense of awareness of corruptive practices and activities is growing in the public as well as in civil realms (Transparency International, 2019).

8.5 CULTURE-SPECIFIC SOLUTIONS

8.5.1 Short-Term Solutions from Chinese Perspectives

Information should be supplied to allay the rumours that some Chinese companies are working informally and invisibly in the fields of minerals and forestry.

Tea ceremonies should be introduced as part of organisational culture in companies. This could lead to communication changes and information transparency.

8.5.2 Long-Term Solutions from Chinese Perspectives

It is recommended that the Chinese be aware and follow the economic targets of both countries, in order to formally create jobs to support the economy of Rwanda in a sustainable way. The Rwandan government has to create a mechanism to investigate opaque activities in Chinese firms to avoid misunderstandings and mistrust on the part of the Rwandans. This would be in the interests of Chinese investors.

8.5.3 Short-Term Solutions from Rwandan Perspectives

The Chinese should improve their environmental responsibility and not overexploit the environmental resources, minerals, forestry and water especially. Invisibility and informality of the Chinese investment in Rwanda should be addressed and dealt with by both parties. Strictly avoid attempts to create *Guanxi* through bribery and corruption. A broad political discussion is needed to draw the red lines for good governance and appropriate organisation culture. The export of raw materials should boost the trade between China and Rwanda. China should export many processed products containing local minerals and woods for the benefit of Rwanda, Cameroon and other sub-Saharan countries.

Rwandans should learn to play the stratagems as well as learning to play the 36 business strategies in workshops and team-building trainings.

8.5.4 Long-Term Solutions from Rwandan Perspectives

Invisibility and informality of the Chinese firms should be addressed and dealt with by both parties. If necessary, Rwandan officials have to create a mechanism to investigate invisible activities in the Chinese firms, making it clear what the win-win situation for both countries will be. Shape awareness of and follow the economic targets of both countries. It is recommended to create jobs in small-scale and medium-scale companies that make intermediate products using own natural resources. This could stabilise the economy of Rwanda to continue on a prosperous course.

8.6 Recommendations for Chinese-Rwandan Intercultural Cooperation

Exchange ideas about making friends in ways Rwandans are used to, and in ways Chinese are used to doing with Rwandans. Avoid mistrust and misunderstanding by setting up truthful relationships. Construct organisations and networks that foster intercultural cooperation not only on the high political levels but also at the level of small-scale or medium-scale enterprises. Private-public partnerships may offer a forum of mutual exchange of culture concepts and strategies. Make the Special Economic Zone in Rwanda, as well as those constructed in other African countries, an open forum for the exchange of international and culture-specific business ideas and international investment for the benefit of both the host countries and the investing enterprises or organisations.

References

Bräutigam, D. (2009). *The Dragon's Gift: The Real Story of China in Africa.* Oxford: Oxford University Press.

Cerutti, P. O., & Tacconi, L. (2006). *Forests, Illegality, and Livelihoods in Cameroon.* Retrieved from https://www.salvaleforeste.it/documentazione/CIFOR_Cameroon_WorkingPaper35.pdf

CIA Central Intelligence Agency. (2018). *The World Fact Book.* Retrieved from https://www.cia.gov/library/publications/the-world-factbook/geos/rw.html

Encyclopedia Britannica. (2018). Luo Guanzhong. *The Three Kingdoms.* Retrieved from https://www.britannica.com/biography/Luo-Guanzhong

Expert Africa. (2018). Retrieved from https://www.expertafrica.com/rwanda/info/rwanda-general-information

Gao, Y. (1991). *Lure the Tiger Out of the Mountains: The Thirty-Six Stratagems of Ancient China.* New York: Simon & Schuster.

Goh, A., & Sullivan, M. (2011). *The Most Misunderstood Business Concept in China.* US-Pacific Rim International, Inc. (www.us-pacific-rim.net). Retrieved from http://www.businessinsider.com/the-most-misunderstood-business-concept-in-china-2011-2?IR=T

Hafsi, T., & Yan, L. (2007). Understanding Chinese Business Behaviour: A Study and Interpretation of the Three Kingdoms Novel. In Z. Jinlong, Z. Wei, X. Xinping, & L. Jainglao (Eds.), *Globalization Challenge and Management Transformation: Proceedings of ICM' 2007, 6th International Conference on Management, August 3–5, Wuhan, China* (pp. 1269–1282). Beijing: Science Press.

Hofstede, G. (2018). *The 6 Dimensions of National Culture. Hofstede Insights.* Retrieved from https://www.hofstede-insights.com/product/compare-countries/

Hofstede, G., Hofstede, G. J., & Minkov, M. (2010). *Cultures and Organizations: Software of the Mind* (3rd ed.). New York: McGraw-Hill.

KT Press Staff Writer. (2017). *China's Xi Jinping Commits to Build Rwanda Economic Zone.* Retrieved from http://ktpress.rw/2017/03/chinas-xi-jinping-commits-to-build-rwanda-economic-zone/

Lumumba, P. (2014). Corruption: The Bane of Africa. In E. Nduku & J. Tenamwenye (Eds.), *Corruption in Africa: A Threat to Justice and Sustainable Peace*. Geneva: Globethics.net. ISBN: 978-2-88931-016-6 (online version).

Price, D. C. (2018). *When Is Giving Gifts Bribery in China Business?* Retrieved from http://davidcliveprice.com/giving-gifts-bribery-china-business/

Richardson, L. B. (2010). *The World in Your Teacup: Celebrating Tea Traditions, Near and Far* (p. 12). Eugene: Harvest House Publishers. ISBN: 9780736925808.

Rotaru, C. (2013). *The Traditional Chinese Tea Ceremony (Part I) – Rivertea Blog*. Retrieved from http://www.rivertea.com/blog/the-traditional-chinese-tea-ceremony-part-i/

Rothlin, S. (2004). *Becoming a Top-Notch-Player.18 Rules of International Business Ethics*. Beijing: Renmin University Press. (Bilingual edition: English and Chinese).

Rwandan Government. (2017). *Rwanda Country Information. Outbreak of Civil War*. 4.5.–4.7. Paragraph 4.2. Retrieved from https://www.justice.gov/sites/default/files/pages/attachments/2017/02/21/uk-country-assess_04-2003_rwanda.pdf

Steidlmeier, P. (1999, June). Gift Giving, Bribery and Corruption: Ethical Management of Business Relationships in China. *Journal of Business Ethics, 20*, 121–132.

Transparency International. (2019). *The Corruption Perception Index (CPI) 2017*. Retrieved from https://www.transparency.org/news/feature/corruption_perceptions_index_2017

World Bank in Rwanda. (2018). Retrieved January 22, 2019, from https://www.worldbank.org/en/country/rwanda/overview

PART III

Intercultural Training Cases: Entrepreneurship, Management Styles, Language and Identity

CHAPTER 9

Case 6: Setting Up Small, Medium and Micro Enterprises by Chinese Entrepreneurial Immigrants in Maputo, Mozambique

Mattheus Johannes Louw, Lynette Louw, and Fiona Geyser

9.1 Case Narrative

Mozambique, a land rich in natural resources, has become a destination for the Chinese to establish entrepreneurial endeavours (Tull, 2006). Accordingly, there has been a significant increase in Chinese entrepreneurial immigrants' presence in southern Africa, particularly in Mozambique (Park, 2010). Mozambique has also become a popular destination for Chinese entrepreneurial immigrants because of the country's healthy business environment and growing economy (Njal, 2012). Over the past decade, there has been an increase in the number of Chinese entrepreneurial immigrants operating Small, Medium and Micro Enterprises

M. J. Louw (✉) • L. Louw • F. Geyser
Department of Management, Rhodes University, Grahamstown, South Africa
e-mail: m.louw@ru.ac.za; l.louw@ru.ac.za

(SMMEs) in the retail sectors of Mozambique (Nhancale, Mananze, Dista, Nhantumbo, & Macqueen, 2009). Entrepreneurship has a very important role in the context of developing the economy of a country such as Mozambique and in confronting problems such as unemployment, overpopulation and poverty (Nieman & Nieuwenhuizen, 2014).

Immigrant entrepreneurs form community groups to assist other immigrants who plan to move to a host country (Light & Bhachu, 2004). According to Light and Bhachu (2004), immigration community groups are interpersonal relationships of kinship and friendship between immigrants, former immigrants and non-immigrants in host countries.

Entrepreneurial immigrants require resources to invest in business opportunities in the host country. These resources are often given by family members or friends, providing the immigrant entrepreneur with the competitive structure to participate in the host country's business market (Light & Bonacich, 1988). Community groups often influence entrepreneurs' choice to immigrate (Light & Bhachu, 2004). The community groups have created employment inside the community, and they provide access to loans as capital for the entrepreneur immigrants (Light & Bhachu, 2004).

Motivation for immigrant entrepreneurs to move from their home country to establish a business can be described as "entrepreneurial intentions" (Marchand & Siegel, 2014). According to Lee, Wong, Foo and Leung (2011), entrepreneurial intention is defined as the decision to start a new business that is assumed to be planned for some time and is followed by the purpose to do so.

Push and pull factors are forces that describe how an individual can be pushed by motivational forces into making a decision and pulled or attracted to a certain destination (Baloglu & Uysal, 1996). According to Kirkwood (2009), push factors are characterised by external forces that drive individuals away from the home country. Push factors are often considered as being negative (Kirkwood, 2009); examples of these are unemployment and overpopulation (Shultz, Morton, & Weckerle, 1998). Pull factors are characterised as influences that attract individuals to start a new business or venture in a host country (Hakim, 1989). Pull factors are considered as being positive, such as the desire for better income and gaining independence (Shultz et al., 1998).

For the purpose of this case study, Tengeh's (2011) framework is used to understand the factors which influence Chinese entrepreneurial immigrants to establish and operate businesses in Maputo, Mozambique. Resources are required as part of the immigration process of moving and starting an SMME in a host country. Financial resources, physical resources, human resources and information resources are all needed to assist and sustain the immigrant entrepreneur (Tengeh, 2011). In order to start and then maintain a successful business, the immigrant entrepreneur also needs motivation, the ability to raise finance, family support, ethnic support and previous experience (Tengeh, 2011). According to Tengeh (2011), there should be a match between these entrepreneurship characteristics and resources for a small business entrepreneur to be successful in a host country.

Study data were collected during 2017 using semi-structured interviews with 12 Chinese entrepreneurial immigrants living in Maputo who own and have operated SMMEs for more than two years in the retail sector. The semi-structured interviews focused on the immigrant entrepreneurship characteristics, types of resources required and the influence of the push and pull factors that led to these Chinese entrepreneurial immigrants starting and operating SMMEs in Maputo. The interviews were conducted with the assistance of a translator who is proficient in Portuguese, English and Mandarin.

9.2 Questions and Points of Discussion

- Explore the immigrant entrepreneurship characteristics that influence Chinese entrepreneurial immigrants to start and operate SMMEs in the retail sector in Maputo.
- Describe the types of resources required by Chinese entrepreneurial immigrants to operate these SMMEs.
- Identify and explain the influence of the push and pull factors on Chinese entrepreneurial immigrants in this situation.
- Develop short- and long-term solutions for this case from a Chinese entrepreneurial point of view.

9.3 Chinese Perspectives

9.3.1 Entrepreneurial Characteristics Needed to Start Up and Operate SMMEs in Maputo

For Chinese entrepreneurs in Mozambique, being able to establish *Guanxi* with locals and having good quality products are regarded as the most important entrepreneurial characteristics to have. *Guanxi* refers to the important relationships with the employees, locals and community in Mozambique. *Guanxi* is a key principle of Chinese Confucian values, as explained by an immigrant entrepreneur in the following way: "Maintain a good relationship with the Mozambican locals, and help develop the economy of Mozambique."

Having good quality products is an important entrepreneurship characteristic as it ensures a good reputation for the business among the locals, which develops customer loyalty. The Chinese interview respondents consider earning money to be the third most important entrepreneurial characteristic, while language ability and motivation are the most important characteristics in terms of immigration assistance. Earning money is defined by the entrepreneurs as the ability to gain or be paid money for the work and services they provide, and to support their families in China. Language is described by the entrepreneurs as the ability to communicate with customers and employees in Mozambique. Finally, the characteristic of motivation means to be determined to earn money, continually grow the business and contribute to the development of the economy of Mozambique.

In comparison to Tengeh's (2011) findings, the Chinese entrepreneurs did not identify ability to raise finance, family support, ethnic support and previous experiences as key entrepreneurship characteristics. Instead, *Guanxi*, good quality products, earning money and language ability were identified as being the most important entrepreneurial characteristics.

9.3.2 Resources Required to Start Up and Operate SMMEs in Maputo

Money is considered as being the most important resource required by Chinese entrepreneur immigrants when starting a business in Mozambique. Having good quality imported products is also perceived as important for the successful operation of a business. It is interesting to note that the immigrant entrepreneurs have an accurate idea of which products will be successful in the Mozambican retail market. This information is supplied to aspirant immigrant entrepreneurs in China by family and friends, before they decide to emigrate and begin such enterprises in an African country such as Mozambique.

The immigrant entrepreneurs describe financial resources as the capital to start up a business. Physical resources are defined by the entrepreneurs as the imported products from China to sell in their SMMEs. Finally, information resources are defined as the community groups that are available in Mozambique, the Internet and reliance on friends and family already living in Mozambique. One of the entrepreneurs interviewed explained that the reason he came to start a business in Mozambique was that the Chinese community in Maputo had told him of the retail opportunities available and also how to start a business in Mozambique.

Findings were very similar to those of Tengeh (2011), in that the Chinese respondents in this study depended on having sufficient financial, physical and information resources. These entrepreneurs spoke of their experiences of the influence of government, costs and language on their businesses. They explained that there are constant checks on foreign businesses by the Mozambican government that include verification of work permits and identification documents. The costs of rates and taxes are also very high for the entrepreneurs who, at times, struggle to pay these costs. In Mozambique, the common language spoken is Portuguese. The overwhelming majority of Chinese entrepreneurs can only speak Mandarin, with the result that their inability to communicate in Portuguese with their customers and the authorities is a limitation and business barrier.

In terms of the success of operating their SMMEs, the majority of entrepreneurs do not regard themselves as successful. They believe that there is always room for improvement. An entrepreneur explained why he does not regard himself as successful when he stated: "Success does not exist, because there are always ways to improve and do better."

9.3.3 Influence of Push and Pull Factors on Chinese Entrepreneurial Immigrants

Unemployment in China is the most important push factor experienced by the immigrant entrepreneurs in Maputo, followed by pollution in the home country. The most important pull factors are favourable job opportunities and the positive living environment in Mozambique. The living environment in China is regarded as hazardous by the respondents in this study, owing to the level of pollution. One participant emphasised how much healthier it is to live in Mozambique because of the absence of smog and air pollution.

The lack of availability of jobs in China has forced entrepreneurs to seek job opportunities elsewhere, and the immigrant entrepreneurs said that Mozambique is one of the easier places to earn a living. One entrepreneur commented that earning a decent living in Mozambique enabled him to use his savings to visit family and friends in China on a regular basis.

The majority of Chinese entrepreneur immigrants interviewed found the actual move from China to be difficult. The main problems they experienced and continue to experience are difficulties in communicating with Mozambicans, absorbing the financial cost of the move and the legal requirements and labour laws as laid down by both the Chinese and Mozambican authorities.

Approximately half of the entrepreneurs stated that things are improving regarding their entrepreneurial endeavours. Most of them advised that because immigrating is a costly move, it is important to have enough money to cover all start-up costs of the new SMME and to have a small reserve fund for emergencies. They also stressed the importance of having savings and being able to request money from friends and family for support, if necessary. Other important factors that are mentioned by existing entrepreneurs are Guanxi with locals, analysing the retail market, familiarising themselves with the local labour laws and learning to speak an Indigenous language as soon as possible.

9.4 Culture-Specific Solutions (Short and Long Term)

This case study indicates that starting and operating SMMEs in Mozambique requires multifaceted immigrant entrepreneurship characteristics and resources. In the short term, immigrant entrepreneurs need to build relationships (*Guanxi*) with their customers, supply good quality products, be motivated and learn the language spoken by the majority of their customers. *Guanxi* is specific to the culture of the Chinese entrepreneurial immigrants, and it involves forming connections with the community and government (Wang, Wang, Ruona, & Rojewski, 2005). It can be acknowledged that Chinese entrepreneurial immigrants display *Mianzi* (face), referring to maintaining trustworthiness with the locals and contributing to the development of the Mozambican economy, in return for a better lifestyle and the ability to earn money (Wang et al., 2005).

In the short term, the immigrant entrepreneurs need financial, physical, human and information resources to successfully operate a business in the retail sector. In the long term, the entrepreneurs believe they need ethnic and family support to ensure the success and sustainability of their retail business. Previous experience in the retail sector will be an added advantage. In the long term, the immigrant entrepreneurs experience better working opportunities, cheaper living costs and are able to earn more money than working in China, while enjoying better living conditions and not being exposed to the air pollution and smog they experienced in China.

Chinese immigrant entrepreneurs living in the host country of Mozambique face particular challenges regarding the laws and regulations pertaining to the retail sector, start-up costs and communicating in Portuguese with their customers.

9.5 Recommendations for Chinese-African Intercultural Cooperation

In this case study, the Chinese entrepreneurial immigrants are found to be greatly influenced by their culture and ethnicity in demonstrating values such as *Guanxi*; they can easily adapt and transform themselves to suit the environment of the host country, and continuously have the drive to improve and grow their businesses to meet the needs of their customers.

Because immigrating is extremely costly, without taking the establishment of the SMMEs into account, it is important for potential Chinese immigrants to ensure they have adequate finances for the start-up process and a little extra for emergencies. Chinese immigrants also need to learn the language of their host country in order to effectively communicate with and relate to employees, customers and government officials. Eliminating the language barrier will strengthen relationships and help to promote loyalty and trustworthiness between the customers and the immigrant entrepreneurs.

Chinese immigrant entrepreneurs could build relationships with locals by offering Mandarin language lessons. By teaching Mandarin, Chinese immigrants may not only build relationships but also contribute to the community at large, while developing their own understanding of the local language, thereby ultimately establishing a cross-cultural bond between the Chinese entrepreneurs and the Mozambican customers. All Chinese immigrant entrepreneurs should become familiar with available resources offered by the host country. In addition, it is recommended that they should become mindful of market opportunities in the economy of Mozambique.

References

Baloglu, S., & Uysal, M. (1996). Market Segments of Push and Pull Motivations: A Canonical Correlation Approach. *International Journal of Contemporary Hospitality Management, 8*(3), 32–38.

Hakim, C. (1989). New Recruits to Self-employment in the 1980s. *Employment Gazette, 97*, 286–297.

Kirkwood, J. (2009). Motivational Factors in a Push-Pull Theory of Entrepreneurship. *Gender in Management: An International Journal, 24*(5), 346–364.

Lee, L., Wong, P. K., Foo, M. D., & Leung, A. (2011). Entrepreneurial Intentions: The Influence of Organisational and Individual Factors. *Journal of Business Venturing, 26*, 124–136.

Light, I. H., & Bhachu, P. (2004). *Immigration and Entrepreneurship: Culture, Capital and Ethnic Networks*. New Brunswick: Transaction Publishers.

Light, I. H., & Bonacich, E. W. (1988). *Immigrant Entrepreneurs: Koreans in Los Angeles*. Berkley: University of California Press.

Marchand, K., & Siegel, M. (2014). Immigrant Entrepreneurship in Cities. World Migration Report 2015. Retrieved from https://www.iom.int/sites/default/files/our_work/ICP/MPR/WMR-2015-Background-Paper-KMarchand-MSiegel.pdf

Nhancale, B., Mananze, S., Dista, N., Nhantumbo, I., & Macqueen, D. (2009). *Small and Medium Forest Enterprises in Mozambique*. London: IIED.

Nieman, G., & Nieuwenhuizen, C. (2014). *Entrepreneurship: A South African Perspective* (3rd ed.). Pretoria: Van Schaik Publishers.

Njal, J. (2012). China's Involvement in Mozambique. *International Policy Digest*. Retrieved from https://intpolicydigest.org/2012/08/02/chinasinvolvementinmozambique/

Park, Y. J. (2010). Boundaries, Borders and Borderland Constructions: Chinese in Contemporary South Africa and the Region. *African Studies, 69*, 457–479.

Shultz, K. S., Morton, K. R., & Weckerle, J. R. (1998). The Influence of Push and Pull Factors on Voluntary and Involuntary Early Retirees' Retirement Decision and Adjustment. *Journal of Vocational Behaviour, 53*, 45–57.

Tengeh, R. K. (2011). *A Business Framework for the Effective Start-Up and Operation of African Immigrant-Owned Businesses in the Cape Town Metropolitan Area, South Africa*. Doctoral dissertation, Cape Peninsula University of Technology, Cape Town.

Tull, D. M. (2006). China's Engagement in Africa: Scope, Significance and Consequences. *Journal of Modern African Studies, 44*(3), 459–479.

Wang, J., Wang, G. G., Ruona, W. E. A., & Rojewski, J. W. (2005). Confucian Values and the Implications for International HRD. *Human Resource Development International, 8*(3), 311–326.

CHAPTER 10

Case 7: Managing a Chinese-Angolan National Housing Project in Angola's Capital, Luanda

Christian Martin Boness, Naiming Wei, and Claude-Hélène Mayer

10.1 CASE NARRATIVE: APPLYING TWO DIFFERENT MANAGEMENT STYLES

Angola is a country in southern Africa in which Portuguese is the main business language. The country gained independence from Portugal in 1975, followed by a long period of civil war until 2002. The war left the country in an economically devastated state; however, since 2004, there has been a phase of restructuring and rebuilding the nation, characterised by an economic uplift (CIA, 2018).

C. M. Boness (✉) • C.-H. Mayer
Department of Management, Rhodes University, Grahamstown, South Africa

N. Wei
Department of Business Administration, University of Applied Science, Nuremberg, Germany
e-mail: Naiming.wei@th-nuernberg.de

© The Author(s) 2019
C.-H. Mayer et al. (eds.), *Managing Chinese-African Business Interactions*, Palgrave Studies in African Leadership,
https://doi.org/10.1007/978-3-030-25185-7_10

Because Angola inherited a huge quantity of oil and diamond resources, this period of rebuilding the country is marked by a strong economic growth rate, and international investment is fostered (CIA, 2018) in the different sectors of Angola's economy (de Morais, 2011). Chinese investors are particularly focusing on nationwide infrastructure projects and housing. As reported by de Morais (2011):

> The China International Fund (CIF), a private company based in Hong Kong, has taken charge of the most ambitious projects, such as the construction of 215,500 low-income social houses, an industrial area in Luanda with 70 factories, an international airport, 2680 kilometers of national railway tracks and 133 depots, and 1500 kilometers of interprovincial roads, with more on the drawing boards.

The most ambitious project carried out by organisations from China is the *Nova Cidade de Kilamba* (Kilamba New City) project, a huge housing development scheme, which is designed to host from 200,000 up to 1 million people (Kilamba, 2018). Kilamba New City is situated 20 kilometres south of downtown Luanda, Angola's capital.

The CEO of the *Nova Cidade de Kilamba* project, Mr Wei, is in a volatile situation. On the one hand, he is very proud of his building and construction organisation having won the competitive bid for this huge investment project in "booming Angola" and initiating it in 2008 (Kilamba, 2018). On the other hand, he is unhappy about the increasing rumours that the Chinese executives' management style is "bossy", "autocratic" and "strict" from the perspective of the Angolan employees. Angolan employees seem to feel uncomfortable with the way he behaves towards them. Mr Wei feels misunderstood and is convinced that his management style is a perfect fit for the success of the organisation, particularly the issues he faces in this African context.

Mr Wei uses two different management styles in the organisation. He explains that one management style is applied to the organisation's Chinese employees, which he describes as the "in-group of the company". According to Mr Wei, this style is

> *similar to the management style used in China ... since more than thirty years I do not use many words; everybody is fully responsible for his work, and the executives have a high level of work specification which in turn requires a medium level of expertise from individuals. ... through the application of this management style, the company cooperates efficiently and ensures that the deadlines of the project are met.*

Mr Wei explains that the second management style is applied to interactions with the Angolan employees. He explains that he has learned from the history of the cultural revolution in China how important education is. This is particularly the case when it comes to managing organisations and leadership. He considers education as a key to increase knowledge, information, moral values and virtues within organisations. Education is also key to fighting poverty, hunger, diseases and ignorance in societies on a long-term basis. Therefore, Mr Wei believes that education is very valuable in both Chinese and Angolan contexts.

Mr Wei believes that his management styles are increasing the life quality of the employees, of the organisation and of society. To do so, management styles need to include the values of discipline, punctuality and achievement. He usually allocates work to the employees and managers in challenging situations by giving guidance and instructions.

The Angolan employees are very unhappy with the fact that different communication and management styles are applied to employees according to their cultural backgrounds in the organisation, creating a split between Chinese and Angolan employees by addressing them in different ways. The Angolans in the company feel unfairly treated, and they have managed to let Mr Wei know about their unhappiness with the two-class system in the organisation. In response, Mr Wei feels hurt and misunderstood, since he experiences his different management styles as being positive contributions to the management of the organisation.

He tries to justify his leadership approach, assuming that different groups of employees, according to their hierarchical levels, need management styles which adapt to the context and the situation. Employees with less education and training need more discipline, moral guidance and supervision, he believes, while middle and top managers also need guidance, but they can develop their ability to work independently more easily because they have already gained experience and guidance.

Based on his extensive working experience in both China and internationally, Mr Wei sees himself as being a *Daoshi*: a master, moral guide and teacher who is responsible for learning, usually in a Chinese learning environment. As a *Daoshi*, he is an educator for others in the organisational system who need to learn and be guided. Mr Wei is convinced that the awareness of *Daoshi* and moral values contribute to success. He is a role model, a boss and a superior who delegates his tasks.

When talking about managing African employees and challenges of management in the Angolan context, Mr Wei refers to the Chinese success stories of *Daqing* and *Dhazai* which he also uses when speaking to Chinese employees to motivate them and to share their common values of discipline, hard work, dutifulness and time management. *Daqing* and *Dhazai* are two legendary models for industrial and agricultural production by practising extreme hard-working self-sacrifice and upright political activity, which became a nationwide campaign driven by Mao Zedong during the period of cultural revolution. Mr Wei compares the actual economic situation of Africa with that of China during the 1970s and 1980s, explaining how a disciplined and hard-working China has reached its impressive economic success today. By telling these two stories to his African employees, Mr Wei intends to motivate them to work in the same way, in order to reach economic success and improve their quality of life.

In addition to sharing the Chinese success stories with his Angolan employees, Mr Wei revisits African and, particularly, Angolan history, in search of economic and political collective success stories, thereby referring to the colonial times in which economic processes were established in Angola by the Portuguese colonial powers. Obviously, Mr Wei is aiming to adjust his Chinese perspective to the Angolan perspective—but does he succeed?

10.2 Questions and Points of Discussion

- Explore the management styles applied by Mr Wei and discuss the cultural background of the management styles and communication within the organisation.
- Discuss Mr Wei's conceptualisation of management from Chinese and African perspectives and reflect on the ways of managing an organisation from Chinese and African perspectives.
- Identify which values play a role in each of the culture-specific viewpoints of Chinese and African employees.
- Relate the case to the socio-historical contexts of Chinese and Africans in their struggle for freedom and development during the past decades and centuries. What do you think: how does the sociocultural history of the collectives influence this case and the behaviour of Mr Wei and the African employees?
- Develop short- and long-term solutions for this case from each of the Chinese and African points of view.

10.3 Chinese Perspectives

Mr Wei is a technically competent executive leader who has undergone many years of training and working experience within the organisation in China and has gained expertise in international collaboration. He makes decisions based on collective experiences in China—which began its economic change and development programmes in the 1980s. He has already spent several years in African countries and sees this experience as a work-in-progress, a lifelong learning task in which he develops himself as an individual (micro-level). His individual experience is also based on the organisational development (meso-level) and on the societal (macro)-level.

Mr Wei is self-confident. Not only does he see himself as knowledgeable with regard to the organisation and the content of his work and leadership, but he also considers himself knowledgeable about how to cooperate with the African employees.

10.3.1 Applying Two Different Leadership Styles

From a Chinese viewpoint, in principle, it is not a mistake to apply two different leadership styles for Chinese and African employees who have different technical and managerial qualification levels and different working experience, as well as different cultural backgrounds. Situational leadership is a widely acknowledged management approach both in academic theory (Hersey & Blanchard, 1969) and in company practice.

It is reasonable to assume that the Chinese managers as well as the Chinese construction workers have more experience and better technical qualifications than the African employees. Therefore, the situational leadership approach is appropriate to the circumstances.

The reason for the Angolan employees' resistance to Mr Wei's leadership appears to lie not in the two different management methods, but somewhere else.

10.3.2 Mr Wei's Management Experience and Value Orientation

Mr Wei has worked for a long time as manager in the Chinese construction company. Typically, company culture in this industry in China is based on a hierarchical organisation structure, hard work, discipline and duty. In this business environment, Mr Wei has developed his personal leadership style: assertive, autocratic and efficiency-driven, which helps him to reach a satisfactory level of working performance and enables good career development within the company.

Mr Wei's primary role in the Kilamba project is CEO of building construction. The major responsibility of a construction manager should be focused on increasing operational efficiency and ensuring project progress in terms of quality, timing and cost. In this role, his previous leadership style was result-orientated. However, faced with African employees, Mr Wei understands his role not only as construction manager but also as cultural educator and even as moral guide (reflected in his *Daoshi* approach). This role understanding is derived from Mr Wei's subconscious conviction of cultural and moral superiority when facing Black African people. This understanding is not only characteristic of Mr Wei, but it is also observed in many other Chinese people, most likely also in Mr Wei's Chinese management team for Kilamba project.

Daqing and *Dhazai* were popular stories during the time of cultural revolution, motivating all Chinese people to sacrifice themselves with extremely hard work and absolute duty to the Communist Party and to the Motherland. Today, no Chinese manager or employee younger than 40 years would be aware of these stories. In the perception of most older Chinese people, the *Daqing* and *Dhazai* models are a faded legend of the past, with a bitter political aftertaste, rather than a proud story of national economic success. It is most unusual for a Chinese manager to still use these stories as a motivational tool for employees in today's business life.

This suggests that Mr Wei has not been exposed to proper modern management tools for employee motivation. He simply takes the story he remembers from his school days and tries to apply it to a totally changed social and economic environment.

10.3.3 Different Perceptions of Mr Wei's Role as Daoshi

Mr Wei's effort to play the *Daoshi* role has created different perceptions. He sees himself as a moral guide who contributes to the African employees' quality of life. But the African employees see him instead as a moral preacher who, together with his Chinese management team, treat them unfairly as second-class citizens.

The situation becomes more complex when Mr Wei speaks about economic progress in Angola during Portuguese colonial rule, without clarifying that he holds a different view regarding the negative aspects of colonialism. This indicates his lack of political sensibility. In this context, the stories of *Daqing* and *Dhazai* are perceived by African employees not as a motivation for a better future life, but rather as a neocolonial education lecture. If this had been an isolated statement from Mr Wei about economic progress during Portuguese colonialism, it could perhaps have been overlooked. But, in combination with their perception of being treated as second-class workers, the Angolan employees' distrust of Mr Wei and his Chinese management colleagues has increased and deepened.

10.3.4 Mr Wei's Strengths and Weaknesses

Mr Wei has good functional competence as a construction project manager. He is efficiency-driven and result-orientated, and he has high positive identification with the company's achievements. He has self-confidence, maintains tight management control and demonstrates goodwill in wishing to contribute to the economic and social development in Angola.

Although he is confident, he overestimates his own social competence and personality. He has an obvious cultural and moral superiority in the face of African people, and his understanding of management practice is traditional and hierarchy based. His knowledge of modern cooperative management tools is limited, and in spite of many years of experience working in Africa, he lacks political and intercultural sensibility.

10.4 African Perspectives

The Angolan employees are particularly irritated by the different management styles used by Mr Wei in managing Chinese and African employees. They also feel uncomfortable about the two languages of instruction—Mandarin and English—used in the organisation. Since the Angolan employees can only speak and understand their own language, they feel left out, marginalised and discriminated against because they do not have access to the knowledge of the Chinese employees, to necessary organisational and management knowledge or to the promotion system. They feel excluded from the resources of the organisation and from forming a closer relationship with the CEO, Mr Wei.

The Angolan employees wonder how Mr Wei can run the organisation successfully by splitting the employees into a Chinese (middle and top management) group and an Angolan (lower employee level) group. They believe that every employee in the organisation should be treated fairly and should have the right to gain organisational knowledge and become part of the organisational family. They do not have a sense of belonging to the Chinese organisational family.

Furthermore, the Angolan employees are reminded of colonial structures and the two-class system created in past centuries by the colonial powers. They refer back to their collective experiences of suppression and oppression in their own country and believe that Mr Wei's management style of discipline, punctuality and delegating tasks, while tightly controlling the overall processes, does not provide them with experiences of equality and opportunities to develop as employees. The Angolans in this company feel dominated by his management style and are of the opinion that they have a great deal of economic and management knowledge to contribute, which could help the Chinese organisation to flourish in the Angolan context. However, their contextual knowledge is ignored by the Chinese management, and they feel marginalised.

The Angolan employees look back at Angola's history of development, political unrest and fight against exploitation from European powers. They are proud of their country's economic development and growth over the past decade and through periods of change referred to as "the wind of change that transforms Africa" (Fleshman, 2010, p. 28). Across the African continent, liberation movements since the 1960s have advanced to move decolonisation forward. The Angolan employees in this case refer to the pan-African role model of Ghana and its valued liberation movement leader, Kwame Nkrumah, who proclaimed: "Our independence is meaningless unless it is linked up with the total liberation of the African continent" (Fleshman, 2010). The President of Tanzania, Julius Nyerere, described the historic incidents in Ghana as "the beginning of the end of colonialism for the whole of Africa" (Fleshman, 2010, p. 28). In 1963, when the Organisation of African Unity (OAU, now known as the African Union) was founded, 32 African countries had successfully gained their independence, mostly through peaceful, non-violent means. The OAU charter emphasised self-determination and majority rule as major guiding principles of resistance and independence from European colonialism, imperialism and rule (OAU, 1963). The Angolan liberation movement is often compared with similar movements in other African countries. These liberation movements have positively impacted on African unity.

Fifty years after decolonisation, the Angolan employees in this company value unity, democracy, self-reliance and equality. They feel irritated by Mr Wei's management style that, in their opinion, is not expressing their values. They are reminded of their collective struggle to liberate their country and experience a similar desire to liberate themselves within this Chinese organisation. From the Angolan employees' viewpoint, the struggle in their own country continues to be accepted, acknowledged and promoted.

The struggle for independence and the civil war have left their mark on the Angolan employees, who now wish for peace and economic growth and the rebuilding of their country into a prosperous new world (CIA, 2018). They would like to play a role in all the processes, which investors are initiating in Angola. They wish to become counterparts of the Chinese employees, being treated fairly and on an equal level with regard to management style and opportunities for promotion.

However, the employees are aware of a split in the organisation and in the management style of Mr Wei, who does not focus on growth through intercultural and international cooperation, but rather on segregated approaches. The Angolan employees want to be treated equally in an international organisation, not only in terms of economic values, moral behaviour and training but also with regard to the behaviour of others. They do not appreciate leadership which primarily delegates tasks; they would prefer a transformational leader who provides direction, safety and security in the organisation and on the job, who would deliver respectful and equal treatment of all employees. Therefore, in response to the organisation's differentiated management policy according to cultural background, the Angolan employees feel humiliated and mistreated.

10.5 Culture-Specific Solutions (Short and Long Term)

10.5.1 Objectives and Solutions

The main objective is to ensure that the construction project progresses smoothly, while existing tension between Chinese management team and Angolan employees is reduced. A mutual understanding of both cultures needs to be enhanced. With this objective in mind, efforts should focus on improving the existing Chinese management team, including Mr Wei. To avoid further escalation of tension between Chinese management and African employees, clearly defined rules for human resource management have to be implemented as soon as possible, otherwise the principal objective could be affected. At the same time, the motivation and pride of the key members of the Chinese management team should be considered in a balanced way.

Enhancing cultural and value understanding for the Chinese management team is a long-term incremental process. If improvements in this area can be linked with company and personal performance achievement, it will be easier to move forward. Result-orientated actions, which will benefit the well-being of all the people involved, are more important than simply talking about good intentions.

10.5.2 Short-Term Solutions from Angolan Perspectives

As a short-term solution, the Angolan employees might ask the Chinese management to call for a general meeting of employees and management. During this meeting, Angolan employees could explain their views on the situation and express their wishes, values and socio-historical background of intercultural and international experiences and cooperation. If such a meeting between the Chinese management and Angolan employees is not possible from the Chinese perspective, the Angolan staff could also ask for an intercultural mediator to mediate between themselves and management. In several Chinese organisations, a job specification for "cultural exchange employee" already exists. Often, this role is played by Chinese employees who have studied African cultures and languages and can support the resolution of conflicts and communication within the organisation across cultural group membership.

10.5.3 Long-Term Solutions from Angolan Perspectives

If there is no position for an intercultural mediator in the organisation, the Angolan employees might ask to install such a position to create a constructive culture of communication. In the long term, Angolan employees would like to see changes in the language policy of the organisation, and to have English as the language of business, without allowing Chinese or Portuguese to take over in the selected employee groupings. To create equality, contracts and management styles should be applied to all employees in an equal way, explaining certain cultural socio-historical aspects and impacts from both sides for both sides.

A common concept of Chinese and Angolan management within the organisation should be established to bridge the gaps in cultural understanding between the two groups. Knowledge should be shared across cultures, and ways to promote individuals should be found which do justice to all employees, while contributing to the aims of the organisation. Chinese and Angolan management styles need to be discussed in terms of advantages and disadvantages. New ways of creating an international management culture need to be established.

10.6 Short-Term Recommendations for Chinese-Angolan Intercultural Cooperation

The short-term solutions mainly aim to restore the relationships between the Chinese managers and Angolan employees. Chinese managers and Angolan employees need to hold meetings on a regular basis in which Chinese and Angolan concepts of management (e.g. *Ubuntu* management), historical impacts (e.g. *Daqing* and *Dhazai*), mastery and education (e.g. *Daoshi*, *Ubuntu* leadership) are exchanged. Later, these meetings need to serve the exchange of values, behavioural collective schemes and communication options, such as Indabas (consensus and decision-making processes), to create mutual understanding. A permanent "improvement box" should be installed near the human resources office to offer employees the opportunity of providing written feedback anonymously.

Intercultural trainings should be conducted for all employees to learn about their own and the other's cultures, the management styles and the core culture concepts to create a mutual understanding. Based on these intercultural trainings, training platforms should be provided to all employees for further education in terms of cultural knowledge of all cultural groups involved, in socio-historic information, language skills as well as networking tasks. Language courses in Mandarin and Portuguese and English as a business language should also be offered to provide all employees with the general ability to begin to understand each other from different (language and cultural) viewpoints.

The three-step action plan recommendations below should be conducted immediately and completed within a short period, in order to create a significant improvement of relationship between Chinese and African employees in an efficient way. An additional step is a long-term-orientated corporate social responsibility programme, which should strengthen the sustainable competitiveness of the company and simultaneously contribute to the social well-being of the Angolan society.

10.6.1 Step 1: Personal Communication with Mr Wei

A personal meeting with Mr Wei should be arranged. Open and careful communication should be used in addressing the actual tensioned relationship between the Chinese management team and the African employees, especially concerning the complaint about "second-class treatment". Point out that the escalation of such conflict has the potential to affect the construction project progress as well as the public image of Mr Wei's Chinese company.

Provide Mr Wei with a personal coaching programme, to help him with handling the conflict potential and to ensure a smooth and efficient implementation of the project. Recognise Mr Wei's goodwill in wishing to contribute to the economic and social development in Angola, in order to explain to him that his *Daoshi* approach and his "education programme" with *Daqing* and *Dhazai* have been negatively perceived by the African employees—indicating a possible deficit in the leadership style and cultural value orientation in his Chinese management team.

Advise Mr Wei not to continue to use previous approaches because there is obviously a mismatch between Mr Wei's original intention and the perceptions of the African employees. The reasons for such misunderstandings are complex and would be time- and resource-consuming to attempt to resolve. It is wise to pursue another more efficient way.

10.6.2 Step 2: Chinese Managers' Meeting and Formation of a Task Force

Mr Wei needs to call a special Chinese managers' meeting, broach the issue of tension in the relationship between Chinese managers and African employees and point out the complaint of the African employees about "second-class treatment" as a critical problem.

Form a task force group with the target to build a harmonious and trusting working environment between Chinese and African employees by retaining previous successful management principles like discipline and hard work, which are demanded of all employees. The task force group of four or five members should consist of Chinese managers and representatives of Chinese and African employees.

10.6.3 Step 3: Introduction of Intercultural Management Rules in the Company

The task force then drafts a document specifying intercultural management rules with the focus on a respectful behavioural code between Chinese and African employees at all levels of the business hierarchy. After approval by Mr Wei, this document is announced officially in a general meeting of employees with an introductory speech made by the company CEO.

Include the requirement: "Work with African employees in a mutual respectful way" in the performance evaluation criteria for all Chinese managers.

In addition to these administrative measures, during the next six months, organise two or three single-day training programmes with follow-up and reflection workshops for Chinese managers and key staff, on the topics of intercultural communication, African culture and history and Angola's recent economic and social development.

10.7 Long-Term Approach to Intercultural Communication

Introduce a tailor-made technical and language-training programme for African employees to improve their professional qualifications as skilled construction workers and team leaders in this international construction company.

Emphasise promotion of qualified and talented training programme graduates to management or key staff or team leader positions in Mr Wei's section of the organisation.

Because the working period for the Kilamba construction project is limited, Mr. Wei's company will only receive part of the benefits resulting from the training programme, which has been paid for in full. However, after completion of the Kilamba project, other Chinese or international construction companies working in Angola, and, of course, the training programme graduates themselves, will receive more benefits from the programme. Therefore, Mr Wei can consider this training programme as a contribution to his corporate social responsibility, in terms of giving back to society.

After the first positive results of the programme (such as the promotion of training programme graduates to team leaders), Mr Wei should bring this practice to the attention of the public, the Chinese Embassy, Angolan industrial and labour associations, universities, reputable charity organisations and the media. Because a best practice such as this is most likely unique in Chinese companies today, a positive response from the society could be expected. With public recognition of the training programme, the Chinese Embassy is likely to be happy to build a good reputation in the country.

For Mr Wei's company itself, the situation offers a unique competitive advantage in the construction industry, which will help them to win future construction projects in Africa and benefit the company's sustainable development. From a long-term perspective, the investment of the company in the training programme will generate a good return.

Considering his contribution to the company, Mr Wei may enjoy improved career development opportunities, which will match his goodwill in contributing to the economic and social development in Angola. The Angolan Industrial Construction Association will be supported in the training of qualified skilled construction workers and managers, and the African employees in Mr Wei's company will have the prospect of a better life, even after finishing the Kilamba project and leaving the company.

If not yet in place, a position should be created for a cultural translator/mediator in Chinese companies that invest in African countries. Employees in these positions should have studied not only their own and the other's culture, management and economy but should also be self-reflective in terms of their own cultural knowledge and biases. Having grown up in a bicultural context would be an advantage for this position.

References

Central Intelligence Agency. (2018). *The World Factbook. Angola.* Retrieved from https://www.cia.gov/library/publications/the-world-factbook/geos/ao.html

de Morais, R. M. (2011). The New Imperialism: China in Angola. *World Affairs, 173*(6), 67–74. Retrieved from http://www.worldaffairsjournal.org/article/new-imperialism-china-angola

Fleshman, M. (2010). *A 'Wind of Change' That Transformed the Continent.* Retrieved from https://www.un.org/africarenewal/magazine/august-2010/%E2%80%98wind-change%E2%80%99-transformed-continent

Hersey, P., & Blanchard, K. H. (1969). *Management of Organizational Behavior: Utilizing Human Resources.* New Jersey: Prentice Hall.

Kilamba. (2018). Retrieved from https://kilamba-info.com/concept

Organisation of African Unity Charter. (1963). Retrieved from https://www.au.int/web/sites/default/files/treaties/7759-file-oau_charter_1963.pdf

CHAPTER 11

Case 8: Language, Culture and Power in the Chinese-South African Telecommunications Sector

June Sun

11.1 Case Narrative

The presence of Chinese technology organisations on the African continent has increased over the past years (Shinn, 2012). In particular, the growth of mobile connectivity in Africa has been strongly tied to the footprint of Chinese telecommunications organisations. Internet connectivity has become a central pillar in supporting economic growth and has been included in the national growth strategies of many countries, including South Africa (South Africa. National Development Plan, 2012). Therefore, China's position as a key global telecommunications provider is relevant to South Africa's economic trajectory. Furthermore, the potential of technology transfer in China's engagement with African countries is often at the forefront of both bilateral and multilateral dialogues (China. Ministry of Foreign Affairs, 2018; Xinhua, 2018a), and the contribution of foreign technology in domestic productivity can be important (Keller, 2004).

J. Sun (✉)
Vera Solutions, London, UK

The meeting place of Chinese and South African managers and employees in the telecommunications sector is particularly interesting, because it ties into existing power structures between the Global North, China and Africa, and it reflects a series of potential obstacles that plague wider Chinese-African interactions. There have always been links between the most powerful countries and the world's channels of communication, from merchant routes to telegram cables, all the way to the IT revolution which placed Europe and North America as global leaders of communications technology (Galtung, 1979; Smith, 1993). China's position as a global superpower in technology, however, is a recent development. For example, even in 1989, of the ten largest telecommunications organisations in the world, eight were European or North American, two were Japanese and none were Chinese (Kaplan, 1990). The case of Chinese-South African telecommunications was selected because South Africa is China's largest trading partner in Africa (Xinhua, 2018b), and it is also one of the most important markets in Africa for Chinese telecommunications organisations. Therefore, expectations of their clients and the South African government are high. However, Chinese-South African interactions are conditioned by barriers that build upon existing power structures and expectations of legitimacy.

Some Chinese telecommunications organisations have set up headquarters in Johannesburg, where they hire both South African and Chinese staff[1] (C2, C5, C8, C14). All organisations operating in South Africa need to comply with South African employment law, which is guided by broad-based black economic empowerment policies. These are a set of employment and corporate ownership policies, which aim to correct historical inequalities stemming from apartheid, by enforcing quotas of employees and owners from demographics that have been historically discriminated against (Horwitz & Jain, 2011; South Africa. Department of Trade and Industry, 2015).

Research interviews showed that language is a central barrier in the interactions between Chinese and South African employees. But research data also showed that the South African telecommunications industry holds up a second benchmark of cultural and linguistic legitimacy, drawn from European and American establishers of the industry. There is considerable

---

[1] Research interviews were conducted in Johannesburg and Cape Town during July to September 2016. References to primary data (interviews) are coded using C for Chinese organisations and S for South African organisations.

power behind the idea of Western "quality" products, as well as Western standards of corporate professionalism (S19, C13). This not only informs South Africa's postcolonial relationship with the Global North but also frames the wider relationship of Chinese and African interactions in recent decades.

When employees of Chinese telecommunications companies approach potential South African clients, they often face serious concerns that their products are not of global standard, thus needing to overcome a "made in China" stigma before being able to sell their products (S16, S18). Sometimes deals are not finalised because of a lack of trust in the quality of Chinese-made products. This both causes and is reinforced by Chinese telecommunications organisations using price as a key differentiator and much lower prices than their competitors.

This is linked to the perception that because most Chinese employees are not native English speakers, this correlates with a lower standard of professionalism (C8). Using Bourdieu's (1986, 1991) and Taylor's (1985) framework of language not as an expressive but a designative system, one can understand language's value as being externally defined rather than as an internally consistent tool for expression. Bourdieu (1991) situates language into contestations of symbolic power. Language, far from being a static "pure instrument of communication", is actually a sign of the socio-economic conditions which form legitimacy and norms in any given setting (Bourdieu, 1991, p. 66).

Central to Bourdieu's analysis is the market in which legitimacy and symbolic power are contested. The market for legitimacy in the ICT industry was established entirely without either Chinese or African agents. Therefore the definition of legitimacy is embodied not only in the use of English but also in the Euro-American precedents of technical and corporate legitimacy in the industry. Subsequently, language plays a dual role: both as a metric of fluency in human interactions and as a metric of a deeper contestation of legitimacy and symbolic power between Chinese challenger firms and European and American market incumbents. In the context of South Africa, the intersection of power and language is particularly important, given the historically colonial role European languages have played in South Africa. In the post-apartheid era, African languages have regained political importance. However, in the realm of corporate culture, power is still given primarily to the language of English, with a lack of fluency being associated with a lack of legitimacy.

Bourdieu's (1986, 1991) concept of *field* provides a useful framework to understand the ways in which Chinese vendors are competing for legitimacy in the telecommunications industry. A *field* is a domain or market in which social agents interact and compete for various forms of power through different forms of capital: economic, social and cultural (Bourdieu, 1986). Economic capital can be reflected through a benchmark like price. On this front, Chinese organisations are particularly competitive, and they have found great success in undercutting the prices of European and American market incumbents. Social capital refers to the social connections and obligations in relationships and networks. Cultural capital refers to non-financial assets, such as language and etiquette competencies. In cultural and social capital, Chinese organisations contest for power against their European counterparts and often fall short. This also fits into a global narrative which tends to see the rise of Chinese corporations as a symbolic contest for power against the Global North.

11.2 Investigative Questions

- What are the origins of Western ideas of professionalism, trust and quality in industries such as telecommunications? Which ideas of professionalism, trust and quality form perceptions of legitimacy? Do they stem from culturally specific histories?
- How do Chinese organisations contribute to existing perceptions about them, and in what ways do they defy them?
- What kind of narratives and power structures are Chinese organisations using when they enter the South African market? In turn, which ones do South African organisations use when observing and interacting with Chinese organisations?
- What kind of narratives and power structures are reinforced or weakened by the emergence of Chinese businesses in South Africa?
- What are some ways to overcome the linguistic and trust gaps and barriers between Chinese and South African colleagues who have limited experience of each other's culture? What might broaden the cultural gap?

11.3 Chinese Perspectives

Despite the rapid globalisation of Chinese multinationals, there is a strong command-and-control culture in Chinese organisations. Many of the decisions are made centrally in headquarters in China and subsequently communicated to local branches in Johannesburg (S7, S17, C13). This contributes to a less flexible organisational structure that is not particularly reactive to local sentiments and less able to address the sense of cultural dissonance or perceived shortfall in legitimacy.

Some senior Chinese managers are aware of the cultural dissonance between their Chinese and non-Chinese employees, but either feel limited in their ability and time to address this or do not think this is an issue of high priority (C13). Chinese managers are also aware that they struggle to compete with Western counterparts in relationship-building, both with clients and with local policymakers. They realise that more work needs to be done to address linguistic barriers in order to make technical training more effective. However, they are often constrained by decision-making hierarchies from headquarters in China. This increases the distance perceived by their South African clients and deepens the difficulty of trust-building.

Some Chinese employees and managers are aware that they engage in gatekeeping practices with sensitive information, and do not hire South African employees for key or managerial positions, owing to a conscious reluctance to "let the fertile water run into other people's pastures", which is a Chinese idiom for the protection of one's own family's interests (C3). Despite the public rhetoric about the importance of technology transfer, some Chinese managers feel protective of technical information, which is also common practice in the wider industry. Some Chinese managers who are aware that their South African counterparts do not get promoted to senior positions (S17) fear that if they train and promote South African employees, they will move to other organisations and not remain loyal, as Chinese employees are more likely to be. This, naturally, confirms South African suspicions that Chinese organisations do not aim to localise, and the lack of legitimacy of professionalism increases.

Both Chinese and South African managers are aware of the price disruption and competition they create for European companies (S7, S18, S20, C12, C13). The fact that Chinese organisations represent a break in the timeline of the telecommunications industry, and play the role of disruptor, means that they are likely to endure higher scrutiny from partners who have not worked with Chinese organisations before.

11.4 South African Perspectives

South African employees at Chinese telecommunications organisations often feel excluded from the decision-making process, which is based in China's headquarters with limited transparency and is then communicated to local subsidiaries (S7, S17, C13). South African employees can often feel locked out of the core of the organisation because they do not speak Chinese (S18). In one case where a particular deal required a Chinese vendor to absorb many employees from a South African client, the majority of South African employees ended up resigning because they felt that their work was becoming less valuable, and they were prevented from doing the same jobs they had been doing before the deal took place (S16, S17, S24).

Although Chinese organisations comply with local broad-based black economic empowerment laws, some South African employees perceive a deeper level of localisation by European organisations, either through a higher rate of local recruitment or through increased autonomy from company headquarters. Some South African employees believe their growth opportunities are limited with Chinese employers. This reinforces the foreignness of Chinese organisations and colleagues in a purely linguistic sense and lowers the legitimacy of Chinese products and practices in the *fields* of social and cultural capital because of a lack of trust and familiarity. It also limits the unity and strength of integrated Chinese-South African organisations, which essentially operate in two cultural siloes.

Senior South African managers working as clients of Chinese organisations are conscious of the challenger role that the Chinese play in the telecommunications industry. Chinese organisations have only entered global markets in the past two decades, while European and American incumbents have been globally active for several decades earlier. For this reason, they are often cautious about the quality of Chinese products. Some perceive products made in China to be more likely to break or to be less sophisticated than Western products (S16). Although many South African clients consider Chinese products to be improving and becoming more adaptable to client-specific needs, initial concern about the quality of Chinese-produced equipment was reflected by almost all interviewees who discussed it.

South African organisations are attracted to the price advantage that Chinese organisations offer. However, some South African client employees find the low price to be an indicator that Chinese products are not credible (S18). In South African organisations that operate in several African countries, some senior managers prefer to try Chinese products in their smaller markets first, before bringing the products to their more important markets. This is a particularly clear reflection of Chinese competition in different *fields*. In the *field* of economic capital, Chinese organisations have used price competition to generally successful ends.

However, in the *fields* of social and cultural capital, they are heavily hindered and have to overcome considerable stigma to operate. The influence of this is so strong that strength in the economic *field* can actually be refracted as a weakness in cultural and social *fields*.

South African employees often feel frustrated by the linguistic gap when their Chinese counterparts are communicating with them in non-native English. Many South African employees speak of struggling to connect with their Chinese colleagues, thus preventing communicating on a project management level (S5, S7). Many South African employees perceive that because Chinese employees speak English as a second language, this indicates they are not as professional, or as good as someone who speaks English more fluently.

Sometimes South African employees find the technical documentation to be less complete from Chinese organisations, compared to their European counterparts (A5,[2] S7, S5, S8). This is sometimes considered as a lack of professionalism or as a signifier of poor product quality. These interactions once again underline the shortages in social and cultural capital in Chinese organisations, when competing in a *field* established by European and American corporations. Chinese employees lack the soft skills and the legitimacy required to build their reputation to the levels of the market incumbents. In a specific case, South African employees have responded positively to decisions from Chinese management in one organisation to hire South African trainers at their training centre (C8). This is a case of active mitigation in cultural and social capital, in that the Chinese managers learned that they could avert direct competition by recruiting local training staff.

11.5 Culture-Specific Solutions (Short and Long Term)

11.5.1 Short-Term Solutions from Chinese Perspectives

As a short-term solution, it would be helpful to hire more local people to occupy key positions, particularly those with communication and training roles. Time should be invested in training such people in these roles to understand the particular difficulties that South African subsidiaries face, to enable them to work closely with senior management in both countries

---

[2] Academic analysts who were interviewed in this research are coded as A.

to effectively address communication gaps. They would hold key positions as communicators between different geographies, cultures and managerial levels. These local staff can assess the situation for the most effective way of communication, whether through town hall meetings, newsletters or webinars. Their most important contribution would be the creation of active and engaging feedback loops, which can be used to sustain improvement. In addition, team-building activities which aim to bring Chinese and South African employees together in social settings can help. Exercises in communication and feedback can be customised from standard business education formats to fit the specific case, and this can create resources and opportunities for common ground.

11.5.2 Long-Term Solutions from Chinese Perspectives

Chinese organisations establishing a presence in South Africa should allow their subsidiaries more autonomy to increase adaptability to the conditions on the ground. A strong central command structure and rigid decision-making mechanisms may be effective for some functions, but it is not always the best way forward to allow for successful localisation.

It is important, in the long run, to integrate non-Chinese employees into Chinese organisations, and provide them with the same trust and opportunities for growth as afforded to Chinese employees. Over time, sustainable construction of autonomous subsidies empowered with their own flexible decision-making mechanisms will be able to cater to the specificities of South Africa.

Trust from clients and partners will come with time, so it is essential for Chinese organisations to continue to invest in sustainable partnerships in South Africa. Actively preempting and responding to concerns about quality can be achieved by more active documentation in local languages, executed with active feedback loops from users. The recruitment, training and use of product champions from local organisations can also mitigate trust issues.

11.5.3 Short-Term Solutions from South African Perspectives

South African organisations can hire Chinese-speaking staff to act as translators of language, and of culture. They can make a stronger case for the needs of South African employees and clients to Chinese organisations. They can help establish best practices in daily project and technical work, setting reasonable expectations from both sides.

Efforts from private and public sector organisations can be valuable in organising events promoting mutual understanding in different cultures and providing opportunities for Chinese and South African partners to socialise and network outside specific work settings. Examples include celebrations of South African and Chinese holidays, as well as town hall sessions facilitated by people who are able to speak to both cultures.

11.5.4 Long-Term Solutions from South African Perspectives

The growth of Chinese organisations in South Africa represents a change, which brings with it expected insecurities and concerns. In this sense, it is a cultural and sociopolitical aspect of change management. Dedicated training programmes which utilise existing change management theories and practices can address different operational norms in corporate culture and provide reassurances in a time of change.

Educational investments will need to be made in South Africa, if it is to take control of a sustainable and equitable commercial relationship with Chinese organisations in the future. Both language and business education materials can be used and customised to better equip staff with content that directly addresses Chinese business culture. Partnerships between South African educational institutions and Chinese educational institutions as well as commercial entities can play a facilitating role. Over time, more South African professionals will become more fluent in Mandarin and more familiar with Chinese business culture. These individuals will be able to act as interlocutors between the two sides.

11.6 Recommendations for Chinese-African Intercultural Cooperation

One of the most important takeaways from this research on the encounter between Chinese and South African colleagues in the telecommunications sector is the limitations upon Chinese-South African relations when the parameters of success are defined by a third culture, in this case, the Global North. This condition is influenced both by Europe's colonial history in Africa and by the core/periphery power division in global technology organisations. The China-Africa encounter is in many ways an interruption of these two existing conditions. Thus, expectation-setting being conditioned by the Global North has been observed in many facets of China-

Africa relations. An explicit awareness of this from both sides can contribute to a more honest dialogue between commercial entities, as well as stronger feedback loops to address concerns and trust issues. High-level training given to senior management by academics who have studied China-Africa relations and postcolonial histories can be a good starting point for more constructive ways of thinking to prevent relationships from becoming strained. Furthermore, for scholars and journalists in specific Chinese-African fields, it is important to frame studies of China-Africa relations in historical context, with these power structures included in the analysis, so as to avoid a historical or polemic accounts that can easily be politicised or misunderstood.

Though often conditioned by existing global power structures, there is nonetheless a novel opportunity within the China-Africa realm of cultural and professional interactions to set fresh and independent norms, in the meeting place of two cultures, which are very different from each other. While norm-setting does not need to be, nor can it possibly be, sealed from outside influences, ideas of respect, equality and excellence should be pursued independent of previous experiences with European and American organisations in South Africa. For example, a typical corporate value such as inclusion can be used in the China-Africa context to respond to specific feedback. HR departments can overcome the excessive use of the term "inclusion" to the point of meaninglessness, by instead creating a culturally specific meaning for the word. Surveys and other feedback tools can be used to measure actual lived experiences of employees and clients from both cultures and can be used to create targeted suggestions for potential improvements. This can then be moulded into actionable feedback and specific policies to put ideas of inclusion into practice. Thus, the inclusion practised in a Chinese-South African setting would take into consideration the very specific cultural and historical contexts of the people in the organisations, as opposed to an idea of inclusion defined on different continents.

In addition, notions such as a lack of fluency in English being equal to poor quality in products, or that South African employees who do not speak Chinese should not be trusted with sensitive information, can be dispelled when the decision to dispel a Eurocentric focus is intentional. The decision to address this should come from senior leadership in both Chinese and South African organisations. One way to overcome reliance on cultural and linguistic biases is to establish and rigorously enforce independent institutions and rules for measuring product quality and only sharing of sensitive or classified information by job grade. The directive should come from senior management and be enacted and protected by strong middle managers. The idea is to wrest decision-making away from culture and language perceptions, while changes are underway. Constructing a strong and independent system to ensure product quality can be a great tool for increasing overall trust and accountability in the organisations.

The new norm-setting for Chinese-African professional encounters will come with time, as cultural paradigms shift slowly. Over a longer time span, the novelty of Chinese organisations in Africa will be replaced by experienced first-hand and best-practice knowledge of how to overcome cultural barriers in their own contexts. However, in the short run, recruiting bilingual and bicultural candidates from both sides can be leveraged to address cultural distrust and language gaps.

Expectation-setting at the offset of projects can mitigate some of the problems down the line. In this case, at the start and during regular intervals of projects, it will be important to run training sessions which explicitly address expected cultural differences, reminding and conditioning colleagues to be mindful of their formed opinions and ways of self-presentation. Being primed of awareness of the added difficulty of working across cultural lines can go a long way. Intentional team- and organisation-building events, aiming for a safe social space for Chinese and South African colleagues to interact, can do much to build trust. From the South African side, reaching a point where they can trust Chinese product quality without the reassurance of Western marketing or a stamp of Western cultural fluency will be key. From the Chinese perspective, overcoming the need to centrally control corporate decisions and to truly localise, beyond local requirements, will be a demonstration of trust. A significant amount of reform will be needed to change Chinese corporate structures to allow for more autonomy in subsidiaries, but this will contribute significantly to the development of local cultures and adaptabilities. A local board of directors or advisers, with locally hired people who are familiar with local conditions and predicaments, can be beneficial. Moving decisions, bringing autonomy to local hubs and making only the most necessary decisions in China can be a helpful long-term goal.

References

Bourdieu, P. (1986). The Forms of Capital. In J. Richadson (Ed.), *Handbook of Theory and Research for the Sociology of Education*. New York: Greenwood.

Bourdieu, P. (1991). *Language and Symbolic Power*. Cambridge: Polity.

China. Ministry of Foreign Affairs. (2018, September 5). *Forum on China-Africa Cooperation Beijing Action Plan (2019–2021)*. Retrieved from https://www.fmprc.gov.cn/mfa_eng/zxxx_662805/t1593683.shtm

Galtung, J. (1979). Towards a New International Technological Order. *Alternatives: Global, Local, Political*, 4(3), 277–300.

Horwitz, F. M., & Jain, H. (2011). An Assessment of Employment Equity and Broad Based Black Economic Empowerment in South Africa. *Equality, Diversity and Inclusion: An International Journal*, 30(4), 297–317.

Kaplan, D. (1990). *The Crossed Line: The South African Telecommunications Industry in Transition*. Johannesburg: Witwatersrand University Press.

Keller, W. (2004). International Technology Diffusion. *Journal of Economic Literature*, 42(3), 752–782.

Shinn, D. H. (2012). *China and Africa: A Century of Engagement*. Philadelphia: University of Pennsylvania Press.

Smith, D. A. (1993). Technology and the Modern World-System: Some Reflections. *Science, Technology, & Human Values*, 18(2), 186–195.

South Africa. Department of Trade and Industry. (2015, May 6). *Broad Based Economic Empowerment Act, Guidelines for the Development and Gazetting of Transformation Charters*. Retrieved from http://www.abp.org.za/wp-content/uploads/2014/11/38766_gen408.pdf

South Africa. National Planning Commission. (2012, March 15). *National Development Plan 2030: Our Future – Make It Work*. Retrieved from https://www.poa.gov.za/news/Documents/NPC%20National%20Development%20Plan%20Vision%202030%20-lo-res.pdf

Taylor, C. (1985). *Human Agency and Language*. Cambridge: Cambridge University Press.

Xinhua. (2018a, July 23). *China-South Africa Ties Model for South-South Cooperation, Says Chinese Ambassador*. Retrieved from http://www.chinadaily.com.cn/a/201807/23/WS5b559974a310796df4df82ce.html

Xinhua. (2018b, July 27). *Eight Major Initiatives Proposed at FOCAC Help Africa Develop: CAR President*. Retrieved from https://www.focac.org/eng/zfgx_4/zzjw/t1599429.html

CHAPTER 12

Case 9: Transforming Employee Conflicts in a Chinese Construction Firm in Kampala, Uganda

Sidney Muhangi

12.1 Introduction to the Case

Uganda is an East African country endowed with natural resources relying on agriculture as its economy's mainstay. The state has a culturally diverse population of over 40 million people of whom 66% are below the age of 35 (United Nations, 2017). As a former British protectorate, Uganda still uses English as its official and business language, since there is a great diversity of languages and dialects spoken. Uganda gained its independence in 1962 from Britain, which was followed by political unrest and military dictatorship from 1971 during Idi Amin's regime, to 1986 when the national resistance government took over through guerrilla warfare (Prunier, 2004).

Currently, Ugandans enjoy a calm political environment which has helped the country to achieve sustained economic growth of 5% and more in recent years (African Development Bank, 2018). Uganda's gross domestic product growth and peaceful political climate are attracting

---

S. Muhangi (✉)
Department of Management, Rhodes University, Grahamstown, South Africa

© The Author(s) 2019
C.-H. Mayer et al. (eds.), *Managing Chinese-African Business Interactions*, Palgrave Studies in African Leadership,
https://doi.org/10.1007/978-3-030-25185-7_12

direct investments from various countries; of these, China is the leading trading partner and foreign direct investor in Uganda (Warmerdam & van Dijk, 2017). China and Uganda also take pride in their traditional political and socio-cultural ties, which is part of the reason for China's strong relationship with Uganda, among other African countries benefitting from Chinese-African business cooperation (Mourao, 2018).

In Uganda, Chinese firms are mostly involved in the extractive, infrastructure and construction industries (Luther & Shinyekwa, 2018). One of the most successful Chinese firms in Uganda's infrastructure and construction industry is China Railway Seventh Group (referred to as "the Group")—a contracting firm involved in a World Bank–funded institutional and infrastructure development project in Kampala to widen and upgrade roads and drainage systems.

Despite the success the Group has previously achieved in Uganda, current employee conflicts between Ugandan and Chinese employees on the project are affecting its smooth operations. The project funder has received reports that "Chinese managers mistreat local employees", which triggered a warning issued to the project manager that further escalation of employee conflicts may lead to termination of the Group's contract. The Ugandan employees accuse the management (most of whom are Chinese) of disrespect, especially of their cultures and religions, and of segregating them from their Chinese colleagues. According to the Ugandan workers, the Chinese managers are selfish, rude people who shout at them and stereotype them as lazy.

Mr Li, the project manager who has been working for the Group in Africa for 13 years, is struggling to save the project and transform these employee conflicts to bring harmony to the project. He acknowledges that the firm has staff conflict challenges, which in his opinion are caused by cultural misunderstandings, with the language barrier being the overriding factor. He says that the company is undergoing conflict transformation which includes promoting authentic relationships between Chinese and Ugandan employees, spearheaded by an independent "grievance-handling committee" set up by the Group to attend to employees' grievances and resolve the conflict.

However, Mr Li is frustrated and says that some of the accusations against the management are unfair; he thinks they are intended to make the company look bad. Mr Li thinks that reducing the frequency of contact between Ugandan and Chinese staff will lead to fewer conflicts. He has therefore decided that the Chinese team dine separately from Ugandan staff and has stopped sports events between Chinese and Ugandan staff, among other actions.

12.2 Questions and Points of Discussion

- From the viewpoints of both Chinese and Ugandan employees, discuss socio-cultural specific factors causing employee conflicts.
- Discuss the conflict management style of Mr Li and the Group, and its effectiveness in resolving and transforming employee conflicts.
- Develop short- and long-term solutions from each of the Chinese and Ugandan viewpoints that Mr Li and the Group's management can employ to manage and transform employee conflict.

12.3 Chinese Perspectives

The Group's human resource manager believes that, unlike Ugandans who take their weekends off, Chinese workers have no time to rest. From their perspective, they only come to Africa to work, and so they pledge their loyalty to their managers and "worship" their work. Most Chinese managers in the Group report that they have no religion; getting the company work completed is their only objective. The Chinese draw their work ethic from Confucianism (Yeh & Xu, 2010), which is their moral doctrine for work, social structures and human relationships (Fan, 2000). They complain that the Ugandans waste time with their friends and attending religious festivals during weekends and holidays, instead of getting the company work done.

Chinese managers want loyalty. According to them, an employee must follow the boss's instructions without any objections. Chinese managers want Ugandan staff to accept this work ethic, but they have found it difficult to achieve.

Mr Li thinks that reducing contact between Chinese and Ugandan staff will minimise conflict. He has formed a grievance-handling committee to mediate the process of resolving employee conflict instead of promoting personal relationships among employees. The committee comprises both Chinese and Ugandans in senior positions. In cases of conflict, individual committee members investigate and submit their report findings back to the committee to deliberate on the matter. After deliberations, the parties to the conflict then give their accounts of what happened, and later the committee makes appropriate decisions in their presence. Mr Li feels proud that the committee is doing well in resolving employee conflicts, but it does not seem to be enough.

Furthermore, Chinese managers have worked comfortably with Mandarin interpreters in Africa to facilitate communication between African and Chinese employees. This method is, however, time-consuming and is becoming unpopular because African employees want to communicate directly with their bosses. Most managers feel comfortable using an interpreter instead of making an effort to learn English or the other official languages used in Africa. In Uganda, Mr Li relies on few Ugandan interpreters to facilitate communication, but this is not effective in the long term. However, one manager is offering free English lessons twice a week in the evenings to his fellow managers who do not understand the language.

12.4 African Perspectives

The Group's African employees complain that Chinese managers are using "colonial tactics" to manage them. However, unlike British colonialists who allowed religious freedom, the company is reported by Muslim and Christian Ugandan employees to interfere with their freedom of worship in not allowing them time to participate in religious activities, including prayers, on Fridays and Sundays respectively. The vast majority of Ugandans are religious people who hold dearly to their faiths.

One of the mid-level Ugandan managers in the Group says that conflict is caused by lack of orientation of Chinese workers in Ugandan cultures, history, traditions and norms. The manager has also observed that Chinese managers took a long time to realise that new Chinese workers needed to know the English language, which most local workers speak and understand. This view is supported by many Ugandan employees of the Group.

The Ugandan workers in the company are unhappy with the tier system, which Chinese management uses to separate them from their Chinese co-workers, limiting their communication and relationships. Ugandan employees say that this is the reason why their Chinese colleagues struggle to integrate, because they only associate with fellow Chinese, in areas which are restricted to Ugandan staff, such as those during meal times.

Ugandan employees' attitude to work differs from that of Chinese employees. While the latter "worship" work, the former believe that there needs to be a balance between work and social life. Ugandan employees want to use their weekends to spend time with their families and friends, attending social events and church. But Mr Li and other Chinese managers require them to work Monday to Sunday, which leads to conflict.

12.5 Culture-Specific Solutions

12.5.1 Short-Term Solutions from Chinese Perspectives

Conflict transformation cannot take place without relationships. Mr Li and the management of the Group need to create opportunities for Chinese and Ugandan employees to interact with each other to develop relationships and close the gap between them. Promoting relationships may include reinstating the sports and games that Mr Li has halted, as well as allowing all employees to eat meals together if they wish to.

Mr Li should stress the need for communication among employees at all levels of the company, as well as the importance of employee collaboration and association at the workplace. Ugandan employees' opinions, suggestions and objections need to be communicated to management, as well as any other relevant or new information that Chinese managers may not know regarding local cultures and behaviours.

12.5.2 Long-Term Solutions from Chinese Perspectives

The language barrier is a severe challenge for employees of Chinese companies in Africa. Mr Li and his management committee need to offer English lessons to Chinese staff who do not communicate well in English. Since most Ugandan employees at the company can speak English, it would be easier for the company to use it as the medium of communication. Effective verbal communication is necessary for building strong and long-term relationships. Chinese managers could also give Mandarin lessons to any interested Ugandan employees. Having Ugandan employees who could speak Mandarin would ease the communication difficulties in the company.

Chinese managers need to consult African employees to learn more about the country's cultures, traditions and religions. For instance, since most Chinese managers claim to have no faith, it will likely be a source of conflict if the company management obstructs Ugandan employees from participating in religious activities. Chinese managers also need to study and be aware of the colonial history of African countries, so as not to repeat the mistakes of past groups of foreigners. For instance, in Uganda, people have a historical bias regarding Indian employee relations and clash of cultures. Chinese managers and new employees coming to Uganda need orientation and information concerning such biases.

It is also vital that Mr Li and the Chinese management understand Ugandans' work ethics and core values. Ugandans do not appreciate being described as "lazy" for having different work ethics and attitudes from those of the Chinese.

12.5.3 Short-Term Solutions from African Perspectives

African employees, through their representatives on the grievance-handling committee, could appeal to Chinese management to convene regular meetings with the Ugandan employees, to enable both groups of employees to learn about each other's cultures, languages and social beliefs. Implementing such meetings would help to build stronger relationships and make communication easier. African employees also, to some degree, need to adapt to the Chinese ways of working, personal behaviour and communication styles. Unless this is done, it could be difficult for Ugandan employees, for instance, to differentiate between a Chinese manager speaking normally or shouting at them.

12.5.4 Long-Term Solutions from African Perspectives

Ugandan employees need to learn to speak Mandarin. China is an important trade and investment partner, and with a view to the future, African and Chinese staff will receive reciprocal benefits from their cooperation. Ugandan employees should request the Chinese management to teach them clear human resource management policies.

Ugandan employees could borrow some concepts from the Chinese work ethic and culture, and need to develop tolerance of cultures different from their own. The Ugandans would benefit from orientation in Chinese Confucianism to learn about the rich Chinese culture, history and work ethic.

12.6 Recommendations for Chinese-African Intercultural Cooperation

Chinese managers need to consider the dynamics of Africa's diverse cultural and institutional contexts, and work to develop the African workforce using cross-cultural human resource management practices (Kamoche, Siebers, Mamman, & Newenham-Kahindi, 2015). Building long-term human resource management practices that take account of African work ethics and values will help to reduce conflicts in organisations and towards the achievement of an Africa-Asia nexus.

There is a need to establish lines of clear communication and reporting. Encouraging communication among employees, according to Eisenkopf (2018), is an effective way of reducing conflicts in an organisation. In conflict resolution processes or negotiations, physical presence and dialogue are essential. Chinese managers need to create social events where employees can regularly meet and interact. Interpersonal conflicts can be adequately resolved with proper communication, but if discussion is avoided, conflict may escalate (Tufano, 2013). Communication problems may be addressed if management supports Mandarin and English lessons being given to the respective employee groups.

It is also recommended that the company's management introduces cultural exchange programmes. Both Chinese and African employee groups need to learn about and respect each other's cultures, traditions and history.

References

African Development Bank. (2018, July 21). *Uganda Economic Outlook*. Retrieved from https://www.afdb.org/en/countries/east-africa/uganda/uganda-economic-outlook/

Eisenkopf, G. (2018). The Long-Run Effects of Communication as a Conflict Resolution Mechanism. *Journal of Economic Behavior & Organization, 154*, 121–136.

Fan, Y. (2000). A Classification of Chinese Culture. *Cross Cultural Management: An International Journal, 7*(2), 3–10.

Kamoche, K., Siebers, L. Q., Mamman, A., & Newenham-Kahindi, A. (2015). The Dynamics of Managing People in the Diverse Cultural and Institutional Context of Africa. *Personnel Review, 44*(3), 330–345.

Luther, M. M., & Shinyekwa, I. (2018, June 24). *Increased Foreign Direct Investment (FDI) from China to Uganda Is Instrumental for Industrial Sector Development*. Retrieved from https://www.newvision.co.ug/new_vision/news/1486496/china-uganda-cooperation

Mourao, P. R. (2018). What Is China Seeking from Africa? An Analysis of the Economic and Political Determinants of Chinese Outward Foreign Direct Investment Based on Stochastic Frontier Models. *China Economic Review, 48*, 258–268.

Prunier, G. (2004). Rebel Movements and Proxy Warfare: Uganda, Sudan and the Congo (1986–99). *African Affairs, 103*(412), 359–383.
Tufano, A. A. (2013). *Conflict Management for Security Professionals* (pp. 107–119). Amsterdam: Elsevier Science.
United Nations. (2017). *World Population Prospects: The 2017 Revision*. Retrieved from https://www.un.org/development/desa/publications/world-population-prospects-the-2017-revision.html
Warmerdam, W., & van Dijk, M. P. (2017). What's Your Story? Chinese Private Enterprises in Kampala, Uganda. *Journal of Asian and African Studies, 52*(6), 873–893.
Yeh, Q. J., & Xu, X. (2010). The Effect of Confucian Work Ethics on Learning About Science and Technology Knowledge and Morality. *Journal of Business Ethics, 95*(1), 111–128.

PART IV

Intercultural Training Cases: International Human Resource Management

CHAPTER 13

Case 10: Sharing Knowledge in a Sudanese Oil Refinery Through Cultural and Language Trainings

Christian Martin Boness

13.1 CASE NARRATIVE

Although Sudan has a rich culture and a long history dating back to 3000 BC, its past decades have been marked by two heavy and enduring civil wars. The last civil war ended on 9 July 2011, when South Sudan became an independent country. South Sudan is also rich in oil and produces 80% of all Sudan's crude oil. A landmark deal was signed between Sudan and South Sudan on the issues of oil pipeline use from South Sudan through Sudan to Port Sudan (Martin, 2012). However, clashes continue; oil production declined at the beginning of 2018, and inflation is about 200%.

For the people of South Sudan, in particular, there is a small hope that the situation can improve; the US has lifted the sanctions imposed on Sudan owing to the Darfur conflict, and the economy has a chance to stabilise after a long period of dramatic decline. South Sudan tries to get

C. M. Boness (✉)
Department of Management, Rhodes University, Grahamstown, South Africa

off the US list of "sponsors of terrorism" (Copnall, 2018), while the United Nations Mission in South Sudan (UNMISS) supports a positive trend to avoid further armed conflicts by running a peacekeeping mission in South Sudan (Mmali, 2018). However, on the list of the most dangerous countries of the world, South Sudan holds the rank of 14 (The Telegraph, 2017).

The World Fact Book edited by the US Central Intelligence Agency (CIA, 2018) contains some interesting data. According to this source, South Sudan has a population of 14 million inhabitants; English is the official language, with some Arabic spoken around the capital, Juba. Educational attainment is very poor owing to a lack of qualified teachers, school materials and school buildings, and only a third of the population is literate (CIA, 2018). The male unemployment rate lies at 20%, and there are approximately two million displaced people in South Sudan (CIA, 2018). The Chinese Ministry of Foreign Affairs (2018) emphasises that China assists with peacekeeping measures in the country, with provision of humanitarian aid, rebuilding schools and improving communication infrastructure. In fact, China plays a pivotal role in South Sudan by making growth possible again. About 40% of South Sudanese oil consortiums are controlled by the Chinese. In Sudan, oil is evidently featured as the most significant component of bilateral Sudan-China economic relations.

In the present case study, Mr Lin is the product manager of a medium-scale topping refinery in South Sudan. He gets crude oil from the South Sudanese oil fields situated along the White Nile. The topping refinery company is equipped with a high standard of technology from China and is producing very efficiently. The paramount goal of the oil production is to provide enough petrol for the entire region of South Sudan.

Mr Lin is aware of the major challenge of knowledge-sharing with the Sudanese staff. He clearly remembers a time when Japan helped China to develop from an agricultural society to a modern economy. A similar goal can only be achieved if, in the long run, skilled Sudanese staff are able to supervise and monitor the refinery processes themselves.

However, there are many other questions to be solved. Sudanese staff find it difficult to be properly trained by the Chinese who move from company to company or even return to China for good. It is true that China has brought skilled technicians to South Sudan for computer science and engineering. However, these experts from China sometimes lack the basic English language skills needed to train Sudanese staff properly. Additionally, the Sudanese concede that they do not have enough experience in the field of refining crude oil, and also lack English language skills, often speaking only Arabic or a local language such as Dinka or Luo. Locals complain that they do not participate in knowledge-sharing and it is said that the organisation is not cross-cultural.

Mr Lin has been ordered by the CEO to collect ideas from his Chinese co-managers and from Sudanese staff on ways to improve language communication and design culture trainings for both staff and management, in order to make the company into a cross-cultural organisation.

13.2 Questions to Consider and Investigate

- How can the problem of knowledge-sharing be solved?
- How would in-house trainings for the South Sudanese staff look? Propose some topics.
- Investigate some basic Chinese language patterns to make communication easier between Chinese management and Sudanese employees.
- What is Chinese communication like? Are there typical patterns of communicating?
- How does African communication take place, especially in South Sudan?
- What do Chinese have to learn from the extremely scarce situation in South Sudan?

13.3 Chinese Perspectives

This case touches issues such as knowledge-sharing, language patterns and other core challenges in the oil refinery controlled by China National Petroleum Corporation. Mr Lin is aware of the official governmental strategies of "aid and trade"; he wants to contribute to the oil trade and sees that he must also contribute to education and skills training to a certain extent. However, he is not sure if it is necessary to train his staff in the oil refinery more than is absolutely necessary. Education is, in his view, a government policy issue to lift the level of literacy in the population. At some stage, the government might approach him to support local endeavours to improve literacy, but he does not care about the issue himself. He also considers knowledge-sharing as unnecessary because it does not support the processing of crude oil. For now, the operational yields are satisfying and meet his expectations. What matters is that the South Sudanese employees do their jobs as he does, working more than 10 hours every day.

Mr Lin is convinced that his staff must first learn some basic patterns in communication and language. This will make it easier to communicate with Chinese experts and managers who are sometimes ordered to move from project to project in South Sudan and other countries. He is certain that the Chinese communication style along with other language patterns makes it possible for the Chinese to be successful in businesses locally and elsewhere in the world.

Chinese communication is characterised by goodwill and humour based on a harmonious, argument-free conversation. Sometimes conversation is loud, cheery and boisterous. People are permitted to finish their statements and are shown due respect. Chinese entertain a culture of listening—rather than speaking. Some examples of the rules of formal communication are as follows: do not interrupt the speaker, use a soft gaze and nod frequently to indicate interest. One should not point out any mistakes made by the speaker; wait for the speaker to finish before commenting or seeking clarification, and keep smiling and maintain a pleasant expression.

Mr Lin knows that it is characteristic of Chinese communication to use an indirect mode of speech. The Chinese often avoid expressing demands, desires, emotions or criticism. In official settings, Chinese people tend to communicate primarily about work-related issues. The personal openness in conversations can be described as "low level". Therefore, Mr Lin suggests that in general communication with Chinese partners, Sudanese people should talk about arts, scenery, landmarks, climate and geography, and even of positive impressions from experiences with the Chinese. But the Sudanese must avoid asking questions about the cultural revolution or about anything remotely political.

Questions must not touch on personal issues for fear of offending: If a Chinese person has been offended by a personal question, a smile in response will indicate a certain range of annoyance or displeasure. As a result of unpleasant contributions to the conversations, the Chinese might later refuse invitations or other offers, but they will not show their embarrassment in the situation.

Mr Lin is convinced that if all staff members follow the Chinese rules of business communication etiquette, his oil refinery will become a more intercultural company. Mr Lin also considers knowledge of greetings and some essential phrases to be mandatory for a good communication culture in the organisation.

13.4 African Perspectives

African communication shares some traits with predominant Chinese communication patterns. Africans would not interrupt the speaker. They would show interest in the speaker's contributions by agreeing to what has been said. They would mirror humour and joy but also sadness and empathetic silence. Positive emotions play an important role in African communication. Africans like to communicate to celebrate their togetherness at work and elsewhere.

Apart from the formal frames of communication, some conversational topics of African communication are quite similar to the Chinese topics mentioned earlier. The most important topic in Sudanese communication is family well-being. It plays an overwhelming role in conversation, followed by news about friends and health. Other appropriate topics are travel and the weather, while talking about work and work operations holds second rank. If a weekend has just passed, religious and spiritual engagements may also be discussed.

In African communication, talking about political issues or topics such as initiation rites is likely to be avoided, unless there is a specific need to exchange ideas regarding these subjects. Senior members of African communities are entitled to supervise communication and to decide which topics are to be discussed.

From an African point of view it appears that in Chinese companies, there is less cooperation and teamwork and a lack of knowledge-sharing. The Chinese seem to keep to themselves in their environments, during meetings and on many other levels of communication. They appear to interact with the local African employees only when it is necessary for work purposes. This can result in information deficits and, in this case, can be interpreted by the South Sudanese employees as not being treated equally. Additionally, many Chinese managers move from project to project, which results in a lack of continuity of any social or reliable relationship-building between the Africans and the Chinese. These conditions can negatively affect the motivation of African workers to engage in hard work (Boness & Mayer, 2013).

In the case study, it is necessary that key features of contemporary Chinese aid and trade must be explained properly by the Chinese management, to give South Sudanese employees a clear view of how the Chinese support schools and vocational trainings to alleviate the poor level of qualifications in the country.

The South Sudanese want to know to what extent natural resources like crude oil are exploited, and how the families of staff members can participate and their infrastructure can be improved. Schools in the area have been raided by the enduring civil war, and there are no paved roads in the entire region. The Chinese are therefore welcomed to improve the situation for local people in the villages along the White Nile in the northern parts of South Sudan. These populations await a visible improvement of education and infrastructure from the government in cooperation with the Chinese management.

13.5 Culture-Specific Solutions

13.5.1 Short-Term Solutions from Chinese Perspectives

Knowledge-sharing should be immediately announced as part of the organisational culture of the oil refinery. Improving the skills of the core local senior staff will stabilise and improve the production and refinery of crude oils. A sound explanation of Chinese trade and aid in South Sudan should be given, showing the benefits for the working staff in the refinery. The quick rotation of Chinese management should be avoided, to emphasise Chinese interest in communicating with the staff and in coming to know the circumstances under which the staff families are living.

13.5.2 Long-Term Solutions from Chinese Perspectives

Offer communication training encompassing English for Chinese and general training on Chinese-African communication to make the refinery a more cross-cultural organisation. Support the Chinese communication style and its rules as well as some basic Chinese language patterns. Found a vocational training centre in cooperation with the local authorities. Obtain qualified teachers from South Sudan and China to offer staff and students basic training modules in the oil refinery industry. Regularly offer aid to primary schools in the region in order to assure literate students with better chances of employment in the oil industry or elsewhere.

13.5.3 Short-Term Solutions from Sudanese Perspectives

Education is highly appreciated by the Sudanese staff. Workers want to get additional in-house trainings in English language patterns and literacy. Besides these trainings, the Sudanese want to know exactly what skills are mandatory for their positions, and even how the modern refineries work. With this in mind, special skills trainings in computer appliances for particular jobs in the industry should be offered, to enable the local staff to receive additional qualifications. Complaints about the Chinese-orientated culture in the oil refinery should be heard and dealt with appropriately.

13.5.4 Long-Term Solutions from Sudanese Perspectives

The Sudanese workforce is interested in attending cross-cultural trainings in order to understand and to have more transparent communication with the Chinese management. The Sudanese also want to secure a basic primary education in the region for their families and other villagers. There is a major need for vocational centres in the region to ensure a qualified workforce. Sudanese employees want to receive Chinese aid more visibly in an open cooperation between local government and Chinese management for the benefit of the Sudanese staff and their families.

13.6 RECOMMENDATIONS FOR CHINESE-AFRICAN COOPERATION

Both Chinese management and Sudanese staff should engage in strengthening their communication in English and Chinese. Also Sudanese people who cooperate with the Chinese should know some idioms and phrases of the Chinese culture to demonstrate their openness to and respect for the culture. English should be the general language for communication in the company as English is the official language in the country. In several Chinese companies two languages are prevailing: English for the use of Chinese-Sudanese communication and Chinese for Chinese-Chinese communication. Basic language patterns should be taught and cross-cultural topics such as food, local and regional geography, mutual friends, the weather, hobbies, news, travel, family, health, work and clothing should be exchanged.

Additionally Chinese management should be informed about the contemporary situation of the war-ridden region of South Sudan. Chinese management and the government of South Sudan should take care of the basic challenges in the educational field and vocational skills trainings in a way that can benefit the local population. The level of literacy can then be improved sustainably and a more skilled workforce can participate in the employment markets.

References

Boness, C., & Mayer, C.-H. (2013). *Chinese-Tanzanian Interactions in International Companies*. Unpublished data, Department of Management, Rhodes University, Grahamstown, South Africa.

Central Intelligence Agency (CIA). (2018). *The World Fact Book*. South Sudan. Retrieved from https://www.cia.gov/library/publications/the-world-factbook/geos/od.html

China. Ministry of Foreign Affairs. (2018, January 13). China and South Sudan Sign Agreement on Economic and Technical Cooperation. *Chinese Embassy in South Sudan*. Retrieved from http://www.fmprc.gov.cn/mfa_eng/wjb_663304/zwjg_665342/zwbd_665378/t1525562.shtml

Copnall, J. (2018, July 11). Why the End of US Sanctions Hasn't Helped Sudan. *BBC News*. Retrieved from https://www.bbc.com/news/world-africa-44711355

Martin, H. (2012, September 27). Sudan and South Sudan Sign Landmark Deal. *Aljazeera*. Retrieved from https://www.aljazeera.com/news/africa/2012/09/201292712585354211 3.html

Mmali, J. (2018, August 6). UNMISS Hails Agreement on Governance as an Important Step in Resolution of South Sudanese Conflict. *UNMISS*. Retrieved from https://unmiss.unmissions.org/unmiss-hails-agreement-governance-important-step-resolution-south-sudanese-conflict

The Telegraph. (2017, October 9). The World's 17 Most Dangerous Countries (According to the Foreign Office). *The Telegraph*. Retrieved from https://www.telegraph.co.uk/travel/galleries/The-worlds-most-dangerous-places/south-sudan//

Today Translations. (2019). *Doing Business in China*. Retrieved from https://www.todaytranslations.com/consultancy-services/business-culture-and-etiquette/doing-business-in-china/

CHAPTER 14

Case 11: Working Conditions in a Chinese-Ugandan Communications Company

Christian Martin Boness and Naiming Wei

14.1 CASE NARRATIVE

Uganda is a flourishing nation in East Africa, with investments from many foreign organisations (Africa Business Pages, 2019). Foreign direct investment has been attracted over the past five years, amounting to more than US$250 million annually (Africa Business Pages, 2019). In 2013, the Vice President of Uganda, Ssekandi, stated that there were more than 7000 Chinese immigrants living and operating economically in Kampala, the capital of Uganda (New Vision, 2013).

The Road and Belt initiative that combines a new Silk Road and a new Maritime Silk Road fascinates both Ugandan and Chinese business people, as well as academics at the Confucius Institute at Makerere University in Uganda (Xinhua, 2018). This Chinese-initiated and Chinese-driven

---

C. M. Boness (✉)
Department of Management, Rhodes University, Grahamstown, South Africa

N. Wei
Department of Business Administration, University of Applied Science, Nuremberg, Germany
e-mail: Naiming.wei@th-nuernberg.de

© The Author(s) 2019
C.-H. Mayer et al. (Eds.), *Managing Chinese-African Business Interactions*, Palgrave Studies in African Leadership,
https://doi.org/10.1007/978-3-030-25185-7_14

project aims to develop Uganda from a farming society into a post-modern industrialised and digitised future country. The fibre-optic project—which is the topic of this case study—is predicted to become the backbone of a transnational network of communication and data transfer in East Africa (PC Tech Magazine, 2015).

A Chinese communications organisation, Huawei, was contracted by the Ugandan government to expand Uganda's fibre-optic infrastructure throughout the country (PC Tech Magazine, 2015). The fibre-optic project is financed by a US$106 million loan from China's Exim Bank (PC Tech Magazine, 2015). In Phase 1 (from 2006 onwards), all government structures should be linked. Phase 2 will link Uganda to Kenya and to the South Sudan, while Phase 3 should link Uganda to Rwanda (PC Tech Magazine, 2015). The Auditor General notes, however, that the procurement was not implemented effectively (PC Tech Magazine, 2015), but work on the fibre-optic project continues, and Phase 2 is nearly finalised.

The public relations manager for the project, Mr Bugeke, is a Ugandan citizen who has been studying in China for about three years. He is interviewed by two students from the Department of Management at Makerere University on certain management and business topics. The students inquire about the working conditions, atmosphere at work and even about neo-Confucian work ethics.

Mr Bugeke is an open-minded manager who has good working relationships with the employees. He confirms that some employees say there are only "small job offers for Ugandan citizens" in this organisation, which leads to some dissatisfaction with the organisation's recruitment policies. Furthermore, the number of holidays seems to be very limited for Ugandan employees in comparison to other local and Western-orientated organisations. But the main issue for employees is "unfriendly treatment by Chinese managers". Mr Bugeke points out that one of his major concerns is to minimise these types of complaints and to build bridges between Chinese managers and Ugandan employees. Sometimes, Mr Bugeke admits, even he does not fully understand the cultural background of the behaviour and approach of his Chinese colleagues, although he has lived in China for more than three years and worked in a Chinese organisation for more than nine years (Boness & Mayer, 2013).

14.2 Questions and Points of Discussion

- Give an idea of the self-image of the fibre-optic company and contrast this image with an African view of the company.
- What do Chinese management expect from the employees in the fibre-optic project in Uganda?
- What is the Chinese manager's understanding of "hard work" and how is this connected to Confucian work ethics?
- What do Ugandan employees expect from holiday benefits and better treatment?
- Identify some characteristics of Ugandan good governance and cooperation with the Chinese company.

14.3 Chinese Perspectives

Chinese organisations employ more Chinese labourers than desired by the Ugandan workforce and the unemployed locals. However, a Chinese organisation in one African country estimated that subcontracting local employees reduced the value of the work done by some 40% (Bräutigam, 2009, p. 153). The ratio of Chinese to African members of the workforce also touches on the implementation of the Chinese "grand strategy" that provides a background to the fibre-optic project in Uganda. This strategy refers to a Chinese cultural principle which affects the organisational strategies of Chinese enterprises. Led by Xi Jinping in 2017, China has entered a new era which aims to transform "riches into strength". In the near future, China will invest about €1 billion to connect 60 countries in Asia, Africa and Europe, building infrastructure, power plants, logistical centres and huge digital nets.

The company Huawei is valued as a highly profitable enterprise, well known for its high standard of corporate governance. The company's management is characterised by a high level of dedication, performance orientation and extremely hard work. Typically, the company exercises a paternalistic leadership style, and salaries in general are above the average for the Chinese staff.

In Uganda, the prevailing ethnocentric staffing model means limited chances for foreign managers to reach top positions. Therefore, a two-system approach is applied in this company: the Chinese staff benefit from the same policy as in China, even if they work in African countries such as

Uganda. Local staff are treated in line with the local environment and its requirements. However, it is not clear whether Chinese management recognises the dominant cultural patterns in a mixed English and Niger-Congo culture where the work–life balance is an important ingredient of work and contracts. Possibly Huawei is not implementing the company's policy correctly in Uganda; the contract issue might not be fully adapted to the country's specific requirements. Chinese managers do not see the necessity of explaining to local employees the policies that they apply. Chinese organisations do not necessarily take labour rights and laws into account. This might be based on the fact that often, labour laws are available but not adhered to in international organisations. Ugandan juridical and administrative authorities seem to provide a favourable business environment for Chinese organisations.

The recruitment of employees in the company depends primarily on the skills and qualifications of the aspirant employee rather than on factors such as marital status or family bonds, as is the case in Uganda. In Chinese recruitment processes, the social network and oral information about applicants are also used to bring qualified workers into the fibre-optic company.

Chinese managers usually expect the full commitment and engagement of employees. To work overtime without extra payment is normal and expected. Managers at the top and middle management levels are usually supposed to stay at work until the CEO leaves the workplace. If Ugandan managers leave before the CEO, they have to face the consequences (Rarick, 2007).

It can happen that contracts given to Ugandan staff do not include holiday and sick-leave agreements, and the labour laws of the country are not necessarily followed. For the Chinese, family relationships usually do interfere neither with work relationships nor with the manner in which the job is done. Family events should not intermingle with the work environment and the commitment at work. In terms of Chinese behaviour in the workplace, greetings are usually quick and friendly, while African employees of lower rank are not necessarily greeted or spoken to in a polite way. The treatment of Ugandan employees differs from that of Chinese managers because the employees are seen as being learners who are not on the same hierarchical level. Chinese managers fulfil the roles of adviser, teacher and educator, which are often associated with Confucian ethics. From this perspective, it is expected that the employee listens and obeys the instructions without comment in response to the fatherly figure of the manager.

Chinese managers and Ugandan employees seem to have different perceptions of the cultural concept of "hard work". The understanding of this concept is mainly influenced by different understandings of work ethics and the historical development of values connected to the workplaces. The Chinese have gained basic work-related values via Confucian ethics. In China, "working hard" means to work as efficiently as expected, while in sub-Saharan Africa it means giving an impression to please a superior. Studies show (Laowei Career, 2019) that there is a growing work–life balance dilemma in China, where 75% of workers report that stress in the workplace has risen in the past year, while only 48% in the rest of the world report having stress in the workplace. The concept of "working hard" nowadays is questioned by Chinese top managers as well as Chinese expatriates (Laowei Career, 2019).

In Chinese organisations, Confucian principles are indigenous since they are related to national culture. These principles advocate respect for work, discipline, thrift, protecting face, order in relationships, duty to family and economic egalitarianism (Hofstede & Bond, 1988; Rarick, 2007). Hard work, frugality and diligence are the values of the Confucian system.

Confucius and Confucianism have had a profound influence on China and major parts of the East and Southeast Asia, generally regarded as the "Confucian culture circle". Concepts of New Confucianism are increasingly being discussed in the context of management, management styles and the validity of classic Confucian principles in a post-modern, globalised world. Neo-Confucianism is a kind of intellectual movement of Confucianism that began in the early twentieth century in Republican China, and revived in contemporary China. Rarick (2007) describes the managerial approach of Chinese leaders: some essential characteristics are "collectivism and harmony, centralised control, authoritarian and paternalistic leadership, expectation of hard working employees". Regarding Confucian social relationships, there is a structural, hierarchical pattern that reflects the perpendicular connection between king and subject, father and son, obedience to elders—and on the horizontal level are husband and wife, as well as trust between friends (Rarick, 2007). Chinese managers are expected to be caring, maintain their dignity and be true to their word (Rarick, 2007). Some Chinese managers working in Africa stick to principles that are also valid in Chinese businesses (Price, 2019). These four Confucian values are family values. They comprise order, respect, hierarchy and harmony (Price, 2019). The concept of family includes the inner circle or loyal subordinates and even government officers (Price,

2019). Whoever belongs to a familial type of in-group is supposed to protect the interests of the family members prior to the public interest (Price, 2019).

14.4 Ugandan Perspectives

In Uganda, the fibre-optic company is highly respected, and Ugandans appreciate the value of Huawei devices such as smartphones in daily life. However, the circumstances under which Huawei is working in Uganda leave some questions unanswered. Recent research on human resource management factors affecting employee retention at Huawei (Abdoulaye, 2017) shows that despite the excellent reputation of Huawei worldwide, there are still some issues in countries of sub-Saharan Africa (Abdoulaye, 2017), including Uganda. Results from this research suggest that Huawei should consider the revision of salary schemes, job security, job contracts as well as better recognition and rewards for better retention of highly qualified staff (Abdoulaye, 2017).

Many Ugandans expect a highly respected company such as Huawei to be steered by values that are rooted in the cultural environment of the people who buy their products. In the fibre-optic project, Ugandan employees expect Chinese management to show much more awareness of the leading values of the Niger-Congo culture. The idiom "sharing is caring" well describes African values across many African countries. Resources are often scarce, and therefore they should be shared to show respect and concern for the other people, as described in *Ubuntu*, the African humanistic philosophy. African work-related values are closely enmeshed with *Ubuntu*, the collective view of humankind.

These Ugandan employees seek a positive working environment with a motivational system in place, enhanced interpersonal communication, monetary and promotional rewards, and performance-related pay. Furthermore, they prefer to have needs-based incentives and open and transparent information policies about incentives and rewards. This would include, for example, an open-minded approach to providing holidays when funerals, marriages or birth celebrations occur. In this way, the connected set of African values concerning family and religion would be respected by their employers.

Although Ugandans often make oral agreements of intention for work according to their traditions, they prefer written contracts with Chinese and other foreign employers, to protect and ensure their rights. Because they have experienced cultural misunderstandings of Chinese employers, they require legal, written contracts that include holidays for family celebrations. Overall, the Ugandan staff experience an unfriendly treatment by the Chinese government, which may reflect an unconscious judgement of the superiority of the Chinese culture. Mr Bugeke may have absorbed this attitude while studying at a Chinese University.

14.5 Culture-Specific Solutions (Short and Long Term)

14.5.1 Short-Term Solutions from Chinese Perspectives

If Chinese managers introduce transparent communication on values, work ethics and the culture-specific concept of "hard work", misunderstandings between Chinese and Ugandan employees can be reduced. Chinese use of Confucian principles should be explained in terms of respect for work, discipline, thrift, protecting face and relationships. As soon as Ugandan employees start to understand these values and can adjust their behaviour accordingly, the easier the intercultural communication should be, and the work atmosphere can improve. Chinese managers' aim to establish harmonious work relationships, with reduced frictions and tensions and are willing to share these Chinese values with the workforce.

Chinese managers should also explain how the creation of a fibre-optic data highway can benefit local employees and the nation, while Uganda is still struggling to create nationwide Internet connections. As soon as Ugandan employees recognise the benefits of the organisation and its purpose, they might be more motivated and work more effectively.

14.5.2 Long-Term Solutions from Chinese Perspectives

Ugandan workers should learn to interpret the behaviour of the Chinese managers from a Chinese perspective. The treatment of employees by the Chinese managers is primarily work related: greetings and small talk rituals do not add value and distract from work (Boness & Mayer, 2013). Treatment is usually related to hierarchy and position, which determine communication styles. Ugandan employees need to follow and learn the work-related hierarchies and their implications.

Confucius is viewed as an important teacher by the Chinese, and his teachings are accepted and still followed. Ugandans should know that the development in China would never have been possible without Confucian work ethics. Confucian values of obedience and thriftiness are major values in work-related settings of the oil refinery. Goals are only achieved if management and staff cooperate. Ugandan employees need to learn that commitment and hard work are traits of employees who develop the goals of the organisation, but who are also part of Ugandan society.

Chinese managers need to provide information to Ugandan employees on the Road and Belt initiative that intends to connect East Africa with China via the Maritime Belt and a huge fibre belt. East African countries such as Kenya, Tanzania and Uganda will be the first to benefit from the fibre belt.

14.5.3 Short-Term Solutions from Ugandan Perspectives

The Ugandan employees have several short-term interests, particularly regarding their work health and well-being. Their security should include the issues of the employee but also issues of close family members. In Uganda, the rate of employment is relatively low, and one contract worker usually nourishes the entire family. Contracts in written form provide security and represent a form of respectful working agreement.

The Chinese management should propel a campaign of mutual respect, showing friendly greetings and listening to the employees and their issues. This will improve the working atmosphere in the short term. Ugandan workers will understand that they are being treated equally and with respect.

14.5.4 Long-Term Solutions from Ugandan Perspectives

Chinese managers need to learn and practise a respectful attitude towards Ugandan locals, expressed in greeting rituals and concern about family matters. This can serve to improve efficiency and productivity of the company in the long run, since it is a sign of relationship-building and trust. Chinese managers also need to be aware of the values of equality and dignity of Ugandan employees in contact with individuals from other ethnic groups. An intercultural mediator can be introduced if conflicts occur which need to be resolved. Third-party intervention is a well-established tool to resolve conflict in many African cultures (Mayer, 2019).

At the level of relationships between the company, government and employees, a change in the long-term structure of the Huawei company in Africa should be considered. The present ethnocentric approach of the company does not attract the employees or their families. They would prefer a company that, step by step, is more culturally aware and opens up to a region-centric management concept, affecting decision-making and leadership style. This would benefit the company regarding its competitiveness and reputation, and the employees would benefit from better mutual understanding.

14.6 Recommendations for Chinese-Ugandan Intercultural Cooperation

It is important to create an open intercultural communication in the organisation and focus on the strengths and the positive aspects of the collaboration.

To increase the mutual understanding of cultural ideas, thought styles, habits and management, the organisation could cooperate with the Confucius Institute of Makerere University in Kampala, Uganda. The Confucius Institute could offer exhibitions, discussion forums, consultancy and research on Chinese-African intercultural cooperation and management. Future research could enrich the understanding of similarities and differences in cross-cultural management, and it should include cross-cultural research teams exploring the intersecting ties of culture, age, gender and language in management. Topics such as work ethics in the Confucian and the *Ubuntu* philosophy should be explored. Research results could be published and solutions for intercultural conflict management could be presented to Chinese-Ugandan organisations. These could focus on the issues that members of both groups encounter, such as contracts, promotion programmes, language competency as well as mutually respectful treatment and its relation to efficiency and productivity in the organisation.

Many African students are currently studying in China in response to African talent-attracting programmes at Chinese universities. For African countries, including Uganda, Huawei should launch a talent-attracting programme at the early stages of study at Makerere University and other tertiary educational institutions. Huawei could also offer jobs or training programmes to outstanding African engineering graduates who have studied in China. Following from this, it is recommended to gradually build up a mixed management team. The Chinese company should internationalise its human resource management policies introducing a more geocentric concept; otherwise, it cannot properly cope with competition and may lose highly qualified key staff to Western competitors. There is a need to modify the ethnocentric approach by adding global-orientated elements to the company, for example, a special programme for keeping and promoting local talents.

Furthermore, it is mandatory to review labour contracts on the basis of labour laws and cultural requirements of the local African country. Chinese staff should be trained to conduct open discussions on critical issues like fair treatment of African employees, cultural sensitivity and corporate governance, including corporate social responsibility.

Finally, data protection in the context of a sensitive fibre-optic project must be secured. This also concerns the main international evaluation of the company in connection with Chinese government and should be taken seriously. In many African countries, there are still no clear government regulations in place owing to weak institutions, lack of skilled personnel and lack of governmental will to enforce laws regarding data protection. The interests of Ugandan civil society and private companies regarding data security should be protected in a project of cooperation between all parties. These measures can improve the image of the company and support the cyber-development of the society, benefitting all citizens in the country and beyond.

References

Abdoulaye, M. (2017). School of Management, Wuhan University of Technology, China. *European Journal of Business and Management, 9*(19).

Africa Business Pages. (2019). *Uganda: Attracting Foreign Direct Investments.* Retrieved from https://www.africa-business.com/features/african-market-uae.html

Boness, C., & Mayer, C.-H. (2013). *Chinese-Tanzanian Interactions in International Companies.* Unpublished data, Department of Management, Rhodes University, Grahamstown, South Africa.

Bräutigam, D. (2009). *The Dragon's Gift: The Real Story of China in Africa.* London: Oxford University Press.

Hofstede, G., & Bond, M. H. (1988). The Confucius Connection: From Cultural Roots to Economic Growth. *Organizational Dynamics, 16*(4), 5–21.

Laowei Career. (2019). *Staying Alive: Work and Life Balance in China*. Retrieved from https://www.laowaicareer.com/blog/staying-alive-work-life-balance-china/

Mayer, C. (2019). *Trainingshandbuch Interkulturelle Mediation und Konfliktlösung. Didaktische Materialien zum Kompetenzerwerb*. 3rd ed. Waxmann.

New Vision. (2013, February 25). *China-Uganda Friendship Association Launched*. Retrieved from https://www.newvision.co.ug/new_vision/news/1314729/china-uganda-friendship-association-launched

PC Tech Magazine. (2015, January 4). *Uganda's USD $100 Million Fibre Optic Project Halted by President*. Retrieved from https://pctechmag.com/2015/01/ugandas-usd-100-million-fibre-optic-project-halted-by-president/

Price, D. C. (2019). Four Confucian Values for Doing Business in China. *The Wall Street Journal*. Retrieved January 21, 2019, from http://davidcliveprice.com/4-confucian-values-business-china/

Rarick, A. (2007). Confucius on Management: Understanding Chinese Cultural Values and Managerial Practices. *Journal of International Management Studies, 2*(2), 8.

Xinhua. (2018). Feature: Uganda's Chinese Language Education Making Solid Progress 21.12.2018. http://www.xinhuanet.com/english/2018-12/21/c_137688182.htm

CHAPTER 15

Case 12: Managing a Chinese-South African Restaurant in Port Elizabeth, South Africa

Zhaoyi Liu

15.1 Introduction

By the end of 2016, there were more than 200,000 Chinese private small- and medium-sized enterprises (SMEs) operating in South Africa, with a total capital outlay of about US$53 million (Lin, 2018). These Chinese investments in South Africa are mostly focused on retail outlets and the service industry, including small factories, tourism organisations, restaurants, catering, and consulting services.

Chinese SMEs have fostered the development of local economy and helped improving local people's livelihood by providing job opportunities, affordable food and necessities, and contributed taxes to local governments. Nevertheless, many of these Chinese SMEs encounter difficulties in dealing with employees from different cultural backgrounds (Liu, 2018). This case study addresses the need for cross-cultural understandings, leading to strategies that can help both knowledge and practice in this neglected but important area.

Z. Liu (✉)
Department of Management, Rhodes University, Grahamstown, South Africa

© The Author(s) 2019
C.-H. Mayer et al. (eds.), *Managing Chinese-African Business Interactions*, Palgrave Studies in African Leadership,
https://doi.org/10.1007/978-3-030-25185-7_15

15.1.1 The Influence of Culture on Work

For this study, a general definition of culture is provided by Hofstede (1991, p. 5), as "the collective programming of the mind which distinguishes the members of one group or category of people from another". Above all, culture includes systems of values that are characteristic of a group of people normally influenced by these values in terms of behaviour and attitude (Aust, 2004; Mead, 1994; Rokeach, 1973). Culture is normally shared by the members of a well-defined group of people, shapes our behaviour, and is passed down to younger generations (Adler, 1997). In a common workplace culture, people "often share extensive background knowledge and experiences and may have similar values and attitudes towards work and the objectives of their orientation" (Holmes & Stubbe, 2003, p. 2). Values are indicators of organisational identity (Aust, 2004). In addition, "identity is arguably more fundamental to the conception of humanity than any other notion" (Aust, 2004, pp. 515–516). According to Rokeach (1973), values are the most central concept existing across all social sciences.

Consequently, in this research, culture is defined as a socio-cognitive composite of values and beliefs. It is these values and beliefs that compose the management style of Mrs K (the owner of the restaurant business in this case study).

Relative centrality of work (RCW) is a concept used in this chapter, referring to the relative importance people place on work compared with other major life domains, including friends, leisure, politics, religion, and family (Feild & Hirschfeld, 2000). In Lu, Zu, and Bond's research (2015), the RCW has been contrasted with the importance of other life domains and across sufficient cultural groups to enable cultural moderation of processes around work centrality to be explored. This research confirms that culture significantly affects people's RCW.

In the present study, to understand South African employees working behaviours, the influence of cultural values on their centrality of work needs to be considered.

15.1.2 Leadership Styles

A leadership style refers to a leader's characteristic behaviours when directing, motivating, guiding, and managing groups of people (Turner & Müller, 2005). Great leaders can inspire political movements and social change. They can also motivate others to perform, create, and innovate. Two leadership styles are relevant to this case study.

Authoritarian (autocratic) leadership provides clear expectations for what needs to be done, when it should be done, and how it should be done (Kiazad, Lloyd, Restubog, Zagenczyk, & Kiewitz, 2010). This style of leadership is strongly focused on both command by the leader and control of the followers. There is also a clear division between the leader and the members. Authoritarian leaders make decisions independently with little or no input from the rest of the group.

Transformational leadership, on the other hand, is often identified as the single most effective leadership style. Transformational leaders tend to be emotionally intelligent, energetic, and passionate. They are committed not only to helping the organisation achieve its goals but also to helping group members fulfil their potential. This style of leadership results in higher performance and more improved group satisfaction than other leadership styles. It is also found that transformational leadership leads to improved well-being among group members (Bass & Riggio, 2006).

15.2 Case Narrative

J's Family Restaurant is a Chinese-owned restaurant located in Port Elizabeth, South Africa. It was established in December 2015, serving traditional Western food and a few authentic Chinese dishes. This business has a large restaurant area, function venues, a Sushi bar, and a children's playground. The restaurant is in a double-story building, with the restaurant area on the ground floor and management offices on the first floor.

There are 27 people working in this business. The owner and general manager, Mrs K, is a 47-year-old Chinese lady with a degree in management, who works from the office on the first floor. On the floor are 6 Chinese and 20 South African employees. According to their expertise, employees work in several sections, each of which has a supervisor (five in all), who take orders from Mrs K, and pass them on to the floor employees.

Mrs K has adopted a typical traditional Chinese autocratic management style in running this restaurant, which is very similar to the Western autocratic management style.

In Confucian philosophy, all relationships are deemed to be unequal. Ethical behaviour demands that these inequalities are respected. The highest person in the hierarchy should automatically receive respect from the senior to the subordinate. This Confucian approach should be seen as the cornerstone of all management thinking. In this way, traditional Chinese management style tends to be directive, with the senior manager giving instructions to subordinates who in turn pass the instructions down the line. It is not expected that subordinates will question the decisions of superiors or give suggestions—such actions would show disrespect.

Mrs K acts as a leader in this "big restaurant family", who gives orders and checks the results. She does not talk to the floor employees because "the only thing they need to do is to follow my orders". The five supervisors (one Chinese and four South African) pass on orders, monitor the work, and report back to her. Mrs K gives trainings and guidance on the specific position when necessary. In situations when work is not done as requested or on time, employees need to face the consequences.

Mrs K uses Mandarin to communicate with six other Chinese employees, as most of them cannot use English at all. The only Chinese person who can speak English fluently is Wang, the supervisor of the Chinese and Sushi Bar section of the restaurant. When she talks to local employees, she uses English. Chinese employees communicate in Mandarin at their workplace, and other employees are allowed to use their own preferred languages to talk to each other. Chinese and South African employees interact very little at work owing to the language barrier, yet they are able to understand each other's basic work-related instructions, like "Please pass me the oil". Mrs K believes this language policy can help employees to become familiar with the workplace and to be friendly to each other.

However, Mrs K has been very confused by Chinese and South African employees, complaining that they "feel neglected" and that "the manager doesn't understand us". The Chinese employees have traditionally been silent and kept a distance from the South African employees, as they feel that their group is somewhat small and isolated in this restaurant. According to Wang, if the Chinese employees are not happy with some instructions, they initially complain within their small Chinese group, but they will still carry out the instructions. On the other hand, according to the other four South African supervisors, sometimes the South African employees complain that "the boss doesn't understand our culture", "she is too strict", and "sometimes we couldn't understand her orders properly but had no chance to ask".

15.3 Questions and Points of Discussion

- Explore the current leadership style in managing the restaurant and discuss the influence of the culture on the manager's leadership style.
- Identify the core cultural values that influence the work-related behaviours, especially the RCW of Chinese and South African employees in this restaurant.
- Discuss and develop short- and long-term solutions for this case from each of the Chinese and South African points of view.

15.4 Chinese Perspectives

In this section, perspectives on the link between leadership style and cultural values in a societal context are established.

Mrs K was born into a large family and grew up in Hangzhou, in the south-eastern part of China, a very traditional region with a long history. As a traditional Chinese woman, Mrs K always keeps Chinese behavioural norms in mind. She dresses modestly and never talks or laughs loudly. She moved to South Africa with her husband and has worked in hotels for more than ten years. She is very strict, knows how to deal with South African customers who visit the restaurant, and has the capability to market the business well.

The traditional cultural values that influence the psyche of the Chinese are harmony and benevolence (Zhang, 2013). Harmony means "proper and balanced coordination between things" (Li, 2016). Benevolence, the core value of Confucianism, flows from the importance of familial ties and blood connections, and is held in high esteem by all Chinese people. "A peaceful family will prosper" (家和万事兴) (Zhang, 2013) is a famous and widely embraced saying. This benevolence, although based in familial ties, also extends to friendships and social relationships.

Nevertheless, it is no secret that China is one of the most hierarchical countries on the planet. Adherence to secular hierarchy, therefore, is the first and most fundamental imperative consciously accepted by all Chinese. In China, hierarchy is everywhere: within the family, father always knows best; in schools and universities, teachers brook no dissent; in the government, the power structure is so layered that obedience is almost instinctive at the lower levels; and in society, the citizen is always subordinate to the policymaker.

"Face" and etiquette have traditionally played an important role in Chinese society. These elements of social interaction are reflected in the way people talk and act. In particular, it has been argued that Chinese people "are much more vague and indirect than Westerners" (Zhang, 2013). In Chinese culture, hierarchy and social roles make it necessary for the individual to be cautious and secretive, to play a complex game in order not to disrupt what is considered the proper social order (Fan, 2000). Every interaction can become problematic if one is not careful enough. This teaches individuals to manipulate language in order to avoid confronting superiors or other people, to keep the "surface-level" harmony, although this strategy may create more misunderstandings and tensions than it averts.

In the case study, Mrs K has developed a supervision system; each section in the restaurant has a supervisor. All requests or problems from the floor are reported to the supervisors, who attempt to solve the problem from their level. Only if they are unable to resolve the problem will they report it to Mrs K, who points out that this supervision system is a strict copy of the Chinese hierarchy structure.

Most local companies in China are either family owned or government run. The hierarchical approach is underpinned by the influence of thousands of years of Confucian teaching and a strongly hierarchical, bureaucratic party structure. Senior managers do not expect or appreciate being contacted by junior staff. Information does not flow freely but follows the hierarchical lines. When information is sent back, it follows the same path in reverse.

According to Mrs K, this supervision system saves her time in not having to listen to everyone from the floor and not being obliged to solve all those small or even "unnecessary" issues. It also avoids possible confrontation or face-to-face conflict. Instead, she is able to use her time to do marketing and administrative work.

15.5 South African Perspectives

In this section, perspectives on the link between cultural values in a societal context and RCW are established.

First, it should be noted that the South African employees form subgroups according to different cultural backgrounds (Xhosa and Afrikaans in this case). Different subgroups always maintain distance from each other, as they have "very little to talk about or share". The management has acquiesced to this situation, as long as it does not affect the work.

This issue is deeply linked to the country's background of history and culture. In South Africa, there is not a single heritage or an easily delineated set of distinct identities. The cultures, languages, and heritages of South Africa are multiple, diverse, and dynamic. In South Africa, the question of definition according to race and culture carries an especially sharp edge to it, which potentially makes it a more contentious issue here than elsewhere (SA History Online, 2013). This is primarily due to the policies of the apartheid government that sought to distinguish and segregate the country according to rigid definitions of race between 1948 and 1994. For this reason, subsequent attempts to define the people of South Africa may easily carry an unpleasant connotation of racist categorisation from the past.

Second, South African employees complain that management is too strict and does not understand their culture. Black African employees in particular sometimes take leave for their family responsibilities (weddings or funerals) without giving notice or returning on time. As a consequence of breaking agreed-upon rules in the enterprise, they have to face salary deductions or written warnings.

One issue relating to this absence-from-work problem is time. Time is not a critical element of black African culture, in the sense that they consider human relations to be far more important than work tasks. Although most black African people value their jobs and do their best to finish work on time with great respect and efficiency, in the conflict between family duties and RCW, black African employees always follow their culture first and choose to fulfil their family duties above work duties.

Another related issue is the collectivism of African culture, in that the individual is part of the group or family. Funerals, for instance, are so important that a member of a community who does not attend them or participate in their rituals faces ostracism (Baloyi, 2012).

Third, South African employees worry about their relationship and communication with the manager. The language difference, cultural barriers, and supervision system of Mrs K's autocratic leadership style make them feel far away from management level. In the meantime, the manager appears to be "too busy" to walk down and visit them on the floor. Sometimes, they want to talk to someone who has power to change a situation, but because of the formal distance, they finally give up and keep silent.

Occasionally, the South African staff fails to understand an order from Mrs K. But for fear of having their motive misunderstood if they were to question her, the South Africans choose to do their work silently, to the best of their ability. They give three reasons for their silence: if they question too much, they might be regarded as being stupid or dull; they could be suspected of trying to shirk duty; and they fear that such behaviour might lead to their dismissal.

Moreover, South African employees report that they feel separated from the Chinese employees' group, as the Chinese have a completely strange language and culture. South African employees suspect that the manager surreptitiously shares some information only with Chinese employees in their own language. This makes the South Africans feel neglected and less motivated to work.

15.6 Culture-Specific Solutions (Short and Long Term)

In the following section, short-term solutions are proposed to guide Mrs K in improving three aspects of communication, with a long-term solution being a change in her leadership style in management. Furthermore, some suggestions are provided to enhance the involvement of South African employees and to achieve mutual respect for all cultures in the business.

15.6.1 Short-Term Solutions from Chinese Perspectives

First of all, Mrs K needs to hold an Indaba with all employees (in Chinese, this is called an open meeting 全员大会 to which everyone in a corporate setting is invited). She needs to listen to the voices from the floor, including all problems, requests and suggestions from the employees. It is suggested that she makes a complete list of all issues discussed in the meeting and has everyone sign the list to ensure there is no mistake or omission in the record. Then relative solutions must be further discussed and followed by action plans, which must also be announced publicly and signed by everyone.

In order to avoid the language barrier and enhance communication between management and employees, and between employees themselves, Mrs K needs to set a rule that English is the only language allowed to be used at the workplace. If there are employees who need help in learning English, language training courses can be arranged by the management, and these will be regarded as a skill development in the enterprise. The Chinese and Sushi Bar Section supervisor, as the only bilingual Chinese employee, needs to assist with the communication when necessary.

Mrs K needs to hold a meeting with black African employees separately and explain to them how to handle the conflict between cultural values and RCW, corporate interests, and professionalism. For attending funerals or other family responsibilities, employees' leave notice must be given 48 hours ahead. And after the leave, employees must be back to work on time. Under all circumstances, enterprise rules must be followed strictly. However, if a delay is caused by unforeseen circumstances, the employee needs to inform management as soon as possible, so that backup arrangements can be made in time.

15.6.2 Long-Term Solutions from Chinese Perspectives

Mrs K needs to alter her traditional Chinese autocratic management style into a transformational style. She needs to walk down from her office and communicate more on the floor with employees, get to know what is happening in the business from observation and participation, encourage and motivate employees, and finally rebuild the trust between all parties.

Participation and involvement of the employees should be encouraged at all levels in the business, including problem definition, crafting of strategies, and solution implementation. Mrs K needs to learn to treat the ideas and suggestions of employees with consideration and respect.

Four processes can be kept in mind to enhance participation and involvement of the employees. These are:

1. Information-sharing, which is concerned with keeping employees informed about the economic status of the enterprise.
2. Training, which involves raising the skill levels of employees and offering development opportunities that allow them to apply new skills to make effective decisions regarding the enterprise as a whole.
3. Employee decision-making, which can take many forms, from determining work schedules to deciding on processes.
4. Rewards, which should be tied to suggestions and ideas as well as performance.

Furthermore, Mrs K should plan a long-term learning session for both Chinese and South African employees on the different cultures present in this enterprise, including symbols, language, norms, values, and artefacts. From these learning sessions, all employees can become familiar with and respect cultures other than their own.

Besides punishment, reward systems need to be in place in this restaurant. Both Chinese and South African employees need to be rewarded in recognition of valuable service and commitment to the enterprise. Salary increments or gifts, and a group or family benefit could enhance the employee's loyalty towards the enterprise, as a function of the collectivism in the values of both Chinese and South African cultures.

Finally, Mrs K should provide opportunities for employees to get together after work and interact in a more relaxing and informal atmosphere. This may help to break the subgrouping and encourage staff to communicate out of their self-protection circle.

15.6.3 Short-Term Solutions from South African Perspectives

As short-term solution, when the manager holds an Indaba (open meeting), all of South African employees should attend and speak. During the meeting, South African employees could share their opinions, explain their views, and express their ideas and suggestions. They have an opportunity to bravely start something new in order to build up trust between management and employees, step by step.

South African employees need to adhere to the business' requirements and strictly enforce "English as the only language at work" rule. If there is difficulty in communicating with Chinese employees who are still busy learning English, the South Africans must not hesitate to ask assistance from the Chinese and Sushi Bar section supervisor, who is the only bilingual Chinese employee on the floor.

Furthermore, South African employees need to understand and embrace modern business concepts such as globalisation and professionalism in following company rules strictly and handling the conflict between RCW and their cultural values wisely.

15.6.4 Long-Term Solutions from South African Perspectives

In the long run, South African employees need to become open-minded, move out of their subgroups, and demonstrate their willingness to share their history, value, and culture with other employees. It is advisable to seek mutual understanding and respect based on a healthy and sustainable communication with others in the restaurant.

South African employees need to know more about other cultures and be more tolerant of other races and traditions. In the meantime, communication and mutual respect can be consciously used as tools to reduce any personal issues triggered by sensitive topics.

Actively attend the enterprise's meetings and be involved in the analysis of problems, development of strategies, and implementation of solutions whether under supervision or not. During contact with management or other employees, to avoid confusion or possible misunderstandings, asking for a repeat of a question or explanation is recommended.

15.7 Recommendations for Chinese-South African Intercultural Cooperation

A well-shaped and sustainable Chinese-South African intercultural cooperation can be gained through diversity training, team building, and conflict transformation.

Utilise the transformational leadership style in managing a cross-cultural Chinese-South African business. Hold open discussions regularly, develop awareness, understanding, and acceptance of diversity. In so doing, let the team experience harmony and teamwork in a transformational team-building environment.

Develop a short list of positive and mutually understood and agreed values and behaviours that must be adhered to by all members of the working team. Develop a list of negative and destructive behaviours or values that must be eliminated from the team's interactions.

Put in place a peer-driven and managed monthly meeting structure to manage all aspects of the agreements and the behaviours of team members. While doing so, ensure that the process is caring, motivational, and empowering while developing understanding and maintaining discipline. The manager who leads this culturally diverse work team to great success will involve each team member in the day-to-day processes of workplace diversity management.

References

Adler, N. (1997). *International Dimensions of Organizational Behaviour*. Cincinnati, Ohio: South-Western College Publishing.

Aust, P. J. (2004). Communicated Values as Indicators of Organizational Identity: A Method for Organizational Assessment and Its Application in a Case Study. *Communication Studies*, 55(4), 515–534.

Baloyi, L. (2012). The African Conception of Death: A Cultural Implication. *Indian Journal of Palliative Care*, 22(4), 369–372. https://doi.org/10.4103/0973-1075.191741

Bass, B. M., & Riggio, R. E. (2006). *Transformational Leadership* (2nd ed.). Mahwah, NJ: L. Erlbaum Associates.

Fan, Y. (2000). A Classification of Chinese Culture. *Cross Cultural Management: An International Journal,* 7(2), 3–10. https://doi.org/10.1108/13527600010797057

Feild, H. S., & Hirschfeld, R. R. (2000). Work Centrality and Work Alienation: Distinct Aspects of a General Commitment to Work. *Journal of Organizational Behavior,* 21(7). https://doi.org/10.1002/1099-1379(200011)21:7<789::AID-JOB59>3.0.CO;2-W

Hofstede, G. (1991). Empirical Models of Cultural Differences. In N. Bleichrodt & P. J. D. Drenth (Eds.), *Contemporary Issues in Cross-Cultural Psychology* (pp. 4–20). Lisse, Netherlands: Swets & Zeitlinger Publishers.

Holmes, J., & Stubbe, M. (2003). *Power and Politeness in the Workplace: A Sociolinguistic Analysis of Talk at Work.* UK: Pearson Education Ltd.

Kiazad, K., Lloyd, S., Restubog, D., Zagenczyk, T., & Kiewitz, C. (2010). In Pursuit of Power: The Role of Authoritarian Leadership in the Relationship Between Supervisors' Machiavellianism and Subordinates' Perceptions of Abusive Supervisory Behaviour. *Journal of Research in Personality,* 44(4), 512–519.

Li, J. (2016). *The Structure of Chinese Values: Indigenous and Cross-Cultural Perspectives.* China: Paths International Ltd.

Lin, S. (2018, February 27). South Africa and China Are Beneficial Partners. *Pretoria News.* Retrieved from https://www.iol.co.za/pretoria-news/south-africa-and-china-are-beneficial-partners-13508542

Liu, Z. (2018). Development Report on Chinese Private Enterprises in South Africa. In *China-South Africa Cultural Exchange Development Report 2017–2018* (pp. 30–45). Zhejiang People's Publishing House.

Lu, Q., Xu, H., & Bond, M. H. (2015). Culture and the Working Life: Predicting the Relative Centrality of Work Across Life Domains for Employed Persons. *Journal of Cross-Cultural Psychology,* 47(2), 277–293.

Mead, R. (1994). *International Management: Cross-Cultural Dimension.* Oxford: Blackwell Publishers.

Rokeach, M. (1973). *The Nature of Human Values.* New York: Free Press.

SA History Online. (2013). *Defining Culture, Heritage and Identity.* Retrieved from https://www.sahistory.org.za/jquery_ajax_load/get/article/defining-culture-heritage-and-identity

Turner, J. R., & Müller, R. (2005). The Project Manager's Leadership Style as a Success Factor on Projects: A Literature Review. *Project Management Journal,* 36(1), 49–61. https://doi.org/10.1177/875697280503600206

Zhang, L. (2013). China's Traditional Cultural Values and National Identity. *Carnegie-Tsinghua Center for Global Policy.* Retrieved from https://carnegietsinghua.org/2013/11/21/china-s-traditional-cultural-values-and-national-identity-pub-53613

PART V

Intercultural Training Cases: Management Practices and Employment Relations

CHAPTER 16

Case 13: Employee Perceptions of a Chinese Heavy-Machinery-Importing Organisation Operating in Uganda

Lynette Louw, Katherine Burger, and Mattheus Johannes Louw

16.1 Introduction to the Case

The noticeable presence of Chinese multinational organisations on the global stage is changing the landscape of international business and politics—especially in sub-Saharan Africa (Alden & Davies, 2006, p. 83). Organisations from the West that once had undisputed command over international resources, finances and the necessary political ties to dominate global business are now being challenged by a host of emerging country organisations, with China at the very forefront of this challenge. Chinese organisations are highly competitive and strongly supported by the state, and they are embarking on an acquisition drive that is capturing key resources and market share across a vast majority of the developing world. In many respects, it is Africa, a land rich in natural resources and

---

L. Louw (✉) • K. Burger • M. J. Louw
Department of Management, Rhodes University, Grahamstown, South Africa
e-mail: l.louw@ru.ac.za; m.louw@ru.ac.za

© The Author(s) 2019
C.-H. Mayer et al. (eds.), *Managing Chinese-African Business Interactions*, Palgrave Studies in African Leadership,
https://doi.org/10.1007/978-3-030-25185-7_16

under-exploited markets, which is serving as the perfect venture for Chinese investment and business opportunities (Alden & Davies, 2006, p. 83; Gill, Huang, & Morrison, 2007).

China is in Africa, and it needs Africa for resources to fuel its development goals, for markets to sustain its growing economy and for political alliances to support its aspirations to be a global influence (Hodzi, 2018, p. 197; Zhang & Daly, 2011, p. 391).

The presence of Chinese organisations in sub-Saharan Africa affects both continents' economies, as well as the local communities and employees who are involved (McNamee, 2012). The significance of the dynamics and synergies of the presence of these organisations still needs to be researched and discussed. Steinacker-Keys (2012) points out that a lack of cross-cultural understanding on the part of Chinese managers working in Africa can create issues that become detrimental to the effective and appropriate management of such organisations.

16.2 Questions and Points of Discussion

- Discuss the general management practices and styles of Chinese managers.
- Explore the management practices and styles of Chinese managers at an organisation in Uganda from an employee's perspective.
- Describe and understand the synergies between Chinese and Ugandan cultures and the implications for managing organisations.
- Develop short- and long-term solutions for this case from each of the Chinese and Ugandan points of view.
- Make recommendations on how Chinese organisations in Uganda (and sub-Saharan Africa as a whole) can modify their management practices and styles in order to enhance employee perceptions of the organisation.

16.3 Chinese Perspectives

The organisation in this case study, as is typical of most Chinese organisations, depends on collectivism and hierarchy as important elements of its organisational structure (Jackson, Louw, & Zhao, 2013). Organisational practices and the profit motive are morally constrained by and consistent with Confucianist philosophy (Cua, 2018). The Chinese are also focused on doing good for the community and society around them (Jackson et al., 2013).

It is the duty of employees to consent and implement, not to question or defy. Relationships in Chinese organisations are seen as more important than rules and procedures. In this context, the CEO runs an organisation like a family and is committed to the subordinates in the organisation, even though the commitment might not be extended uniformly. Since relationships are so important in Chinese organisations, a sense of belonging and being a part of a social group is important and motivational to all staff members.

Chinese organisational strategies are heavily influenced by national strategies (Goodall & Warner, 1999; Warner, 1995). China's economic restructuring in 1987 also caused substantial change in human resource management at organisational level (Shen, 2006, p. 295), predominantly seen in the disappearance of life employment (*tie fan wan*) and fixed salaries (*tie gong zie*), which have been substituted by employment contracts (*lao dong he tong*) (Child, 1994; Nolan, 1995; Peng, 2000). In recent years, industrialisation in China has advanced to the point where the nation is now known as "the world's manufactory" (Shen, 2006, p. 296).

According to Warner (2011a, p. 401), there is little doubt that Chinese organisations have a sound, well-equipped infrastructure of management training. It has achieved in less than three decades what it took a century for the US to create (Jenster, 2009, p. 173). In China it is therefore important, according to Gan (2014, p. 208), for organisations to have long-term plans in place for human resource development and implementation.

As more large Chinese organisations expand their activities to other countries, particularly in Africa, there may be a greater need to train Chinese managers on local sites, in order to best cope with the specific business environments in which they operate. It has been suggested that even large and sophisticated Chinese multinational corporations are struggling to operate on a global scale (Bartlett & Ghoshal, 1998). This is a consequence of not enough senior staff being familiar with foreign markets, foreign language skills and the experience of managing large-scale activities overseas— in other words, of cross-cultural management (Warner, 2011a, p. 401).

Chinese companies do not have a good track record regarding low wages, excessive overtime and bad working conditions, even outdoing such underdeveloped countries as Vietnam and Cambodia (Thorborg, 2006, p. 895). Explanations for this state of affairs include China's unlimited supply of labour and the lack of freedom to organise independent trade unions. Before 1978, labour markets did not exist, and urban workers were paid according to wage grades. With the development of economic reforms, the traditional compensation system faded out and was replaced by hybrid, market-orientated, performance-based reward systems (Warner, 1996). More recently, it has been found that opportunities for career progress, employee empowerment and compensation are the most effective motivators for Chinese workers (Gan, 2014, pp. 254–255) in organisations such as the one cited in this case study.

16.4 Ugandan Perspectives

The organisation in this case study is the market leader in its sector in Uganda. The organisation has a total of 30 employees, 20 of whom are Ugandan and 10 are Chinese. The study is based on data analysed from nine participants: six female and three male Ugandan employees.

The Ugandan employees describe their experience of the organisation's culture as hiding from the Ugandan government and being scared of the law. Amid accusations that the organisation is not properly registered and not paying taxes, the employees say that is easy for Chinese organisations to operate in Uganda because Ugandan policies are not really strict and laws are easy to manipulate.

All Ugandan employees in the company agree that the Chinese managers have difficulty understanding local Ugandan culture, especially religious ceremonies. Chinese managers are considered "not religious … they have no God". The managers do not observe national holidays or grant leave to local employees wanting to celebrate family occasions in their villages.

The local employees working in this organisation describe their jobs as "multipurpose". An employee explains: "I was employed as an electrician but I am doing different things … they give you a variety of work". Employees appreciate this arrangement because it informally broadens their skills base, knowledge and experience, but they are extremely dissatisfied that Chinese employees occupy all managerial positions and Ugandans hold lower positions without power in the organisation. The Ugandan employees also find their working conditions harsh, resulting in a negative workplace atmosphere. Working long hours, not receiving proper meal intervals, poor medical and sick benefits, and absence of safety standards are common occurrences. The Ugandan employees see Chinese employees in the organisation as being valued, listened to and treated with more respect than they are. This is also the case when decisions are made pertaining to granting of sick and compassionate leave.

The Chinese managers are experienced by the Ugandans as "dictatorial, controlling, abusive, uncompassionate". This is in stark contrast to general Chinese managerial principles, which include internal and external focus on fairness, humanity, social hierarchy and paternalism (Jackson et al., 2013, p. 14).

Because the local labour laws are not adhered to and no formal staff records, contracts or payslips are kept, the Ugandans fear that their services could be terminated at any time. Combined with this situation, and in the absence of any formal training, mentoring or workshops, their performance, motivation and effectiveness are compromised. The Ugandan employees want to be able to use their own initiative, and to learn from their mistakes.

The salaries received by the Ugandans are inadequate and barely cover their basic needs. They report that the Chinese organisation regularly makes deductions from their salaries when they are absent from work, even during times of sickness or bereavement. The company basically follows the principle of "no work, no pay".

Because they are not consulted at all when managers make decisions on the shop floor, the Ugandans do not trust management. Employees feel as though they are being monitored all the time and cannot use their own initiative to perform work. The organisation also has no policies for managing grievances, discipline and disputes in the work environment. Nonetheless, the Ugandan staff do perceive the Chinese managers as "hardworking" and totally committed to the parent organisation, with profit being the important driver in this process. This commitment appears to energise the managers' performance, enhance their work satisfaction and eliminate harassment and corruption in the workplace. The employees admit that Ugandan organisations could learn from the work commitment shown by Chinese managers as this could result in higher levels of performance and less corruption.

The organisation, according to the employees, does not make use of teams in the fundamental way in which it does business. However, the Ugandans create informal teams to execute their work more effectively. This informal teamwork benefits the employees when dealing with customers who ask difficult questions. Employees point out that language is a barrier to forming Chinese/Ugandan teams at the workplace. The language barrier issue is also problematic for effective communication between employees and managers.

16.5 Culture-Specific Solutions (Short and Long Term)

16.5.1 Short-Term Chinese Perspectives

The Chinese company needs to address a wide array of human resource management issues. It needs to implement formal training and development programmes, formal teamwork systems, issue employment contracts, allocate staff numbers and adhere to the local labour laws. The implementation of a commission-based pay structure can result in a unified and hardworking workforce. It is essential for the Chinese line managers to accept the Ugandan working culture and not to hold stereotypical and negative views of the Ugandan employees' abilities.

Chinese managers must involve Ugandans in daily decision-making. This will motivate employees and increase their sense of responsibility for the work they do. Incentives such as being valued, given a transport allowance, being allowed to learn Mandarin and being granted paid leave for religious festivals or compassionate reasons will increase employee motivation.

If Chinese managers increase wages or provide a transport and food allowance, decrease the employee turnover rate (increasing job security) and value employees as fellow workers in the organisation, management will achieve organisational effectiveness more easily by creating a productive and committed workforce.

16.5.2 Long-Term Chinese Perspectives

The Chinese managers should conduct a human resource audit of their organisation with the assistance of local consultants. In the audit, they need to look at human resource planning, job analysis, staffing, onboarding, training and development, performance, compensation, management of discipline and labour relations. If the necessary human resource outcomes are achieved, they will lead to the long-term success of the organisation. The Chinese managers will soon realise that engaged, committed employees will make the organisation effective—and effective organisations have the best chance of long-term success.

16.5.3 Short-Term Ugandan Perspectives

The Ugandan employees should attempt to improve their understanding of the Chinese culture and work ethic. It is also imperative that they demand to be treated fairly and according to the local labour laws and working conditions of employment. The employees could possibly join a trade union to protect them from unlawful dismissals and economic reconstruction, and ensure improved wages, training and development, and fair conditions of service.

16.5.4 Long-Term Ugandan Perspectives

It is clear that the Chinese managers are hardworking and money-driven, corresponding with a high sense of responsibility, focus and minimal corruption (Jackson et al., 2013). In the long term, Ugandan leaders could learn from this hardworking and focused attitude and avoid practising corruption, which has unfortunately become an accepted part of everyday business in most sub-Saharan African countries (Van Zyl, Dalglish, Du Plessis, Lues, & Pietersen, 2009, p. 150). The effects of corruption are insidious, and they extend far beyond requests for bribes and favours, as espoused by employees in the case study.

16.6 Recommendations for Chinese-Ugandan Intercultural Cooperation

The Chinese managers should attempt to learn English and understand the Ugandan work culture; the Ugandan employees should likewise learn Mandarin and attempt to understand the Chinese work culture.

Management should take cognisance of the importance of Ugandan employees' security needs. With random firing of employees in the Chinese organisation, job security is very low, which translates into low motivation. When granting (or denying) sick and compassionate leave, the Chinese managers' responses should be uniformly extended to all subordinates, whether Chinese or Ugandan.

Ugandans should respect and learn from the Chinese management's awareness of time and their honesty regarding finances. If African managers are more hardworking, driven and time-conscious, they can achieve their goals more easily (van Zyl et al., 2009, p. 150).

Formal company training and development is normal practice in China, where implementation is a closely monitored process (Warner, 2011b, p. 3232). This should be applied in the Ugandan context. It is also recommended that the Chinese organisation reformulates its human resource management policies and general working conditions. This is based on research findings that Chinese organisations have a bad reputation in terms of fair working conditions and paying equitable salaries (Thorborg, 2006, p. 895). The Chinese managers of the organisation can greatly improve Ugandan workers' motivation by including a mix of incentives both financial (such as commission-based pay) (Grobler, Wärnich, Carrell, Elbert, & Hatfield, 2011, p. 418) and non-financial (such as learning Mandarin) in their compensation system (Mathauer & Imhoff, 2006).

This study concludes with a comment from one of the Ugandan employees:

> I would say concerning all human resources, they really need to learn a lot. Because, the way they treat their workers is not the way really we wish to be treated ... it is not convincing at all!

References

Alden, C., & Davies, M. (2006). A Profile of the Operations of Chinese Multinationals in Africa. *South African Journal of International Affairs*, 13, 89–96.

Bartlett, C. A., & Ghoshal, S. (1998). *Managing Across Borders: The Transnational Solution*. Cambridge: Harvard Business School Press.

Child, J. (1994). *Management in China During the Age of Reform*. Cambridge: Cambridge University Press.

Cua, A. S. (2018). *Confucian Philosophy, Chinese*. Routledge Encyclopedia of Philosophy. Retrieved from https://www.rep.routledge.com/articles/thematic/confucian-philosophy-chinese/v-1. https://doi.org/10.4324/9780415249126-G003-1

Gan, S. (2014). *How to Do Business with China: An Inside View on Chinese Culture and Etiquette*. United Kingdom: Author House.

Gill, B., Huang, C. H., & Morrison, J. S. (2007). Assessing China's Growing Influence in Africa. In T. Jackson, L. Louw, & S. Zhao (Eds.). (2011). *Chinese Organisation and Management in Sub-Saharan Africa: Towards a Cross-Cultural Research Agenda*. The Seventh International Symposium on Multinational

Business Management – Enterprise Management in a Transitional Economy and Post Financial Crisis. Nanjing, China, June 5–6.

Goodall, K., & Warner, M. (1999). Enterprise Reform, Labour-Management Relations and Human Resource Management in a Multinational Context. *International Studies of Management and Organisation, 29*(3), 21–36.

Grobler, P. A., Wärnich, S., Carrell, M. R., Elbert, N. F., & Hatfield, R. D. (2011). *Human Resource Management in South Africa* (4th ed.). Hampshire: South-Western Cengage Learning.

Hodzi, O. (2018). China and Africa: Economic Growth and a Non-transformative Political Elite. *Journal of Contemporary African Studies, 36*(2), 191–206. https://doi.org/10.1080/02589001.2017.1406191

Jackson, T., Louw, L., & Zhao, S. (2013). China in Sub-Saharan Africa: Implications for HRM Policy and Practice at Organisational Level. *The International Journal of Human Resource Management, 24*(13), 2512–2533. https://doi.org/10.1080/09585192.2012.725067

Jenster, P. V. (2009). *The Future of Management Education and Business Schools in China*. London: Routledge.

Mathauer, I., & Imhoff, I. (2006). Health Worker Motivation in Africa: The Role of Non-Financial Incentives and Human Resource Management Tools. *Human Resources for Health, 4*, 24.

McNamee, T. (2012). Africa in Their Words. A Study of Chinese Traders in South Africa, Lesotho, Botswana, Zambia and Angola. The Brenthurst Foundation Discussion Paper 2012/13. Parktown: The Brenthurst Foundation. Retrieved from http://www.thebrenthurstfoundation.org/files/brenthurst_commisioned_reports/Brenthurst-paper-201203-Africa-in-their-Words-A-Study-of-Chinese-Traders.pdf

Nolan, P. (1995). *China's Rise, Russia's Fall*. London: Macmillan.

Peng, M. W. (2000). *Business Strategies in Transition Economies*. London: Sage.

Shen, J. (2006). Factors Affecting International Staffing in Chinese Multinationals (MNEs). *International Journal of Human Resource Management, 17*(2), 295–315.

Steinacker-Keys, J. (2012). Yes, Laoban, No, Laoban, Three Bags Full, Laoban: Challenges Faced by Foreigners Working in China and Chinese Working for Foreigners. International Waters: Far East Focus. *HR Future*, 12–13.

Thorborg, M. (2006). Chinese Workers and Labor Conditions from State Industry to Globalized Factories: How to Stop the Race to the Bottom. *Annals of the New York Academy of Sciences, 1076*, 893–910.

Van Zyl, E., Dalglish, C., Du Plessis, M., Lues, L., & Pietersen, E. (2009). *Leadership in the African Context*. Cape Town: Juta.

Warner, M. (1995). *The Management of Human Resources in Chinese Industry*. London: Macmillan.

Warner, M. (1996). Managing China's Enterprise Reforms: A New Agenda for the 1990s. *Journal of General Management, 21*(3), 1–18.

Warner, M. (2011a). Management Training and Development in China Revisited. *Asia Pacific Business Review, 17*(4), 397–402.

Warner, M. (2011b). Society and HRM in China. *The International Journal of Human Resource Management, 22*(16), 3223–3244.

Zhang, X., & Daly, K. (2011). The Determinants of China's Outward Foreign Direct Investment. *Emerging Markets Review, 12*, 389–398.

CHAPTER 17

Case 14: Hiring and Firing in the Chinese-Zimbabwean Mining Industry

Christian Martin Boness

17.1 Introduction

Zimbabwe is a landlocked country in south-eastern sub-Saharan Africa. The country is rich in resources such as gold, nickel, chrome and uranium (Zimbabwe. Ministry of Mines and Mining Development, 2016). The government of Zimbabwe has the vision to provide a world-class mining environment and to promote sustainable management in mining for the benefit of all Zimbabwean citizens by 2020 (Zimbabwe. Ministry of Mining and Mining Development, 2018).

In the past, until 1980 when Zimbabwe became independent, the former Southern Rhodesia had an apartheid-style educational system of a high international standard with a low number of illiterates and—in comparison with other African countries—a high number of A-level students (Ernstes, 2014). The country therefore fostered high international expectations to soon become an industrialised country with a strongly growing (GDP) owing to its rich resources, on the one hand, and a well-educated and highly skilled workforce, on the other. Between 1980 and 1990,

---

C. M. Boness (✉)
Department of Management, Rhodes University, Grahamstown, South Africa

© The Author(s) 2019
C.-H. Mayer et al. (eds.), *Managing Chinese-African Business Interactions*, Palgrave Studies in African Leadership,
https://doi.org/10.1007/978-3-030-25185-7_17

primary schools grew by 43% in number and secondary schools by more than 600% (Ernstes, 2014). However, during the past decades, from 1995 onwards, governmental policies changed drastically and influenced the country's development on all levels (Ernstes, 2014).

In education, economy, governance, and international and foreign policies, Western countries such as the United Kingdom imposed wide sanctions, and Zimbabwe was excluded from the Commonwealth in 2003 (Taylor, 2005). During this time, Zimbabwe lacked an efficiently productive mining industry, and investors, who were willing to modernise the mining industries in terms of equipment and strategies, could exploit the gold and platinum resources as effectively and sustainably as possible (Ojakorotu & Kamidza, 2018). During the political and economic changes in the country, almost 2000 Western mining organisations either left the country voluntarily or were dismissed by the government and were banned from the international scene of collaborators (Ojakorotu & Kamidza, 2018). This ban of collaboration between Zimbabwean and Western mining companies is contemporarily still in place, and Western (mining) organisations are still not admitted to mining activities in Zimbabwe (Ojakorotu & Kamidza, 2018).

Since the country needed mining machinery, expertise and collaborators, the Zimbabwean government searched for new collaborators and investors to save its mining industry. Chinese investors started to invest in the country's mining industry and filled the void of expertise. The refurbished Zimbabwean mining industry was mainly built up by Chinese private and parastatal mining organisations and their collaborators. They invested successfully to gain their share of Zimbabwe's natural resources.

Zimbabweans have different views on the new collaboration with Chinese organisations in the mining industry. The political change and the loss of power of President Mugabe and his retrenchment from the presidency in 2017 have also impacted on the attitude towards China's influence in Zimbabwe. Especially from the side of opposition leader Chamisa, there are now political voices to be heard, calling for China's withdrawal from its major activities in Zimbabwe (Perper, 2018).

Since 2003, Zimbabwe's "Look East" policy (Perper, 2018) has invited China to be a major investor in the country, with more than purely economic influence. China appears to have gained influence in politics by investing in major development projects that impact on the improvement of infrastructure such as airports, water supply, hydraulic systems and mining. Growing criticism of the political opposition to Mugabe's party emphasises China's policy of "asset-stripping" of Zimbabwe's resources (Perper, 2018).

17.2 Case Narrative

The region of Mashonaland West in Zimbabwe is home to a large number of mines (Zimbabwe Ministry of Mines and Mining Development, 2016). The region is situated 120 kilometres north of Harare, Zimbabwe's capital city. The gold mines are connected with Harare by dirt road and the infrastructure in Mashonaland West and, in general, seems to be underdeveloped for the increasing mining activities. The mines are mainly operated by Chinese governmental and private-owned companies. These organisations use primarily Chinese building and mining equipment, as well as Chinese management capacities. The company, however, employs a strong Zimbabwean workforce in the mines and aims at maintaining the security of the mines. In the central mining office, a Zimbabwean security guard wears security company outfit, highlighting "People's Republic of China—Security" in Chinese letters. An election poster for the Chinese President Xi Jinping hangs near the entrance.

The Chinese-Zimbabwean mining organisation is known for having created jobs for about 2000 Zimbabwean workers in the region. The job creation is much appreciated by the Zimbabwean government as well as by the Zimbabwean employees. However, the workers often complain about their treatment by Chinese managers in the organisation. The organisation is managed by 12 Chinese managers who cooperate closely with the Zimbabwean government. The international cooperation between the Zimbabwean government and the Chinese management flourishes, while the workers complain about the recruitment policies, the treatment at work and the abuse of labourers by the Chinese organisation (Mangirazi, 2016).

Zimbabwean journalists have arrived to explore the circumstances and the work conditions in the Chinese-owned mines in this region of Mashonaland. They point out that since the change in ownership of the mines, the salaries paid to the Zimbabwean workers are significantly lower than the salaries paid previously by the British mining company. Further, journalists report a breach of labour laws and rights of the employees, and that the expectations of the workers with regard to human rights, fair treatment and endurable work conditions are not met. This includes the facts that workers can be released from their positions at any point in time—a kind of "hire-and-fire" policy—and that a reason for dismissal does not need to be given. However, if reasons for prompt dismissal are given, they are usually: "dishonesty" and "bad performance". Zimbabwean employees complain about the work conditions and the abuse of labour (unpaid overtime hours in the mines), a lack of adequate clothing, security measures and the casualisation of labour contracts. Zimbabwean employees assert that they have to pay US$50 per month to the mining company to secure their work contracts (Mangirazi, 2016).

Based on the research and reports, Zimbabwean investigative journalists have approached the human resources manager of the Chinese company, Mr Peng, for an interview to receive an official statement on the situation. Mr Peng accepts the interview, and he is asked why a large number of workers have been dismissed from their jobs in the gold mine without prior notice, and under non-transparent circumstances.

Mr Peng comments diplomatically:

> Well, you know, we've got a huge number of labour and want to give them a chance to work for their families and their country. Actually we need about a thousand more workers in mining. However, it is very difficult for the organisation to find appropriate employees. What we need are honest workers who respect the properties of the company. Workers have to listen to what Chinese management orders. If there is performance not complying with our standards we are forced to shift the worker to a more appropriate place. We now do our best to hire work power from other regions in Zimbabwe, since the local workers often do not meet our expectations. A lot of workforce we get through informational channels and recommendations. We even offer trainings to improve the skills of our work force to comply with the expectations of the Chinese management.

The Zimbabwean journalists thank Mr Peng for the interview. Back in their editorial office, they discuss the meaning and implication of the positive statements. The journalists contrast the official statement with the grievances of the Zimbabwean staff in the gold mine.

17.3 Questions to Consider and Investigate

- What do you think the journalists discuss on recruitment policies in the Chinese organisation in Zimbabwe?
- What are the Chinese organisation's core values that are reflected by Mr Peng? What are the core values of the Zimbabwean workers? What do you think are the core values of the Zimbabwean government in this situation?

- How can a positive solution be found for both parties: the Chinese organisation, including the Chinese managers, and the Zimbabwean workers?

17.4 Chinese Perspectives

Chinese-owned organisations often display huge Chinese emblems and symbols on their premises. They are proud of their country of origin, the "Middle Kingdom" (*Zhong Guo*). Usually Chinese organisations establish a consistent, stable and good political relationship with the governmental elites and present themselves as Chinese organisations investing in African countries to the benefit of both countries. President Mugabe's "Look East" policy makes Chinese investment and engagement a core issue between Zimbabwean elites on the one hand and Chinese governmental and private organisations on the other.

The management of Chinese mining companies usually is usually in the hands of national Chinese managers. These managers expect the Zimbabwean employees to listen to the instructions, comply with the organisational standards and work hard. If this is not done, dismissal of the employees can be the consequence. However, from a Chinese perspective, local employees usually do not meet their high levels of expectations in terms of skills, effectiveness, efficiency and ability to comply (Mayer & Boness, 2016).

Chinese management often emphasises that honesty is one of the most important ethical work values in Chinese companies (Inglehart & Welzel, 2010). Chinese ethics and work values are strongly connected to social values of honesty, obedience and best performance. Besides these values, the World Value Survey shows that Chinese prefer secular rational values. This includes a low emphasis on family values and religion (Inglehart & Welzel, 2010).

Mr Peng is responsible for the "hire-and-fire" policy of his organisation and shows a low tolerance of theft (Inglehart & Welzel, 2010). In China, theft of material and property is viewed as organisational sabotage and can be punished with a death penalty, owing to the fact that public safety is not secured. If theft occurs in the organisation, Mr Peng usually shifts employees to other places or dismisses them straight away. In Chinese organisations, firing is an instant process (Mayer & Boness, 2016). In firing processes, Chinese organisations will instantly confiscate the properties of the dismissed person such as computers, other hardware and files. This happens to avoid any further contact with or possible interference by the dismissed person. By these means, Chinese management aims to secure stability in the organisational structures and to maintain the core values of the organisation.

17.5   AFRICAN PERSPECTIVES

Zimbabwean employees working in Chinese organisations often experience and highlight the breach of national labour laws. Additionally, they consider the different quotas of Chinese in management versus Africans in labour as unfair and inappropriate, particularly since Chinese organisations invest in African countries. The payment system does not appear to be transparent for Zimbabwean employees since it is not openly accessible, and if available, it is usually written in Chinese. As previously noted, Zimbabwean employees are sometimes required to pay certain fees to the organisation on a monthly basis, such as "security fees" of US$50 to guarantee themselves a secure and enduring position within the organisation. The security fee is then deducted from salary. For the workers, this deduction often pushes them below minimum living standards, because one person's salary is usually required to finance the worker's own needs and those of the family. This necessity of family support reflects values that are favoured and strongly supported by employees in Zimbabwe.

In the understanding of Zimbabwean workers, hiring and firing are formal processes, which should follow specified legal procedures. For example, before firing an employee, a warning letter should be issued to provide that person with a chance to improve performance or change behaviour. Most Zimbabwean workers expect the mining company to abide by these procedures, including mandatory termination benefits which should be issued to workers to sustain them until their next job. This is why Zimbabweans agree to the involvement of labour unions in their employment, to be assured that basic conditions of contracts, dismissals and labour laws are observed by Chinese superiors.

It can be assumed that Zimbabwean workers have no major interest in serving a Chinese company in Mashonaland West other than to support their extended families and clans, to enable them to survive in habitable conditions. This is why the issue of having salaried, permanent contracts instead of casual employment is of utmost importance to them. Zimbabweans will agree to work overtime—but in return expect to receive extra payment. Zimbabwean workers also do not wish to work in times of family events such as marriage, burial or baptism. It is a basic expectation of Zimbabweans to leave work to attend such family occasions or religious celebrations. As studies show, spirituality is a highly ranked value for many Zimbabweans (Mbiti, 1990).

Focusing on the global cultural map of the World Values Survey (Inglehart & Welzel, 2010), it can be seen that survival values of economic and physical security are leading values in many African value systems. These values are linked to ethnocentric world views and low levels of trust and tolerance (Inglehart & Welzel, 2010). Additionally, in Zimbabwe, values such as social tolerance, life satisfaction, public expression of feelings and liberty are important (Inglehart & Welzel, 2010).

17.6 Culture-Specific Solutions

17.6.1 Short-Term Solutions from Chinese Perspectives

The Chinese management should emphasise the compliance of Chinese investment and organisational goals with official development goals of the Zimbabwean government. The mining company should re-evaluate their policies with regard to imposed payments by employees (such as security fees) to the mining company. The same re-evaluation applies to all types of dismissals which occur without providing reasons to the Zimbabwean workforce.

17.6.2 Long-Term Solutions from Chinese Perspectives

Chinese management should, in terms of long-term investment planning and the development of the employees, design trainings for the Zimbabwean employees, provide information on promotion of employee status and get a deeper insight into the values of the Zimbabwean employees. Chinese managers need to learn that other values like family, spiritual engagement, fair treatment, celebrations and social responsibility have a higher ranking in other value systems than their own top-ranking values of hard work, punctuality and best performance.

17.6.3 Short-Term Solutions from Zimbabwean Perspectives

Zimbabwean staff need to receive clear guidance concerning the reasons and procedures for dismissals by the Chinese management, in an effort to more easily adapt to the casual conditions. Zimbabweans should ask

Chinese managers to take their combination of working and religious duties into account, understanding the significance of funerals, baptism, marriages and church-orientated celebrations in their lives.

Chinese managers must respect the overall power of survival values in the Zimbabwean value system. This applies especially to working hours, days off, contracts and treatment issues.

17.6.4　Long-Term Solutions from Zimbabwean Perspectives

From the perspective of Zimbabweans, their trade unions must guarantee labour rights, fair treatment of employees, improvement of work conditions and formal work contracts. Zimbabwean employees should advocate the inclusion of family members in the workforce to enlarge the family income. They need to convince the Chinese management of the benefits of job creation and the impact of job creation on the wider public.

17.7　RECOMMENDATIONS FOR CHINESE-ZIMBABWEAN INTERCULTURAL COOPERATION

It is recommended that basic business ethics, encompassing the following rules (Schulman, 2006), are followed and enforced:

Strive to understand the values of different cultures, in order to find points in common.
Analyse the facts, which show that honesty and reliability are of benefit.
Respect your colleagues; this is the best investment possible.
Increase productivity by providing safe and healthy working conditions.
To inspire trust, make your performance transparent.
Downsizing your labour force is only beneficial when you respect each stakeholder.
Reduce the gap between the rich and poor by developing a new social security system.
Know that a public relations strategy will only secure your reputation if it witnesses your drive for quality and excellence.
Care for your business by caring for society.

References

Ernstes, C. (2014). Education in Zimbabwe. *The Borgen Project*. Retrieved from https://borgenproject.org/education-zimbabwe/

Inglehart, R., & Welzel, C. (2010). Changing Mass Priorities: The Link Between Modernization and Democracy, World Values Survey. *Perspectives on Politics, 8*(2), 551–567.

Mangirazi, N. (2016, September 11). Workers at Chinese Mine Raise Hell Over Abuse. *The Standard*. Retrieved from https://www.thestandard.co.zw/2016/09/11/workers-chinese-mine-raise-hell-abuse/

Mayer, C.-H., & Boness, C. (2016). "Somehow It Is Like The Military …". Experiences of Chinese and Tanzanian Cooperation in a Chinese Organisation in Tanzania. In T. Jackson, L. Louw, D. K. Boojihawon, & T. Fang (Eds.), *Chinese Organisations in Sub-Saharan Africa: New Dynamics, New Synergies*. Routledge.

Mbiti, J. S. (1990). *African Religions and Philosophy* (2nd ed.). Portsmouth, NH: Heinemann.

Ojakorotu, V., & Kamidza, R. (2018, January 24). Look East Policy: The Case of Zimbabwe-China Political and Economic Relations Since 2000. *India Quarterly: A Journal of International Affairs*. Retrieved from https://journals.sagepub.com/doi/full/10.1177/0974928417749642

Perper, R. (2018, May 3). Zimbabwe's Opposition Leader Has Pledged to Rid the Country of Chinese Investment. *Business Insider. Deutschland. International*. Retrieved from https://www.businessinsider.de/chinese-investment-in-zimbabwe-opposition-leader-2018-5?r=US&IR=T

Schulman, M. (2006). *Business Ethics*. Markkula Center for Applied Ethics. Santa Clara University, California. Retrieved from https://www.scu.edu/ethics/focus-areas/business-ethics/resources/business-ethics-in-china/

Taylor, I. (2005). 'The Devilish Thing': The Commonwealth and Zimbabwe's Dénouement. *The Round Table, 94*(380), 367–380. https://doi.org/10.1080/00358530500174630

Zimbabwe. Ministry of Mines and Mining Development. (2016). *Mashonaland Central. Important Minerals and Potential*. Retrieved from http://www.mines.gov.zw/?q=mash-central/194

Zimbabwe. Ministry of Mining and Mining Development. (2018). *Our Vision. Our Mission*. Retrieved from http://www.mines.gov.zw/

CHAPTER 18

Case 15: Managing Chinese-Cameroonian Daily Interactions in a Company in Douala, Cameroon

Jocelyne Kenne Kenne

18.1 CASE NARRATIVE

Cameroon is a Central African state, which is bordered to the west by Nigeria, to the north-east by Chad, to the east by Central African Republic and to the south by Equatorial Guinea, Gabon and Congo. It is known as "Africa in miniature" due to its linguistic, cultural, ethnic and geographic diversity. This diversity present in Cameroon is a mixture of linguistic, geographic and cultural elements found in other African countries (Siebetcheu, 2012). As a matter of fact, on a linguistic level, in Cameroon three of the four families of languages spoken in Africa are spoken. At a cultural level, Cameroon has various ethnic groups. The main ones are the *Fang* (around 20%), the *Bamiléké* and *Bamoun* (around 20%), the *Douala* and *Bassa* (around 15%). On the geographic level, Cameroon has the continent's major climatic areas and natural features such as white beaches, coastal plains, mountainous areas, hills, tropical forest and deserts.

J. K. Kenne (✉)
University of Bayreuth, Bayreuth, Germany

© The Author(s) 2019
C.-H. Mayer et al. (eds.), *Managing Chinese-African Business Interactions*, Palgrave Studies in African Leadership,
https://doi.org/10.1007/978-3-030-25185-7_18

Cameroon has a unique historical configuration in the whole African continent. This is due to the fact that it is the only African country which underwent a triple colonial experience: German, French and English (Siebetcheu, 2013, p. 2). The singularity of Cameroon is also determined by its official bilingualism with French and English as official languages. Besides the official languages, there are 283 indigenous languages spoken (Simons & Fennig, 2018).

The linguistic and cultural situation in Cameroon is more complex with the settlement of migrants. Chinese migration to Cameroon is a topic which is receiving unprecedented attention. Their presence goes back to the 1970s (Röschenthaler & Socpa, 2017, p. 167). Over the years and more specifically from the 1990s, Chinese migration has accelerated to the point that studies estimate between 20,000 and 50,000 Chinese people are living in Cameroon (Cabestan, 2015, p. 17). This growing presence of the Chinese is the result of the *zou chuqu* or "Go Out" policy, which is a strategy promoted by the Chinese government to encourage investment abroad. That said, a considerable number of Chinese have settled and opened organisations and shops in Cameroonian cities.

Mr Li belongs to the recent Chinese migration. He is the owner-manager of a large organisation that manages the distribution of Chinese products from the commercial port to individual Chinese shops in Douala, Cameroon's capital. He was the leader of this organisation in China for over 20 years until three years ago, when he left China and settled in Douala where, together with his wife, he opened a subsidiary of the Chinese company. Mr Li thinks that the long experience he has as a leader in China gave him enough experience to know how to successfully lead in Douala. He is personally satisfied with the evolution of the business. Nevertheless, he is surprised by the regular complaints of his employees regarding his leadership style. As a matter of fact, they find his behaviour too overbearing and they regret that no space is given to them to share their views in the decision-making process.

However, according to Mr Li, he is doing what a leader should be doing. He therefore assumes that his employees should be fully satisfied. When referring to his leadership style, he affirms that he is applying the same style he was using in China. He does not understand why there are so many complaints from his Cameroonian employees, while those in China never did so.

18.2 Investigative Questions

- Analyse the leadership style used by Mr Li in the organisation.
- Examine the complaints of the employees and explain the position of Mr Li regarding those complaints.
- Define the values that are fundamental for a good collaboration between leader and employees from a Chinese and an African perspective.
- Examine short- and long-term solutions to solve the case from a Chinese and African perspective.
- Make recommendations for a successful Chinese-African intercultural cooperation.

18.3 Chinese Perspectives

Mr Li's leadership style is based on the authoritarian leadership, which is referred to as the paternalistic leadership (Cheng, Chou, Wu, Huang, & Farh, 2004; Farh & Cheng, 2000). It is also considered as the main leadership style used in Chinese business organisations (Cheng et al., 2004). It combines three main principles: authority, benevolence and moral values (Farh & Cheng, 2000). This way of leading gives absolute power to the leader, and its authority is uncontested. This involves giving rules and instructions to the employees, even if those rules can sometimes be very strict (Cheng et al., 2004; Wang, Chiang, Tsai, Lin, & Cheng, 2013).

Mr Li finds his employees very disrespectful. He thinks that, as the leader, he deserves more respect. Mr Li comes from a hierarchical culture where the notion of superiority and the respect attached to highest ranking person is strictly observed. In fact, it is a significant value in the Chinese traditional context. Moreover, Mr Li thinks that as a leader he should neither be debating with his employees nor should he be considering their views—otherwise the roles would be confused and the hierarchy would not be respected. Wang, Greg, Wendy, and Jay (2005) define respect for the hierarchy as a very important Confucian value, which implies that the people placed in higher positions expect respect from their subordinates. Mr Li is therefore disappointed, as he does not receive enough respect from his Cameroonian employees.

As China is a high power-distance culture (Hofstede & Bond, 1984, 1998), power distance plays an important role in Mr Li's leadership. Again, as the leader and figure of authority, Mr Li expects to be followed without questioning. He should not be justifying the reasons for his decisions. He finds it important to ensure that the power distance is maintained between the leader and the employees, simply because the employees might not always understand what the leader is referring to.

Mr Li also complains that his employees confront him in the workplace, which is, he adds, very embarrassing and threatens his reputation. He asserts that it is a sign of disrespect he never experienced in China. The concept of saving face or giving face, which means keeping someone's reputation or dignity is very important in the Chinese context. It occupies an important place in Confucianism; saving face is a sign of respect, especially in a social hierarchical framework such as the one in China (Cardon & Scott, 2003). Mr Li therefore insists that he should not be ashamed in front of others or "lose his face" (Brown & Levinson, 1987). He expects his employees to avoid confronting him in public.

Finally, Mr Li complains about the lack of discipline the Cameroonians display and about their regular delays in accomplishing tasks. He considers it a threat to the business if they do not finish the work on time.

18.4 African Perspectives

The Cameroonian employees in the company are very irritated by the language their managing director uses to communicate with them. In particular, they complain about his lack of proficiency in any of the languages spoken in Cameroon. The employees speak of the "Chinese invasion" and consider his use of Chinese when speaking to them as another form of colonialism. It reminds them of their colonial history with the Germans, the French and the English who ruled Cameroon and imposed the use of their respective languages to the detriment of the local languages. They therefore find it frustrating when Mr Li asks them to learn the Chinese language so that they can efficiently communicate with him. They feel that Mr Li is just looking for profit and does not care about them or what is happening around him.

They wonder how he can successfully manage the organisation while ignoring the languages spoken by his employees and the national languages used in Cameroon. In a similar vein, they find it frustrating when he gets angry with them because they do not understand him, or when a task is not correctly done due to miscommunication. In short, Cameroonians would like to be able to have proper communication with the managing director using the same linguistic code.

Furthermore, the Cameroonian employees complain about the leadership style used by Mr Li. They consider it too dictatorial. According to them, he does not need to dictate rules, which are very strict at times (Cheng et al., 2004). On the contrary, he should allow more space for discussion. They regret their passivity and their inability to share their views or make suggestions. They are dissatisfied by the lack of communication and find the atmosphere at the workplace too cold to create a peaceful setting and harmonious working environment. Finally, they regret that Mr Li does not encourage them or congratulate them when a task is well done or when they take initiatives, which decreases their spontaneity. In their opinion, the only thing he cares about is getting tasks done, and done quickly.

18.5 Culture-Specific Solutions

18.5.1 Short- and Long-Term Solutions from Chinese Perspectives

Mr Li should hold an informal session where grievances can be shared. In order to have a harmonious team, he should be ready to listen to his employees and take note of their complaints. As a long-term solution, Mr Li should consider revising his leadership style, and most importantly, he should avoid reproducing the same leadership style he was using in China, given that the cultural context is so different in Cameroon. As highlighted by Hofstede (1980), Farh and Cheng (2000) and Cheng et al. (2004), leadership styles differ across national and even regional boundaries. In other words, what is permitted in a leader's behaviour in one culture may be counterproductive in another; what is required is the ability to adapt a leadership style to the culture.

In the same vein, Mr Li should be ready to introduce new elements in his leadership style. To achieve this, he should be more open, ready to accept suggestions or negotiate when necessary. Moreover, he should get into the habit of integrating his employees into the decision-making of the organisation, and also, he should encourage them to take initiatives. Mr Li can therefore combine different leadership styles. He could take elements from autocratic leadership and from democratic or participative leadership, which implies decentralising authority and integrating the active participation of the employees in the decision-making process. In doing so, the creativity and the satisfaction of the employees will certainly increase.

Mr Li could also approach other Cameroonian organisational leaders to learn about their leadership behaviour. It would be important to observe how they integrate Cameroonian values into their leadership style, to understand which elements are crucial for successful leadership in a Cameroonian context. Likewise, he might ask them for advice to improve his own leadership style.

With regard to the language used during interactions with staff, it is important for Mr Li to learn the main language spoken by his employees. This would help to avoid miscommunication and conflicts caused by language barriers. He could also ask them to teach him some important values attached to the Cameroonian culture as this might help to avoid conflicts induced by culture. It would also be useful for Mr Li to organise regular meetings to evaluate the team and hear their views.

18.5.2 Short- and Long-Term Solutions from African Perspectives

Cameroonian employees should attend the meetings called by Mr Li. They should avoid passive resistance by pretending conflicts do not exist, but they should share their concerns in a clear and precise way. They should also avoid confronting Mr Li directly as he might consider it as a sign of disrespect. After all, after sharing their concerns, they should give him time to consider their views.

Additionally, they should learn about the main leadership styles used in China and more specifically the one used by their managing director. This would help them to understand him better and might help to avoid confusion related to Mr Li's behaviour. The employees should learn about and be aware of the important Chinese cultural elements in a business context. These include an understanding of the concept of face (*Mianzi*) in order to prevent Mr Li from experiencing a loss of his reputation and social standing. Another important concept they could learn about is *guanxi* (relationship) so as to build and nurture good relationships from a Chinese perspective. Another important value like *renqinq* (exchange of favours) should be explained to them.

However, if miscommunication and conflicts still occur, the Cameroonian employees should find a translator who is not only bilingual but also bicultural, and who could effectively promote communication between the two cultures.

18.6 Recommendations for Successful Intercultural Cooperation

As highlighted by Hofstede (1980), in cross-cultural contact, an effective leadership and team should combine their cultural specificities. It is important for each culture to understand their cultural differences, and it is crucial that this understanding is integrated into the leadership style. To do so, both the leader and the employees should be conscious of the main values attached to the culture of the other, especially the values related to the business setting.

Again, insofar as it is possible, the same language should be used by the leader and the employees. This would save time-taking explanations and avoid conflicts related to miscommunication, which could result in mistrust, bad moods, stress and lack of motivation.

Regular meetings should be organised to evaluate personal satisfaction, which allows a safe space for successful teamwork. It may also be important to consider hiring a linguistic and intercultural mediator within the organisation to intervene in conflict situations.

References

Brown, P., & Levinson, S. (1987). *Politeness: Some Language Universals in Language Use.* Cambridge: Cambridge University Press.

Cabestan, J. P. (2015). China–Cameroon Relations: Fortunes and Limits of an Old Political Complicity. *South African Journal of International Affairs.* https://doi.org/10.1080/10220461.2015.1014930

Cardon, P. W., & Scott, J. C. (2003). Chinese Business Face: Communication Behaviors and Teaching Approaches. *Business Communication Quarterly,* 66(4), 9–22. Retrieved from https://doi.org/10.1177/108056990306600402

Cheng, B. S., Chou, L. F., Wu, T. Y., Huang, M. P., & Farh, J. L. (2004). Paternalistic Leadership and Subordinate Responses: Establishing a Leadership Model in Chinese Organizations. *Asian Journal of Social Psychology, 7,* 89–117.

Farh, J. L., & Cheng, B. S. (2000). A Cultural Analysis of Paternalistic Leadership in Chinese Organizations. In J. T. Li, A. S. Tsui, & S. E. Walton (Eds.), *Management and Organizations in Chinese Context* (pp. 95–197). London: Macmillan.

Hofstede, G. (1980). *Culture's Consequences: International Differences in Work Related Values.* Newbury Park, CA: Sage.

Hofstede, G., & Bond, M. H. (1984). Hofstede's Cultural Dimensions: An Independent Validation Using Rockeach's Value Survey. *Journal of Cross-Cultural Psychology, 15,* 417–433. https://doi.org/10.1177/0022002184015004003

Hofstede, G., & Bond, M. H. (1998). *Masculinity and Femininity: The Taboo Dimensions of National Cultures.* Thousand Oaks, CA: Sage.

Röschenthaler, U., & Socpa, A. (2017). Facing the China Challenge: Cameroonians Between Discontent and Popular Admiration. In K. Young-Chan (Ed.), *China and Africa: A New Paradigm of Global Business* (pp. 155–188). London: Palgrave.

Siebetcheu, R. (2012). Comportamenti Linguistici Delle Famiglie Immigrate in Italia. In L. Zanfrini (Ed.), *Famiglie che migrano, si dividono, si ritrovano, si disperdono. Atti della Summer School "Mobilità umana e giustizia globale"* (pp. 69–90). Rome: Centro Studi Emigrazione.

Siebetcheu, R. (2013). Lingua ed emigrazione italiana in Camerun. In M. Fondazione (Ed.), *Rapporto Italiani nel Mondo 2013* (pp. 119–128). Todi: Tau.

Simons, G. F., & Fennig, C. D. (Eds.). (2018). *Ethnologue: Languages of the World* (21st ed.). Dallas, Texas: SIL International. Retrieved from http://www.ethnologue.com

Wang, A. C., Chiang, J. T. J., Tsai, C. Y., Lin, T. T., & Cheng, B. S. (2013). Gender Makes the Difference: The Moderating Role of Leader Gender on the Relationship Between Leadership Styles and Subordinate Performance. *Organizational Behavior and Human Decision Processes, 122*(2), 101–113. https://doi.org/10.1016/j.obhdp.2013.06.001

Wang, J., Greg, G. W., Wendy, E. A. R., & Jay, W. R. (2005). Confucian Values and the Implications for International HRD. *Human Resource Development International, 8*(3), 311–326. https://doi.org/10.1080/13678860500143285

CHAPTER 19

Case 16: A Cross-cultural Conference in the Mozambique Confucius Institute

Christian Martin Boness and Naiming Wei

19.1 CASE NARRATIVE

In 2011, a delegation of Mozambican and Chinese officials agree to establish a Confucius Institute in order to promote Chinese-African intercultural cooperation. The institute opens the following year and hosts a cross-cultural conference on understanding cultural biases of Chinese and African employees in joint ventures and on the impact of cultural bias on future cooperation.

Dr Mei, from the Chinese Academy of Social Sciences, speaks about Chinese perceptions of Mozambican culture. She draws on her interviews with Chinese managers from a Chinese-owned iron and steel corporation, which develops coal reserves for export to China. The other invited researcher, Prof. Mareleta from the University of Lubumbashi in the

---

C. M. Boness (✉)
Department of Management, Rhodes University, Grahamstown, South Africa

N. Wei
Department of Business Administration, University of Applied Science, Nuremberg, Germany
e-mail: Naiming.wei@th-nuernberg.de

Democratic Republic of the Congo (DRC), speaks about interviews with Congolese workers in Chinese-owned mining companies in Katanga.

In her presentation, Dr Mei reports that the Chinese managers she interviewed who live in Mozambique find that Mozambicans are very friendly and welcoming towards strangers; they laugh a lot, celebrate, enjoy life and build sustainable social relations. So, in general, Chinese expatriates can feel at home. The company's Chinese managers consider Mozambicans to have a far better work–life balance than they do, in the sense that the local people are very relaxed about their work and their output. They are perceived by the Chinese managers as being team orientated and they cooperate easily with each other.

On the other hand, Dr Mei explains that the Chinese managers also think that Mozambican culture does not appreciate knowledge and expertise. From the viewpoint of Chinese management, the Mozambicans should increase their organisational commitment, dedicate all of their energy to their work and should have a greater sense of responsibility. Additionally—and that is a pressing issue from a Chinese perspective—the local workers lack efficiency because they do not value punctuality or time management.

Dr Mei then speaks of various work situations in Mozambique that deeply challenge Chinese feelings and beliefs. Some Chinese employees report racially motivated attacks and feel threatened; Chinese organisational compounds are often targeted by thieves and the Chinese face harassment from Mozambican officials in addition to corruption in official settings, which makes it difficult to do business. The Chinese managers think that the Mozambican government should act to protect the human rights of the Chinese community in the country. She pauses, and then adds that there is much work needed to resolve these challenges. However, the way forward is not too dark. Some Chinese managers consider Chinese and Mozambican cultures to be similar in nature. Overall, it is understood that Chinese and African individuals have a good working relationship that is rooted in cultural respect. The Chinese managers believe that Chinese and Mozambicans can learn from one another's cultures.

When Dr Mei concludes her lecture, she calls on the director of the Maputo Confucius Institute to take these findings into account, and to improve the relationship between Chinese and Mozambicans by exchanging ideas and discussing different cultural and organisational perspectives. Dr Mei is convinced of the need for both Chinese and Mozambicans to attend seminars, information sessions and workshops to be aware of and understand the most important Confucian work ethics and those of

African *Ubuntu* management, as well as recent research and inputs concerning intercultural and cross-cultural management. The members of the audience look interested, applaud and then prepare to listen to the next invited speaker.

Prof. Mareleta takes the stand, and reports on his interviews with workers from 15 Congolese mining organisations, mainly at the Kolwezi Depot and the Lubumbashi smelter. He points out to the audience that everything he says is based on the interviews, and he does not reflect his personal views. He explains that he would not like to embarrass Chinese citizens, managers or employees working in African countries, nor does he wish to embarrass representatives of the People's Republic of China. On the contrary, Prof. Mareleta praises the good relationship and friendship between the Chinese and Congolese governments at top levels, emphasising that the majority of Congolese citizens view the Chinese culture as being geared for success and cooperation. Chinese managers and employees appear to be getting the work done and are viewed as hard-working and results-driven. The Chinese employees' dedication and their punctuality appear to be desirable characteristics for Congolese employees. Congolese employees would therefore be willing to adopt these Chinese values and behaviours in order to improve their work performance.

Members of the audience are beginning to see a criticism behind these words regarding Chinese-Congolese cooperation. Prof. Mareleta mentions that subgroups of Congolese workers in the mining organisations say that the Chinese culture tends to be "foreign, aggressive and male-dominated" and as a result, many Congolese people think Chinese managers are disrespectful and unfriendly to the Congolese mineworkers. These employee subgroups see the Chinese managers as separate, creating a kind of glass ceiling in the organisation, not mixing with Congolese employees, just keeping to members of their own culture. This attitude does not fit with African cultures, and it is unacceptable that interviewed employees should feel that Chinese organisations and their employees should stay in China rather than permeating the Congo with an attitude of separation and their foreign ways of behaviour.

As soon as Prof. Mareleta ends his lecture, one can hear the unrest in the auditorium and feel the discomfort of the attendants. In a feedback session after the presentations, Chinese business people admit that they do not know enough about *Ubuntu* management, and the Mozambican politicians seem to be more interested in the characteristics of Confucian ethics.

19.2 Questions and Points of Discussion

- How do Chinese view the Congolese workers, according to Prof. Mareleta's research?
- What are the specific views given of the Mozambican workforce according to Dr Mei's presentation in the Confucius Institute?
- Which essential concepts of Chinese Confucian ethics can be identified?
- Which aspects of the African *Ubuntu* concept are presented in the speeches?

19.3 Chinese Perspectives

How Chinese perceive Mozambicans is not only a matter of ascribed characteristics of personality but also a matter of culture and cultural perceptions. Based on their Chinese value set and self-awareness, Chinese managers often judge the Mozambican employees. These judgements and stereotypes are frequently generalised to all Africans and culturalisation takes place. The interview findings referred to in the case study are largely true. According to research by Fidelys and Liang (2015) at the Wuhan Iron and Steel Company, the overall feeling of the Chinese managers working in Mozambique is not positive. The "friendly working relationship" reported by Dr Mei seems to be a politically correct statement rather than a reflection of the truth. These Chinese managers are facing challenges in their daily business lives, such as dealing with the lower-than-average qualification levels of Mozambican employees, different understandings of and attitudes to work ethic and organisational behaviour, as well as the bureaucratic harassment of local officials. Other difficult aspects of the working relationship for the Chinese management arises from the unconscious cultural predominance of a Chinese "master" over the African people, and from unrealistic expectations of enjoying a "good business life" in Mozambique.

Chinese managers working in African contexts often see their own culture as solemn, ancient, traditional, huge and very powerful. A Chinese executive director explains (Boness & Mayer, 2013):

> You know, the Chinese culture is the only culture in the world that has lasted for the longest time without a break. There have been like the dynasty changes, like wars and a lot of killing and revolutions—but the culture like

passing down did not break. So Chinese culture we can say that it is a long culture, it is like a big ball so everything that is mixed with Chinese culture: you get inside and it is like a circle circling together. So we can say like where there is Chinese culture you always feel like a part of that. It almost feels like it is similar with your own (sub-)culture. And you may say, Chinese culture resembles the spinning ball of the dragon.

This Chinese narrative also applies to Chinese-owned Mozambican organisations. They are like small constructions of the Motherland China, including communication styles, structures and ethics. So, if Mozambicans meet Chinese managers in a joint venture organisation, they are likely to encounter culturally distant features in communication, structure and treatment. The tendency will be to create as much Chinese atmosphere as possible. For Mozambicans, this is a huge challenge.

In comparison to Chinese cultures, African cultures have few historical written records; artefacts show that heterogeneity and diversity are valued in African cultures. However, a plethora of ancient writings and philosophies exist in Chinese cultures, from Confucius and others who left multiple legacies, not only to the Chinese, but globally. In sub-Saharan Africa, scriptures have been spread since colonisation of the continent about 500 years ago, while Chinese scripture is several thousand years old. These facts may foster pre-emptions, pre-assumptions and even prejudices of Chinese managers and employees towards African employees. This is based on the ideal of China during past decades, to assist in developing countries in Africa in a similar manner to the way China developed from an agricultural society to a highly industrialised and post-modern service society.

Based on recently conducted in-depth interviews with Chinese managers and employees (Mayer, Boness, & Louw, 2016), one can recognise some typical features of self-imaging. Regarding industrial virtues, Chinese managers see themselves as serious, efficient, cooperative, punctual, hardworking and "chance-taking in the shortest time possible" (Mayer, Boness, & Louw, 2016).

With regard to Chinese culture, the concepts of truth and truth-telling are cornerstones of Chinese self-esteem. Family and elders are respected. The philosophy of Confucius is highly valued (Mayer, Boness, & Louw, 2016). Based on these values and the self-concept they create, Chinese managers highlight that in African cultures, economic goals might not be reached because these goals are not prioritised as they are in Chinese cultures.

On encountering the African lifestyle, a Chinese manager narrates the following short story (Mayer, Boness, Louw, & Louw, 2016):

> One Chinese couple works very hard to buy a big house, but—you know—because they are working very hard, they have got to find someone to take care of the house, right? ... So they find like a house girl to help keep that house clean and whatever. So basically it looks like this young couple works from eight am to midnight every day and their house girl sitting on the couch playing with the pad. And she sees the sunrise and sundown; that is it.

In this short story, the Chinese manager targets the balance between life and work in both cultures; he speaks about two different lifestyles. The Chinese lifestyle aims to work hard, to earn money in order to achieve one goal: to buy a luxury house for living a luxurious lifestyle. However, the Chinese couple cannot find the time to indulge their desires. They restrain their wish to enjoy themselves, while the house girl, working from sunrise to sunset, has the use of the fancy house and finds happiness in the comfortable situation and gorgeous natural surroundings.

Hofstede (2010) developed a useful model of six culture dimensions that differ between cultures: high or low power distance, individualism or collectivism, masculinity versus femininity, high or low uncertainty avoidance, and short- or long-term orientation. Hofstede (2018) also identified a varying cultural dimension as the extent to which people control their desires and impulses, based on the way they were raised. Relatively weak control is "indulgence", whereas relatively strong control is "restraint" (Hofstede, 2010), therefore cultures can be described as indulgent or restrained. The indulgence factor in China is very low while the same factor in most sub-Saharan countries is remarkably high. People in societies classified by a high score in indulgence generally show a willingness to realise their impulses and desires with regard to enjoying life and having fun (Hofstede, 2010). They possess a positive attitude and have a tendency towards optimism. In addition, they place a higher degree of importance on leisure time, act as they please and spend money as they wish. By contrast, China is a restrained society with its low indulgence rating. Such societies lean towards cynicism and pessimism, do not put much emphasis on leisure time and control the gratification of their desires. People with this orientation have the perception that their actions are restrained by social norms, and they feel that indulging themselves is somewhat wrong (Hofstede, 2010). This is one major reason why Chinese employees and managers admire the work–life balance (Mayer, Boness, & Louw, 2016) of the majority of Mozambicans, including their teamwork skills.

19.4 Mozambican and Congolese Perspectives

Similar to Dr Mei, some politically correct statements were made by Prof. Mareleta in his opening speech, but the problems he reported are a generally accurate reflection of reality.

In research by Goethals, Mbaya, and Okenda (2009)—based on interviews held with Congolese mineworkers at the Congo Dong Bang Mining Company—it was found that the employees did not understand the labour regulations and felt these were inadequate in their Congolese context. The research by Goethals et al. (2009) confirms that the environment was not respected by the Chinese managers in charge, injured workers did not receive adequate medical attention and there was insufficient protective work clothing available for the Congolese mineworkers. Further, illegal mining and child labour was occurring in the organisation; Congolese employees were dismissed for trivial offences (such as being late for work) and any complaints about health and safety measures led to dismissal (Goethals et al., 2009). Racial discrimination was experienced by the Congolese workers and some Chinese managers appeared to be "above the law" (Goethals et al., 2009).

Chinese companies appear to have an increasingly serious problem with their public image in Mozambique and other African countries. However, in general, both Congolese and Mozambicans meet the Chinese in deep respect with a positive attitude.

Mozambicans, if questioned, would often reframe Chinese opinions on Africans in general. They would reject stereotypic assumptions, for example: "Laziness is not our concept, but while working we need to understand each other, to understand what we are doing, the processes, for which purpose we are doing what and for whose benefit" (Mayer, Boness, Louw et al., 2016). In many African ethnic and cultural groups, consensus-building processes are important. These processes are part of *Ubuntu*, an African humanistic philosophy which underlies many African organisational and management practices. *Ubuntu* and communalism in African educational discourse are anchored in a long tradition of sub-Saharan ethics. Communal affairs come first. The main values of *Ubuntu* are interdependence, sensitivity to others and caring for others. Humanness, as with the dignity of mankind, is also a core value connected with recognising human needs (Le Roux, 2000; Venter, 2004).

African work ethics differ from those of the Chinese, and they might improve the work–life balance more than the Chinese "hard-working" ethic can do. Concepts of time can also have very different meanings. The English word "punctuality" has no equivalent in many Bantu languages, and in Mozambique, there are more than 20 Bantu languages spoken (Banda & Canhanga, 2017). This phenomenon indicates that time in the African view is usually and primarily bound to social interaction and not to objective and linear timeframes of running hours (Mbiti, 1990). Mozambicans may assert that they have a rich and satisfying time management that enables them to live their lives in a profoundly spiritual way (Mbiti, 1990). The vicissitudes of life weigh much more than obligations or responsibilities in work-related contexts. Attending a funeral of a family member, for instance, is always prioritised above presence at the workplace. Building sustainable relationships and contact with the ancestors is valued over relationships at work or the individual success of an employee in an organisation (Mbiti, 1990). Teamwork in particular is highly valued in East African work ethics.

A representative survey which was carried out in East Africa during 2013 to 2015 (Mayer, Boness, & Louw, 2016), shows that African views of Chinese people, and perspectives of the Chinese on African people, are heterogeneous. For Chinese managers in the Congo, hard work has several meanings. Some of these are: to work longer than the minimum hours, to be available to superiors—even under harsh circumstances, and to find a solution for any problem in a clearly defined timeframe, even if fellow employees have already left. Timeliness and hard work go together. This often results in the convincing performance of Chinese planning and implementation. "Getting the work done" appears as an attractive and desirable value or virtue for many Africans, which can and should be learned. That would create reliability, confidence and a positive sense of their own power. If the Congo is ever to build up an independent industry and service sector, this kind of confidence is urgently needed.

Also present in this scenario are ethnic and cultural Congolese groups who might take an opposing stand and assert that the growing dependency on Chinese skills and performance can create a feeling of cultural weakness (Mayer, Boness, Louw et al., 2016). This group would emphasise the foreignness of the Dragon culture, which would further underpin the "aggressive" character (Mayer, Boness, & Louw, 2016) of Chinese investment in Congolese resources and the aggressive and often unfriendly way subordinates are treated. Congolese workers perceive Chinese managers as disrespecting Congolese culture and people, as they follow their own cultural imperatives (Mayer, Boness, & Louw, 2016). Moreover, the Chinese would segregate themselves from Congolese citizens, living in separate settlements and not mingling socially with local people, but grabbing their natural resources to be shipped to China.

Views such as these often culminate in the call to reduce African economic engagement with Chinese enterprises. However, it is largely recognised that Chinese economic activities are part of bilateral or multilateral agreements. Western countries or India would not so easily offer their investments and services under the same conditions. Additionally, the bartering of "mines for infrastructure" reflects China's policy not to make the Congo and other African countries indebted through loans and credits that would ultimately contribute to the ruin of state budgets.

On a more interpersonal level, some Chinese attitudes are distant from the dominant values of African culture. Being aggressive can be interpreted as being goal-focused, taking a straight course and fighting obstacles that might block the way. Being unfriendly can be translated as the Chinese not putting emphasis on greetings, family-orientated chat or on creating a pleasant atmosphere wherever they are. Chinese might find it normal to first of all see the work, and only then see the relationships with people. They might have observed that greeting in African contexts can take up much time, time that is necessary for good performance of a task. That is why Chinese want Africans to obey and follow their instructions or commandments. Chinese are convinced that they know better how to perform. And good performance leads to more benefits, first for the company, second for the country and last but not least, for the individual.

A lesser-known fact is that Chinese people who are working in Chinese enterprises in sub-Saharan Africa observe how peaceful the locals are (Mayer, Boness, Louw et al., 2016). Soft in words and smooth in approach, Africans also appear, to the Chinese, to be prepared for positive cooperation with others. Beyond that, they all know how to celebrate life, in singing, laughing, chatting and praying. The vast majority of Africans believe in God as the main source of their coming to being and existence (Mbiti, 1990).

19.5 Culture-Specific Solutions

19.5.1 Short-Term Solutions from Chinese Perspectives

Mozambicans need to acknowledge that the Chinese feel pressure to conform with timeframes and deadlines, to plan properly and efficiently, and to achieve goals. Mozambicans can see how supportive Chinese management are in explaining and teaching the basics of Chinese work ethics. Africans should observe and acknowledge that the majority of Chinese citizens in Mozambique do not need churches or a belief in God to find meaning in their lives regarding work, family and society. Mozambican employees and all African staff should learn to see Chinese culture "as a big ball that spins and absorbs from all other cultures, mixing them with Chinese culture until it is like one Chinese culture". Chinese employees should be offered intercultural preparation courses before they are sent to Africa. Wuhan Iron and Steel in particular is a large-scale company that can afford to provide trainings for managers who are destined to work in Mozambique. They must be given a realistic introduction to the circumstances of business in south-east Africa as well as the social and economic environment. This type of intercultural course should be more fact-based and constructive than ideologically driven. Information should be presented without obscuring or misrepresenting the reality of life in Mozambique. The company is required to define rules for constructive intercultural communication and cooperation with Mozambican employees in an employee handbook.

19.5.2 Long-Term Solutions from Chinese Perspectives

Chinese managers would prefer African employees to learn from the impact of Chinese work ethics and general behaviour through seminars and intercultural training. That includes cross-cultural training on management principles and styles to be applied in the organisation. Follow-up activities should be offered concerning the rules defined in preparational courses for Chinese as well as African workforces. This would include the evaluation and reflection of intercultural communication on a quarterly or semi-annual basis. Improvement activities should be noted and undertaken in an appropriate way.

Chinese managers would like their Mozambican counterparts to understand Chinese culture, learn basic Mandarin and be informed about the

Chinese history. Then Mozambicans could participate more easily in communication with Chinese managers, employers and improve their understanding of the organisational culture.

19.5.3 Short-Term Solutions from African Perspectives

For Chinese managers who migrate from China to sub-Saharan Africa, to Mozambique or to the DRC it will be essential to learn about African lifestyles, tribal culture, dressing and food habits. In addition to knowledge of external cultural phenomena, the fundamental question of intercultural values and behaviour in encounters should be understood. Mutual respect is the leading value in Mozambican cultures, using an appropriate language and greeting. This should be acknowledged and absorbed into daily behaviour. From African perspectives, Chinese managers should recognise that a majority of inhabitants of African countries are religious and believe in God or another higher power, and they believe that all their actions are connected to their belief in God.

Mozambicans would like to see Chinese managers take care of their personal and natural environment. Africans should also be given opportunities to learn to cope with Chinese ideas for future collaboration with Africans. This could be facilitated in offering proper in-house trainings or collaboration with the Confucius Institute.

19.5.4 Long-Term Solutions from African Perspectives

Learning from each other means for Mozambicans a permanent mutual contact and exchange of ideas and the building up of a sustainable relationship. Facilitate an organisational culture where Mozambicans and Chinese can contact each other. Avoid seclusion and language barriers that create uncertainty and misunderstandings of the views of numerous African workers. Invite African staff to officially expose ideas on topics of intercultural communication. Mainly focus on time concepts in Africa, work ethics, family bindings and spirituality. Give all your commitments a spiritual base. Acknowledge and learn the last hundred years of African history, its struggles and heroes, its defeats and victories. Accept that people in sub-Saharan countries will not easily follow Chinese concepts due to unconscious culture concepts and biases. Strive for freedom and harmony in your organisation.

African employees would like to see their Chinese managers using English, Swahili and Portuguese (Banda & Canhanga, 2017) or other African languages of their permanent residents so as to learn about ethnic and language-related cultures, in order to build sustainable work relationships and to understand the host culture in which Chinese managers and employees live while they are in African countries.

19.6 Recommendations for Chinese-African Intercultural Cooperation

At various levels of interpersonal relations within organisations, the following ideas are presented to improve the organisational climate, creating increasingly satisfying cooperation between Chinese and Mozambicans or Congolese staff.

At the micro-level of interaction, avoid xenophobic attitudes. If these occur at the workplace, all anti-Chinese and anti-African utterances must be identified, and discussed, even fought, if severe. The goal is to maintain peace between African and Chinese staff in organisations. Offer transcultural trainings with tandem trainers, Chinese and Africans. This might help to change the viewpoint from African to Chinese and vice versa on personal and group-related issues. Language courses are very necessary for both cultures. Establishing language and culture organisations like Confucius institutions is recommended. Culturally skilled staff who are based in these institutions can be invited to offer opportunities to medium- and large-scale companies. Basically, be open to learning formally and informally from each other's cultures to recognise cultures equally and to build mutual understanding.

At the meso-level of the organisation and the macro-level of governments, some major improvements are recommended. The Chinese-owned companies should comply with environmental management plans as far as possible in the respective African countries. Awareness of environmental management should be publicised, even in the local companies and on websites.

Chinese and African institutions such as the Confucius Institute can develop a plan of action to improve intercultural dialogue and build a climate of mutual trust. Chinese managers and supervisors should consider being better prepared in language skills to facilitate integration and communication between the two communities.

At the macro-level, the Chinese government should prepare a set of national guidelines for responsible behaviour in Chinese-African organisations. These guidelines should be in line with internationally recognised standards. The DRC government is obliged to increase awareness of codes of conduct, especially legislation of labour in order to ensure health and safety. The prohibition of child labour should be highlighted and included. Both African and Chinese authorities need to investigate all complaints of ill-treatment and abuse of workers and take action. Even compensations for abused or injured workers are appropriate.

Set up a corporate social responsibility programme for the Mozambican communities and a human resource development programme for Mozambican employees. Wuhan Iron and Steel Company can consider introducing a corporate social responsibility programme in order to change the negative perception of many Mozambican people towards Chinese companies. "Doing good things" for African communities should be talked about it in the print media and television and by governmental bodies. The intercultural cooperation could be triggered through creating a human resource development programme that targets outstanding African employees who could break the "glass ceiling" barrier in the company. Traditional mindsets should be changed to judge such social responsibility not as a cost factor for the organisation, but rather as an investment in the future of cooperation, with mutual respect and benefit.

REFERENCES

Banda, M., & Canhanga, V. (2017). Education Language Policy in Mozambique: A Critical View. *International Journal of Humanities, Social Sciences and Education,* 4(5), 12–21. https://doi.org/10.20431/2349-0381.0405002. Retrieved from https://www.arcjournals.org/pdfs/ijhsse/v4-i5/2.pdf

Boness, C., & Mayer, C.-H. (2013). *Chinese-Tanzanian Interactions in International Companies.* Unpublished Data, Department of Management, Rhodes University, Grahamstown, South Africa.

Fidelys, R., & Liang, Y. (2015). Analysis of African Iron and Steel Market for Wuhan Iron and Steel. *American Journal of Industrial and Business Management,* 5, 235–257. https://doi.org/10.4236/ajibm.2015.55026

Goethals, S., Mbaya, R., & Okenda, J.-P. (2009). *Chinese Mining Operations in Katanga Democratic Republic Of The Congo.* Field Research in Katanga. Retrieved from http://www.raid-uk.org/sites/default/files/drc-china-summary.pdf

Hofstede, G. (2010). Dimensionalizing Cultures: The Hofstede Model in Context. *Online Readings in Psychology and Culture, 2*(1). Retrieved from https://scholarworks.gvsu.edu/cgi/viewcontent.cgi?referer=https:// search.yahoo.com/&httpsredir=1&article=1014&context=orpc). https:// doi.org/10.9707/2307-0919.1014

Hofstede, G. (2018). *Indulgence vs. Restraint – The 6th Dimension*. Retrieved from https://www.communicaid.com/cross-cultural-training/blog/indulgence-vs-restraint-6th-dimension/

Le Roux, J. (2000). The Concept of 'Ubuntu': Africa's Most Important Contribution to Multicultural Education? *Multicultural Teaching, 18*(2), 43–46.

Mayer, C-H., Boness, C., & Louw, L. (2016). *Perspectives of Chinese and Tanzanian Employees on Intercultural Cooperation in a Private Chinese Organisation in Tanzania*. The 2016 China Goes Global Conference, University of Macerata, Italy, July 26–28.

Mayer, C.-H., Boness, C., Louw, L., & Louw, M. J. (2016). *Intra- and Inter- Group Perceptions of Chinese and Tanzanian Employees in Intercultural Cooperation*. Department of Management, Rhodes University, South Africa. Competitive Paper. SAIMS Conference, September 4–7. University of Pretoria.

Mbiti, J. (1990). *African Religions and Philosophy* (2nd ed.). New York: Heinemann.

Venter, E. (2004). The Notion of Ubuntu and communalism in African Educational Discourse. *Studies in Philosophy and Education, 23*(2–3), 149–160. Retrieved from https://link.springer.com/article/10.1023%2FB% 3ASPED.0000024428.29295.03

Index

A
Africa, 3, 5, 19, 30, 37–42, 45–48, 50, 51, 53, 71, 73, 80, 86, 90, 101, 102, 107, 119, 121, 127, 138, 141, 142, 148–150, 159, 162–165, 181, 183, 187, 205–207, 225, 237, 242, 243
African and Chinese socio-history, 138
African Renaissance, 38, 40, 45–48
Angola, 85, 135–148

B
Balanced scorecard, 97, 98
Bourdieu, P., 151, 152
Business management, 21, 26, 29, 30

C
Cameroon, 114, 116, 119–122, 225–231
Cameroonian and Chinese cultural values, 226, 230
Centrality of work, 192

China, 4, 19–26, 37–40, 48, 64, 66, 67, 73, 86, 87, 90, 93, 97, 101–104, 106, 107, 112, 114–122, 130, 131, 133, 136–139, 149, 150, 152–154, 159, 162, 166, 172, 176, 180, 181, 183, 186–188, 195, 196, 205–207, 212, 216, 219, 226–230, 233, 235, 237, 238, 241, 243
China-South Africa, 191, 193–195, 199–201
Chinese-African interaction, 3–5, 10, 11, 13, 37, 72, 75, 76, 82, 150, 151, 158
Chinese and African cross-cultural perspective, 233
Chinese culture, 20–23, 25, 26, 28, 31, 38, 40, 71, 73, 77, 79, 88, 89, 103, 104, 107, 112, 113, 115–117, 120, 166, 177, 185, 196, 211, 235–237, 242
Chinese idioms, 88, 90, 91, 97, 115, 153, 177

INDEX

Chinese-style management, 21–29
Communication, 3, 4, 6, 7, 9, 11, 22,
 28–29, 31, 37, 41, 44, 47, 49,
 50, 63, 66–68, 71–82, 88–90, 95,
 97, 102, 103, 108, 113, 115,
 121, 137, 138, 144–148, 150,
 155, 156, 164–167, 172–177,
 179–188, 197, 198, 200, 209,
 228–230, 237, 242–244
Conflict, 3, 7, 8, 13, 28, 76, 79, 80,
 87, 91, 121, 144, 146, 161–167,
 171, 172, 186, 187, 196, 197,
 199–201, 230, 231
Conflict management, 163, 187
Confucian ethics, 180–183, 186,
 234–236
Confucianism, 5, 20–22, 25, 27, 77,
 103, 104, 113, 163, 166, 183,
 195, 228
Cross-cultural management, 166, 187,
 207, 235
Cultural misunderstanding,
 108, 162, 185
Cultural stereotypes, 4, 40, 236
Cultural value, 42, 44, 76, 106, 146,
 192, 195, 196, 199, 200

D

Decision-making, 27, 29, 38, 51, 63,
 65, 67, 68, 85–98, 145, 153, 156,
 159, 187, 199, 210, 226, 229

E

Ethics, 21, 23, 40, 43, 77, 92, 113,
 116, 163, 166, 167, 180, 181,
 183, 185–187, 211, 219, 222,
 234–237, 239, 240, 242, 243

F

Future cooperation, 106, 233

H

Hierarchy, 21, 24, 27, 51, 52, 77, 78,
 89, 90, 106, 141, 147, 153,
 183, 185, 193, 195, 196, 206,
 209, 227
High-context culture, 102–104, 107

I

Immigrant entrepreneurship, 129, 132
Intercultural communication, 3, 4, 37,
 44, 47, 66, 67, 71–82, 147–148,
 185, 187, 242, 243
Intercultural communication
 awareness, 71, 75, 78–82
Intercultural competences, 4, 5, 7–11
Intercultural cooperation, 39–40,
 68–69, 82, 97–98, 108, 122–123,
 133, 145–147, 157–159,
 166–167, 187–188, 201,
 211–212, 222, 227, 231, 233,
 244–245
International management, 5, 6, 145
International success, 90
Interpersonal relationship, 20, 21,
 27, 28, 30, 31, 104–108, 115,
 128, 244

L

Language, 4, 9, 38, 40, 43, 46, 49,
 75, 89, 106, 111, 118, 130–133,
 135, 141, 144, 145, 149–159,
 161, 164, 166, 171–177, 187,
 194, 196–200, 207, 209, 225,
 226, 228, 230, 231, 240,
 243, 244
Language barriers, 29, 31, 133, 162,
 165, 194, 198, 209, 230, 243
Leadership style, 24, 27–28, 30, 41,
 139, 140, 146, 181, 187,
 192–193, 195, 197, 198, 201,
 226, 227, 229–231

M

Management styles, 26, 40, 42, 135–138, 141–145, 163, 183, 192–194, 199
Meaning of colours, 89–91, 93, 97
Mozambique, 85, 127–133, 233–245
Multinational organisation, 205

O

Organisational culture, 6, 7, 94, 121, 176, 243

P

Push and pull factors, 41, 91, 128, 129, 131–132, 220

S

Share value concept, 95, 96
Social culture, 22, 38, 49–50
Social etiquette, 152
South Africa, 41, 42, 48, 61, 86, 92, 119, 149–151, 156–158, 191–201

T

Technology, 19, 20, 25, 39, 48, 149, 150, 153, 157, 172
Telecommunications, 19, 149–159

U

Ubuntu, 5, 38, 40, 43–45, 49, 51, 78, 81, 91, 92, 97, 145, 184, 187, 235, 236, 239
Uganda, 161–167, 179–188, 205–212

V

Values, 4, 6, 9, 21, 23, 26–29, 31, 38, 42–44, 50–52, 63, 67, 68, 76–80, 95, 103, 105–107, 115, 116, 118, 129, 133, 137–140, 142–146, 151, 158, 166, 167, 181, 183–186, 192, 195–197, 199–201, 210, 218–222, 227, 230, 231, 234–237, 239–241, 243

Z

Zambia, 61, 85–87, 93
Zimbabwe, 78, 85, 215–218, 220, 221